A DARK
HISTORY
—— OF ——
SUGAR

For Mum and Dad.

A DARK HISTORY OF SUGAR

NEIL BUTTERY

PEN & SWORD HISTORY

AN IMPRINT OF PEN & SWORD BOOKS LTD.
YORKSHIRE – PHILADELPHIA

First published in Great Britain in 2022 by
PEN AND SWORD HISTORY
An imprint of
Pen & Sword Books Ltd
Yorkshire – Philadelphia

ISBN 978 1 52678 365 3

Typeset in Times New Roman 11.5/14 by
SJmagic DESIGN SERVICES, India.
Printed and bound in the UK by CPI Group (UK) Ltd.

Pen & Sword Books Limited incorporates the imprints of Atlas, Archaeology,
Aviation, Discovery, Family History, Fiction, History, Maritime, Military,
Military Classics, Politics, Select, Transport, True Crime, Air World,
Frontline Publishing, Leo Cooper, Remember When, Seaforth Publishing,
The Praetorian Press, Wharncliffe Local History, Wharncliffe Transport,
Wharncliffe True Crime and White Owl.

For a complete list of Pen & Sword titles please contact
PEN & SWORD BOOKS LIMITED
47 Church Street, Barnsley, South Yorkshire, S70 2AS, England
E-mail: enquiries@pen-and-sword.co.uk
Website: www.pen-and-sword.co.uk

Or
PEN AND SWORD BOOKS
1950 Lawrence Rd, Havertown, PA 19083, USA
E-mail: Uspen-and-sword@casematepublishers.com
Website: www.penandswordbooks.com

Contents

Acknowledgements...vi

Introduction..vii

Chapter 1   Innocent Times.. 1

Chapter 2   Enter the White Man..................................... 13

Chapter 3   Pioneers of the New World: The Spanish and
Portuguese Sugar Industry 21

Chapter 4   Life on the Sugar Colonies 34

Chapter 5   Making Sugar... 53

Chapter 6   Fear of Freedom 65

Chapter 7   The Slave Trade.. 80

Chapter 8   Abolition and Aftermath 99

Chapter 9   Sugar States... 118

Chapter 10 Sugar Takes Hold in Court............................. 129

Chapter 11 Sugar for All... 139

Chapter 12 The Rise of Junk Food 151

Chapter 13 Fifty Words for Sugar................................... 168

Chapter 14 Legacy.. 175

Afterword: A Brighter Future?.. 188

Notes 192

Index 229

Acknowledgements

This was a book written during the Covid-19 epidemic and I am so grateful to the wonderful and patient staff at Manchester Central Library, the British Library, the National Maritime Museum and the International Slavery Museum, who all worked so hard keeping me and everyone else safe.

I'd like to thank too Karen Foltyn for helping me to locate some tricky to find manuscripts, and Richard Fitch and Elise Fleming for their Tudor sugar craft advice. I am eternally grateful to my editor Alan Murphy and the supportive staff at Pen & Sword for their advice and for entrusting me with such a complex and important topic.

A huge thanks to my forever supportive family and friends, especially my mother and father, Sandra and David Buttery, Stuart Kinlough and Brian Mulhearn for the encouragement, humour and humouring required of them throughout the project. But the biggest thanks must be ladled upon Hugues Roberts for his unabashed help, emotional support, and constructive comments upon and criticism of the text; I really could not have done it without you.

Introduction

The use of sugar has increased every day, and there is no household in the civilised world which can do without it.

Mrs Isabella Beeton[1]

Sugar is a nutrient that makes up a vital part of our diet, but it is more than just a food group; our lives revolve around it, even if we don't know it. Sugar is a food desired, a food to be adored: our appetite for it is huge, and our want of it has shaped the modern world in every sense – physically, politically and culturally. Wars have been fought over it, and countless millions exploited, enslaved and murdered just so that we can spoon it onto cereals, beat it into cakes or stir it into macchiatos. That's how *good* it is.

In the English language the word 'sweet' is older than the word 'sugar' because in Europe sweetness was experienced first; before sugar, sweetness came fleetingly in seasonal fruit gluts, tree saps and honeycombs. The word 'sweet' was typically used in Old English in combination with the word 'honey', the sweetest natural substance, to make the word *hunigswēte* (honey-sweet).[2] Sweetness *without* honey? Impossible. But when sugar did slowly trickle into Europe at the turn of the twelfth century people were amazed that the sweetness they were tasting could be provided by a plant without the aid of bees. Sugar and honey were one and the same, and were therefore revered as such, though sugar would eventually displace honey to become the top-ranking symbol of goodness. Sweet little girls are made of 'sugar and spice and all things nice' after all.

Sugar is good because it is sweet, and things that are sweet are pure and they are lovely. Someone described as 'sweet' is nice, polite, pretty, innocent even, your romantic partner is your sweetheart, and if you are an exemplar of virginal godly goodness, you are all sweetness and light.

To be sweet is also to be pure and clean, like sweet mountain air or sweet-smelling freshly laundered sheets, and don't we all want a sweet-smelling sweetheart who is all sweetness and light? That would be a sweet life indeed. And when things are not so sweet, and we have to tell others bad news, we sometimes help things along by sugar-coating it. But sweetness is not always a positive thing. There are phrases such as the back-handed compliment 'arm candy' – used when someone's partner is very good-looking but has little else going for them. If sweetness is ladled on too thickly (like in many a romantic comedy) it becomes sickly sweet, syrupy or cloying, and if a sweet smile is discovered to be insincere, it is not made of sugar, but of bittersweet saccharine.

The word sugar has ancient roots, coming from the Sanskrit word *karkara* meaning 'sand gravel'. As sugar spread through Asia, then the Middle and Near East, the word changed as sugar muscled its way into new cultures and new languages: *sakkara* in Prakrit and then *sukkur* in Arabic, finally becoming *sugar*; the word was first spotted in English in the thirteenth century.[3]

This was not food of the everyday. In Europe sugar was 'an extravagant luxury'[4] at this time, appearing on the banquet tables and medicine chests of kings and their cronies. We get glimpses of the ways sugar was eaten from early manuscripts such as *Forme of Cury* (c1380), the first cookbook in the English language, written by the master cooks of Richard II. In attendance at many of Richard's opulent banquets was one Geoffrey Chaucer[5], who included several descriptive accounts of sugar and sweet foods in his writing, as illustrated in this description of a banquet from the *Tale of Sir Topaz* (*Thopas*):

> They fetched him first the sweetest wine,
> Then mead in mazers they combine
>   With lots of royal spice,
> And gingerbread, exceedingly fine,
> And liquorice and eglantine
>   And sugar, very nice.[6]

Sugar and honey are particularly revered in religion: Ancient Egyptians ate honey at the Festival of Thoth and welcomed each other with the greeting 'sweet is the truth',[7] and it has been discovered amongst the array of burial goods in the tombs of long-dead pharaohs (sometimes still perfectly edible). Early well-off Christians even preserved their dead in honey.[8] The Roman poet Virgil described honey as 'heaven's gift'[9], and many a Roman grave has been found to contain honey cakes placed to nourish the dead as they travelled to the afterlife.

Sugar and honey frequently appear in the Old Testament. Whenever manna from heaven is discussed, it is invariably in terms of milk and honey, both reckoned to be found in vast amounts in the Promised Land. Sugarcane was evidently important too because it was included in rituals such as sacrifice. In Isaiah (43:24), God makes clear his disappointment to Jacob when he did not include sugarcane in his sacrificial offerings: 'Thou hast bought me no sweet cane with money, neither hast thou filled me with the fat of thy sacrifices; but thou hast made me to serve with thy sins, thou hast wearied me with thine iniquities.' But then in Jeremiah (6:20) He takes the exact opposite view: 'To what purpose cometh there to me incense from Sheba [frankincense] and sweet cane from a far country? Your burnt offerings are not acceptable, Nor your sacrifices sweet to Me.'[10] God was obviously in two minds Himself as to the virtuousness of the stuff.

Religion and reverie have put sweetness – in every form – on a pedestal, making our cravings stronger and compelling us to seek it ever more readily. Sweetness is not just nice or pure, it is positively godly, and literally heaven-sent. There can be no higher regard.

But what substance are we talking about when we speak of sugar? If we mean the sugar we stir into tea or beat into a sponge cake batter, then we are talking about the sugar derived from either sugarcane or sugar beet: sucrose. The suffix '-ose' is used in biochemistry to tell us the compound is a sugar and 'sucr-' is taken from the French *sucre*, so literally, it means 'sweet sugar'. Sugars are a simple type of carbohydrate, and there are several types. The simplest are the monosaccharides, a single ring-shaped molecule; fructose and glucose are examples of this, meaning 'fruit sugar' and 'sweet sugar' respectively (the 'sweet' coming this time from Greek[11]), and they taste very sweet. Indeed, the latter is commonly found as high fructose corn syrup in American sodas, and it is to blame for the lion's share of type-2 diabetes cases in the United States.

Monosaccharides join with a partner to form disaccharides, of which sucrose – the star of the show – is one, but there are others such as maltose, which is extracted from malted barley and is found in beer and a range of sweet drinks and desserts, and lactose, the sugar found in milk. Lactose is present in particularly high concentrations in human breast milk. The reason? Our large, energy-thirsty, rapidly developing brains need a lot of food, but they are choosy organs and insist upon sugar as their energy source. The upshot of this is that it gives us a taste for sweetness from the very day we are born. Monosaccharides can form very long chains to make polysaccharides, also called complex carbohydrates, and their purpose is energy storage. The most familiar of these is starch, present in large amounts in our daily bread or baked potato. In animals, excess carbohydrates are turned not into starches but instead go through a complex metabolic ordeal in the liver before being transported via the bloodstream to be deposited as fat in adipose tissue that forms our muffin tops, beer bellies and love handles.

Saccharides are our energy source and therefore a fundamental food group, and without them we simply could not function. In nature, sweet mono- or disaccharides are rare, precious, desired and fleeting. Back in the day when seasonal fruits really were seasonal, humans gorged themselves on them – and still do, if given the chance. Notice, however, that we do not gorge ourselves on broccoli or lettuce. We are predisposed to get sugar while we can: evolution has gifted us with the capacity to put away vast amounts of the stuff. But evolution did not gift us with an off switch. Indeed, quite the opposite: it gifted us the ability – the adaptation – to carry on eating well after we feel full.[12]

The ingenuity of the human species, and its need for sugar, led us to work out ways to make things sweeter and to taste sweetness more often: apiculture was made more sophisticated, and fruits were selectively bred to contain more sugar, and fruit juices and tree saps were boiled down into sugary syrups.

When sugarcane juice was transformed into very pure sugar crystals in the Near East and picked up by crusading Christians, it was so successful that its manufacture spread around the world, creating with it globalisation and capitalism. It fuelled the British Empire and it made the West rich. It has shaped the world economy, meaning that 'Big Sugar', as it is known, had – and still has – huge political influence. Now sugar is made in massive amounts. Something that was once divine is now a commodity that costs us – on a personal level – very little, yet requires a complex process to transform the cane juice into those pure white, glistening granules that sit in paper bags in our supermarket shelves. We take sugar for granted, but now we are paying the price, and have been for some time. With cheap and plentiful sugar came centuries of exploitation, slavery, racism, diabetes, obesity, rotten teeth, and mistreatment of an exhausted planet.

The heavenly sweetness sugar provides has made a third of the world's population obese and is the catalyst of a slave trade that snatched ten million Africans from their homelands to be worked to death in servitude. Without sugar the 2020 Black Lives Matter protests may not have been needed, because the slave trade that displaced so many Africans to the Americas would never have existed. Without sugar, the British Empire probably wouldn't have existed either, and the British couldn't be exposed as being ruthless, cruel and exploitative to its colonies' inhabitants. Without the slave trade and the money made from it, the United States would not be the greatest superpower on the planet. Without sugar, we wouldn't have to spend countless billions on healthcare treating the diseases associated with consuming it.

Many white Europeans and Americans feel they are currently overly scrutinised, singled-out and blamed for what their ancestors have done in the past, complaining that history is suddenly being rewritten. Well, history *is* being rewritten, because we have come to realise that the previous Western-centric perspective was wrong; it wasn't looking at the broader picture, and many facts are false, missing, misinterpreted and in dire need of updating. As a result, the view of our past and how it created the present will be richer, more inclusive, nuanced and reflective. Of course, there is a lot to be done, and sugar has a lot of explaining to do, and I hope to do sugar's job by telling you the dark history of this most contradictory of substances, warts and all. This is not a discourse in modern racism or economics, and I am not a journalist, nor do I pretend to be. My task is to trace the line from sugar's innocent origins and connect the dots through the murky world of its past to finally emerge at the present day. Whenever possible, I have used the words of the people who were there: it is their story, and their voices need to be heard. This makes some parts of the book rather quotation heavy, but I make no apologies for that; it is not my place as a white man from England to put words in other people's mouths, not when I can use theirs.

The history of sugar is a complex one, and to tell it I have decided to tell it twice: first, I look at its production, and second, at its consumption. I do focus upon England's colonialism, sugar plantations and exploitation over other countries. The English were not the first to invent[13] any of these by any means, but they did eclipse all others with the scale of their ruthlessness and cruelty. In doing so, they set a new (im)moral benchmark for all other nations' sugar plantations, both contemporary and future, including the United States. I have tried not to dwell upon or repeat the details of the cruelties of these other plantations. I feel it would be both gratuitous and repetitious of me. Instead, I have highlighted what was different about their regimes.

Though my version of sugar's dark history is split into two distinct points of view, it is important to bear in mind that one is always informing the other; all of this exploitation and cruelty existed so that Europeans could fill their fattening faces with cake, candy and coffee. It was the Europeans' desire for sweetness and for status symbols that fuelled the entire industry. Capitalism increased production and dropped the price, allowing sugar to sprinkle down evenly through the classes, so that by the twentieth century the working classes were eating more than the middle classes. To achieve such a thing, Big Sugar manipulated how we think about this commodity, and then, just as we were getting wise to its effects on our health, it used fat as a scapegoat to get away, temporarily at least, unscathed. Not that it matters now we are all hooked, myself included. At times you may think of me as a little too disparaging towards the human race and its poor diet choices, especially in the twentieth and twenty-first centuries, but when I am waving the finger, I resolutely include myself in the telling-off. I am a person with an incredibly sweet tooth and a love of confectionery, puddings and patisserie. Sugar is my downfall; indeed, it is everyone's downfall. That is why its history is so dark.

Chapter 1

Innocent Times

> Collecting wild honey is not for the lazy, and greed alone is no guarantee of success.
>
> *Maguelonne Toussant-Samat*[1]

In a world before sugar the only sweet things available to humans were the fleeting seasonal fruits of summer, and honey; a sporadic source of large numbers of easily digestible calories. Complex carbohydrates were found in cereal grains or the roots and tubers of plants, but they are difficult to digest into a form the body can assimilate.[2] They are difficult because the body's own energy is needed to break the food down, whether it be masticating it or producing digestive enzymes; it also usually required time and energy to cook it. In Europe fruits such as raspberries, bilberries and blackberries were essential sources of sugar, their sweet taste making them highly prized and actively hunted out, but they too needed digesting, and although they do contain sugar, their main constituent is water. Honey, though, requires no further digestion. The bees that collect the nectar in the first place digest any disaccharides into monosaccharides with their salivary enzymes, and then helpfully concentrate the sugars by slow evaporation in honeycombs until it becomes a viscous syrup containing up to ninety-five per cent sugar.[3]

Evolution has shaped our behaviour to hunt out any high-calorie foods in the environment. The social groups of hunter-gatherers who could find and collect sugars more frequently or harvest them more deftly than others tended to do better. In Darwinian terms the group would be fitter because they would have more offspring compared to other groups that did not display those behaviours. The human brain has adapted over time to put sweetness, and the acquisition of it, to the forefront of our minds and seek out anything sweet and therefore calorific. These foods are also rare, so bingeing was a perfectly reasonable strategy. In this way the group gets the calories and prevents any others from benefitting from it. Any heritable trait that gave the individuals within groups an edge over others would be selected for as well, whether it was a greater capacity to problem-solve or a more avaricious pleasure centre in their brains. In other words, we've evolved to really enjoy eating sugar, *and* to think about the next chance to eat it again.

This unconditional love is the driving force behind our appetites and desires today.[4] It is worth pointing out here that evolution works not on a gene or an individual, but a population, and it occurs when there is a change in the frequency of a gene or genes over time due to natural (or some other) selection. The problem with evolution, however, is that it is not concerned with the future, only with what is 'best' to do right now.[5] Runaway selection for brains that could problem-solve and seek out honey acted on the proto-human, changing how it thought about sugar on a fundamental level. Our predilection for sugar addiction was an evolved adaptation just as much as the ability to find and collect it.

Craving sweetness makes us what we are. The pleasure we derive from consuming sugary foods causes our brains to produce endogenous opioids, a family of analgesics that includes heroin, methadone and codeine.[6] In turn, these pleasures produce a physical craving inspiring early humans to develop more elaborate and ingenious ways of getting their hands on it. In other words, our ability to plan, discuss, think laterally and cooperate within groups was fuelled by sugar. However, so were less savoury character traits like ruthlessness and greed, especially between groups. It is the interaction between these 'good' and 'bad' behaviours that is the root of the dark side of sugar: it brings out the best and the worst in us.

***

That humans have been eating honey throughout their entire existence is beyond doubt. Indeed, that we can observe some of the great apes today using tools to extract honey from the hives of angry bees suggests that it was going on a long time before *Homo sapiens* had been knocking about on the planet.[7] It has been hypothesised that there was an explosion of creativity around 2.5 million years ago when our hominid ancestors the Australopithecines learnt to make and use stone tools, including those to extract honey efficiently.[8] Evolutionary palaeontologists are very aware of the hominids' love of sugar, yet few have assessed the importance of honey in fuelling the evolution of these energy-thirsty big brains.[9] Certainly, an ability to deftly and swiftly crack into hives with such tools must have been a game-changer, putting the tribes that acquired these new skills head and shoulders above the rest.

The first real evidence for well-planned complex honey raids comes from Palaeolithic (40,000 to 8000 BCE) art found in caves in India, Africa and Europe, particularly Spain. Art in the Arana Cave in Valencia clearly depicts a person clinging onto ropes, their free hand thrust into the centre of a hive surrounded by many bees. Others show that they have brought with them a basket to fill with stolen honey-laden combs. The Altamira Cave paintings show a person on spindly ladders precariously placed against a tree leading up to the honeycombs.[10] Raiding hives was obviously not for the faint-hearted: skill and bravery were required by the bucketload, and because of this fact, it appears that for many hunter-gatherer societies it was considered a form of hunting.[11]

The lengths people were going to, and the fact that Palaeolithic man felt compelled to make art of this most dangerous activity suggests strongly that the acquisition of honey was very important indeed, and there are plenty of modern anthropological studies to support this. In the Democratic Republic of Congo the Efe people collect honey in small family groups during the brief summer season and share their spoils with the rest of the group upon their return. The Efe are very proficient in this and bring back so much honey they eat nothing else during its

Cave art from Arana Caves, Spain, depicting a honey gatherer collecting their quarry from a bees' nest in a tall tree as the bees buzz around them, 6000 BCE.

season. In Nepal some hunter-gatherers can gather 40 *l* of honey per hour, enough for each member to receive over 1000 calories from the sweet stuff every day. Indeed, the Ache people of Paraguay consider honey to be the second most desired foodstuff after meat, and the Hadza of Tanzania prize it over and above anything else.[12] The Hadza have also formed an endearing relationship with a bird called the honeyguide. When one of these little birds finds a beehive it flies to the closest village and signals frenetically, hopping and fanning its tail and emitting a flurry of chats and whistles in a bid to get the Hadza's attention. As soon as it does, it flies to the hive, guiding them to their bounty. When the bird reaches the hive, it stops and falls silent, patiently waiting for them to smoke out the bees. The hunters remove the honey from its combs, casting aside the wax which the little bird hops down to eat for itself.[13]

As ingenious, thrilling and rewarding it may be raiding bees' nests for honey, it is also perilous, so any strategies that reduced injuries or fatalities in man's quest for sweetness were going to be favoured. It would be much easier for starters if the honey was at a sensible height

Egyptian Honey Cakes. Egyptian bakers remove freshly-baked honey cakes from clay ovens in this tomb painting from the Tomb of Rekhmire, Thebes, c.1450 BCE. (Nina de Garis Davies)

from the ground. One approach from the middle Bronze Age was to relocate hives by cutting them out of a tree, surrounding bark and all, and setting them in clay at an easy-to-reach height.[14] This may have been less treacherous, but it still made honey an opportunistic energy source and by around 7000 BCE the Egyptians were fully exploiting the honey bee. They made their own beehives that imitated trees, and there are reliefs in tombs dating to 2600 BCE showing the pressing of honey.[15]

Of course, the honey-hunters were not the only people to find ways to get a sugar rush. Over the millennia *Homo sapiens* has selectively bred plants for increased sugar content, and concentrated sugars by sun-drying, making sugar-rich syrups, or extracting the malt sugars from grains such as barley. Still, nothing was quite as immediate, bountiful or delicious as honey. Not until sugarcane came along.

***

Cultivated sugarcane, *Saccharum officinarum*, does not exist in the wild. In fact, it only exists at all because humans have exploited it, growing and selectively breeding wild species far beyond their natural form. The *Saccharum* genus of perennial plants belongs to the Poaceae family of grasses, which includes other grasses naturally high in sugars like maize and sorghum.[16] If you have ever sat in a field and dissected a stem of grass with your fingers, you may have noticed that some types are filled with white foam-like pith. In *Saccharum* species it is in this pith that sweet cane juice sits. Modern cultivated sugarcane is around twenty per cent sucrose by weight, grows up to 5cm a day, reaching a height of 6m, and has a thin rind that can be crushed easily. *Saccharum officinarum*, like its wild relatives, is very well adapted to life in the south-east Asian islands; its ideal growing temperature is between 27 and 38°C but will grow in temperatures as low as 21°C.[17] Though built for tropical climes, *Saccharum* species have a broad altitudinal range meaning that they can grow at any height as long as the soil is rich and wet enough. Being a grass means that *Saccharum* species can reproduce asexually by vegetative propagation, rather like strawberry and spider plants. Indeed, anyone who has ever planted bamboo – another type of large grass – in their garden will know that these types of plants can spread quickly and aggressively and are surprisingly mobile. This ability to grow at most

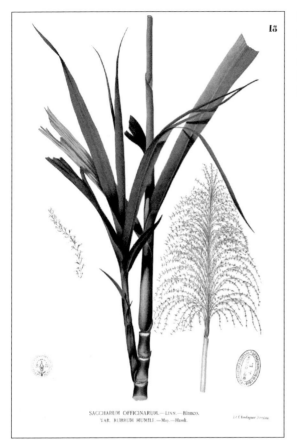

Botanical plate (c.1880) of sugarcane, *Saccharum officinarum* from *Florade de Filipinas* by Spanish botanist Francisco Manuel Blanco. (Rawpixel)

SACCHARUM OFFICINARUM.—LINN.—Blanco.
VAR. RUBRUM HUMILE —Moy.—Hassk.

altitudes, its readiness to reproduce asexually and its perennial growth are the secrets to its success.

There are disagreements about just how many *Saccharum* species there are – plant genetics is a murky world with much inbreeding, outbreeding, hybridisation and chromosome duplications. This produces gradients of variation between 'species' that are not discrete entities but a huge 'species complex' where all species can potentially interbreed.[18] However, it seems that the first wild species to be cultivated was *Saccharum robustum*, its Latin name suggesting it is somewhat stouter than its domesticated cousin. Archaeological evidence indicates that it was cultivated in New Guinea around 8000 BCE.

The New Guineans were one of the world's first agriculturists, responsible for domesticating many food plant species, including another future commodity, the banana.[19] *S robustum* was grown as a snack food rather than a primary carbohydrate source.[20] The New Guineans considered sugarcane important because, according to their myths and legends, it spawned the entire human race.[21] *S robustum* originally grew wild in the Philippines. It is not clear whether it found its own way to New Guinea or whether it was physically brought over by, say, a trader, though going by the voraciousness of the farming on the island, one might assume the latter. However they got their hands on it, the New Guineans cultivated *S robustum* over time for sweeter juice and a softer, less fibrous rind so it could be chewed easily, altering it from its natural form so much it is deemed *S officinarum* or least a proto-version of it. Eventually and somewhat inevitably, it grew so well that it escaped and grew ferally, spreading like wildfire around the surrounding areas. Trade with the Philippines, Indonesia and the Solomon Islands made it even more cosmopolitan before it hit the mainland and spread to India and China around 6000 BCE, even reaching Hawaii in the first millennium AD.[22]

The next stage in its domestication history is unclear; it is not easy to track genes and their genomes when there is such ready geneflow between related species. The result is a tangled mass that isn't easy to unknot, but it seems that when the feral proto-*officinarum* reached India, it hybridised again with another species, *S spontaneum*.[23] When two species successfully hybridise, the resultant hybrid offspring (and the new species it creates) are often fitter than the parent species – a concept known as hybrid vigour – and this is what seems to have happened with *S officinarum* which is both hardy and fast-growing, two characteristics that would go on to make it perfect for cultivating on a large scale.

***

In 325 BCE part of Alexander the Great's army was exploring India with plans to invade the region. It was during one particular reconnaissance mission that they came across a very curious crop that produced a substance with almost mystical properties. Nearchus, one of his generals, described 'a reed in India [that brings] forth honey without the help of bees, from which an intoxicating drink is made, though the plant bears no fruit.' His wonder reflects the limited opportunities to experience sweetness in the wider world at this time. Nearchus could not imagine something that sweet could come from neither honey nor fruit. News of this exciting plant, along with a few samples, were sent to Macedonia, but there it seemed to stop – just a mere curiosity from a faraway land. Any stories you may have heard of Alexander being so excited about sugarcane he cultivated it in Egypt are, sadly, apocryphal.[24]

What Alexander would not have realised is that sugarcane had been cultivated and harvested in India for 600 years before Nearchus happened upon it,[25] its thin skin making it easy to crack open and crush to extract its juice. Then the juice was boiled over wood fires to produce brown sugar.[26] The sugar is called *gur* and is still produced and eaten in India today where it often goes by the name *jaggery*, the African word for the same product, a word introduced to the country during its second wave of sugarcane cultivation when it was ruled over by the British Empire. *Gur* is a Sanskrit word meaning 'ball', presumably because of the dark treacly mass that forms during the final stages of sugar-making.[27]

By 325 BCE *gur* was being mixed with rice, barley and wheat flours and a variety of spices to produce an array of confections, sweet drinks similar to those drunk by Nearchus, and even a type of rice pudding. Two hundred years later there are mentions in manuscripts of different grades of sugar where a whole vocabulary surrounding sugar and sugar-making had developed.[28] Even today sugar-making is highly regarded by followers of the Hindu religion where sugar is considered *sattvic*, pure enough that everyone is allowed to eat it, including holy people.[29] Sugar is thought to have medicinal properties: it soothes the stomach and is essential for a healthy reproductive system,[30] an idea that spread via the Middle East to Europe where physicians prescribed it to patients in the springtime to balance the humours and soothe one's loins during Lent.

Aside from Nearchus's fleeting interest in it in the fourth century BCE, there had only been one other connection with Indian sugar, this time by invading Persians led by Emperor Darius two centuries previously. But again no real interest seems to have gathered around the plant or the substance produced from it[31] and there would not be another mention of sugar or sugarcane by the Persians for another thousand years.[32] When it was mentioned again in sixth century AD, cultivation, extraction and refining were already underway in earnest, so they must been familiar with the entire process of making sugar for a considerable amount of time. In the sixth century the Persian Empire had a well-established, efficient and wide-ranging central authority which, among other things, had developed an excellent irrigation system that they had been tinkering with since the second century AD. They used it for watering other thirsty crops such as rice, so when a viable sugarcane cutting did arrive, cultivation of it could begin immediately, as could a burgeoning sugar business.[33]

There is a legendary tale that recounts how sugarcane arrived in Persia. The Sassanian king Chosroes I was on campaign in India in the sixth century. One particular day he wandered away from his troops. Hot and thirsty in the stifling temperatures, he came across a farmhouse with a beautiful garden and seeing a girl outside tending to it, he called her over to ask for a drink of water. Being courteous, she obliged and retreated into the house only to return not with a cup of water, but with one of sugarcane juice. It was so delicious, he asked for a second cup. And so, sated (and probably somewhat lightheaded) from drinking the delectable nectar, he found his troops and, like any emperor worth his salt, came back with a garrison and took the farm and garden for himself.[34] The girl was probably very anxious about this turn of events, but she need not have worried because he allowed her to marry him (though I'm not sure that would count as an appropriate resolution today). True or not, the story suggests that the Persians transported the plants from India along with the methods of cultivating it and extracting its juice.

The seventh century saw the beginning of the great expansion of the medieval Islamic Empire through Syria, Egypt and Palestine, and wherever the empire went, so did sugarcane. The Nile Delta was particularly conducive to the cultivation of the plant because it was uncommonly rich in nutrients that were continually topped up with runoff from the river. Egypt became renowned for its high-quality sugar, which was considered 'the best in the world, white as snow and hard as stone'.[35] Obviously, they were no longer making brown *gur* but something much more refined. Not only were they producing a purer product but sugarcane cultivation and sugar making had gone from a small cottage industry to something much larger in scale. By the tenth century the first sugar plantations as we would think of them today were being constructed. We get a lot of information about them from *gazetters* – early Arab travel writers – who tell us that the plantations could be found all along the banks of the Euphrates and had even spread eastwards in the direction of India west of the Indus Delta. It also spread northwards to the south coast of the Caspian Sea in what is now Afghanistan.[36]

Islam's success in the Near and Middle East was a catalyst for its rapid expansion west, initially along the south coast of the Mediterranean and many of its islands.[37] The Islamic Empire expanded out of Syria in the 630s before moving on to Egypt and Northern Africa in 640, Rhodes in 658 and Morocco in 682. They moved onto the Mediterranean islands too, invading Cyprus in 644 and Sicily in 655, and reached Spain in 711. Of course, it took time to occupy and stabilise these lands fully, but once established, they took Crete in 823 and Malta in 870 in a second wave.[38]

Although territories were gained and lost, the Muslim Empire remained relatively stable for centuries, allowing them to improve the sugar-making process. As a result, these early years of expansion saw 'more experimentation in sugarcane cultivation than any subsequent period until the nineteenth century'.[39] The methods upon which they settled would remain almost unchanged for a millennium: short pieces of sugarcane, two joints long, called 'setts' were planted horizontally in rich heavily irrigated earth. The setts were planted on their sides so that several stalks emerged from each piece, producing sugarcane fields that were so dense workers could not even enter them to weed. Canes were cut, collected and transported to the pressing factories to be crushed by water-driven mills to extract the juice which was then boiled down in copper tubs over wood fires. Time was of the essence. The whole process up until the point of boiling had to be completed within twenty-four hours; left any longer and enzymes in the canes and extracted juice would convert sucrose into its constituent molecules, glucose and fructose, which cannot crystallise and can only form a syrup. Boiling the juice denatured the enzymes and forced impurities to the surface which were skimmed off. Eventually, the super-saturated sugar syrup would be concentrated enough for crystals to form on its surface; these were gingerly removed with a long wooden spoon and packed into wicker baskets to slowly dry and harden.[40]

As the empire expanded west into Europe so did its knowledge and techniques in farming a whole host of novel foodstuffs in a great agricultural revolution. It was not only food that was transformed, but also medicine, mathematics and philosophy. The Muslim Empire was a very successful trading bloc by the tenth century; not only did it have a monopoly on sugar and sugarcane cultivation, but it also controlled the spice trade from Asia. Baghdad had become the centre of trade for the whole empire – a warehouse city for exotic products sold at a king's ransom to all four corners of its empire. It wasn't just the spices and sugar either, but also confections such as marzipan and caramel.[41] Much of this growth was spurred by Venetian traders who saw the potential profits that could be made. They were perfectly positioned to trade between Europe, North Africa and the Middle East, and being both shrewd and tenacious, they quickly formed a business relationship with the Muslims. As a consequence they were responsible for the majority of the trade in sugar between the diaspora of the Muslim Empire.[42]

***

Sugar's part in standard histories of the Mediterranean in the Middle Ages is not typically focused upon, except for a note that it was picked up and handed around by returning Crusaders as a bit of a 'curiosity.'[43] This is odd bearing in mind that they created the blueprint for a sugar industry that would last for centuries.[44] Also, sugarcane was being grown along the entire length of the Mediterranean coast, making North Africa and Southern Spain the most important centres of production outside of the Near and Middle East by the early eleventh century.[45] Spain's earliest account is contained in the Calendar of Cordoba, dated 961, which lists the various perennial activities and events of that year where sugarcane cultivation appears to be well-established and fully integrated into the Spanish-Muslim economy. Eventually their sugar wasn't just being traded within their empire; by 1300 Muslim Malagan sugar was available for purchase in European cities such as Bruges.[46]

The secret to the Muslim Empire's success in the cultivation of sugarcane is down to their knowledge and skills in irrigation. Before sugarcane was being cultivated they had already pioneered a technique of running canals alongside rivers to divert water to flood the fields, or along extensive networks of underground conduits via *norias* – belt-fed buckets transporting water directly to the field.[47] The Egyptians intensified the system, irrigating the land up to twenty-eight times per growing season[48] and keeping the fields productive in the summer months when they would ordinarily be too dry for sugarcane. The limiting factor was climate. This was not tropical New Guinea and there was nothing that could be done about the cool winters where temperatures dropped too low for sugarcane to grow.

Just as pre-existing irrigation methods were applied to sugarcane cultivation, the same approach was taken with milling and extraction.

The cane mill was both the literal and metaphorical fulcrum of the plantation. Wheat had been milled under stone, and olives and grapes pressed to yield their oil and juice for centuries.[49] There were two types of mill: the first consisted of a large circular static millstone laid horizontally with another set on top that could be turned; the other, called an 'edge runner', was a circular millstone set vertically in a shallow depression which was turned to crush canes. There were two downsides to these mills: first, the sugarcane had to be cut down into short lengths, which was time-consuming; and second, the extraction process was inefficient, so the canes had to be pressed twice. Even after two pressings, only half of the juice was extracted, but this method would not be improved upon until the mass production of sugar on the island of Madeira at the end of the fifteenth century.[50] The sheer weight of sugarcane (the majority of it being woody biomass and water) and the rapidity with which it had to be processed meant that sugar was refined in the same place it was harvested until the Portuguese eventually uncoupled the processes in the fifteenth century.

As sugarcane spread with the rest of Islamic agriculture from East to West, so did their ways of managing land and labour. When the Muslim Empire was in its more formative years, the land was managed by tenant farmers, but as sugar demand accelerated within the empire, extra hands were needed quickly. They solved this problem by turning to forced slave labour, and it appears that this is the first time it was used on sugar plantations. However, there is an important distinction to be made between the slavery here and that of the much more ruthless European regimes of the future. The slaves in the Muslim Empire were there to supplement an existing workforce who were finding it difficult to meet demand. Not that any of this is *excusing* slavery of course – there is no excuse – but that was the *reason* for this demographic change. As William D. Phillips puts it: '[Iberia] was home to societies with slaves, not slave societies.'[51]

For many, slavery is slavery and they resolutely point the finger at the Muslim Empire as the germ of the association between slavery and sugar, while others, because of the distinction Phillips makes, resolutely believe it is not. Either way, sugar's history achieved its first dark stains, but there was worse to come and the indelible association between sugar and slavery would not form until much later.

Chapter 2

Enter the White Man

It must be emphasised that the union of black slavery and
sugarcane had a European origin.

Stuart B. Schwartz[1]

It is a commonly held belief that Western Europe didn't get its first
taste of sugar until the Crusaders brought some back from the Holy
Land along with a whole load of strange and exotic foodstuffs. This
is not precisely true. A few decades before the First Crusade a small
army of Normans invaded Muslim-occupied Sicily after some of their
predecessors who, after living on the island in what seems to have been
a relatively peaceful multicultural community, sent out samples of sugar
and other goods alerting their kin to the bounties available for the taking
should they fancy.

Though it took a few false starts, the Normans took control and picked
up sugar production where the Muslim administration had left off, often
keeping the same workers. Now there was a very small, but steady,
trickle of sugar reaching the West. This did not kick off the European
sugar boom as one might expect. In fact, it was largely ignored by the
merchants who were far more interested in the Muslim Empire, which
was where big money was, which distributed its sugar within its own
sprawling borders. There was a little trade with neighbouring Europe
from Muslim Spain, so some sugar did appear in the Christian West.[2]

It took the conclusion of the First Crusade in 1099 for sugar to be
brought back in sufficient quantities that enough high-ranking people
could experience the taste *and* ask for more. Norman Sicily remained a
small producer because it was not on the Crusaders' route to the Holy
Land. They picked up their first modest haul of sugarcane during the
Siege of Acre in 1104 when they were forced to chew it to prevent
starvation.[3] By the time the Crusade had ended, they had developed a

taste for sugarcane and sugar itself. Eventually, the Crusaders would come to occupy Acre and Egypt, Syria and Tyre and by the twelfth century these cities were producing large quantities of sugar, especially in the Levant region where the first Christian-made sugar exports left for Europe. However, it took a further century for the first large shipment of sugar destined for England to leave port.[4]

Although the Near East had, for the most part, changed hands – the same Italian merchants continued to trade and export sugar – they simply adjusted their direction of trade towards Christian Europe. Many Europeans travelled to the Holy Land on Crusade and here we find the first European accounts of sugarcane *in situ*, such as the celebrated French chronicler Jean de Joinville, who followed King Louis IX on the Seventh Crusade and mentioned in his accounts, 'very fair canes, from which they obtain that which makes sugar.'[5] The number of plantations

A fourteenth century depiction of the Siege of Acre, the first time Crusaders found a taste for sugar and sugarcane. From BL Royal 20 C VII, f. 24v. (British Library/Picryl)

grew exponentially with many financed by Venetian merchants, the Knights Templar, the Hospitallers and the Teutonic Knights.[6] A system for efficient export quickly emerged: sugar was formed into blocks, wrapped in palm leaves and stamped with the maker's trademark to make *cassonade* (meaning literally 'packed in crates') and large conical sugar loaves. To fit the loaves into boxes more easily, their tips were removed and ground down to a fine powder which sold at a premium. There was also a hard, transparent sugar candy produced in various shades from almost colourless to a deep brown.[7]

Some structural changes to the sugar industry by Christians had some adverse effects in cities. Sugar refineries had been moved from the plantations into urban centres to enable multiple plantations to feed fewer and larger refineries in a bid to increase efficiency. As a result, however, the air rapidly became heavily polluted and the cities over-populated.

The Holy Land's Christian occupation was not to last of course, with Saladin and his nephew leading the attacks that displaced the Crusaders from Syria, where the inner-city refineries were immediately dismantled.[8] The loss of this occupied territory was a massive blow to the Crusaders from the point of view of religious conquest, but it only affected their sugar production temporarily. In hindsight, it was perfect timing. Output in this area was beginning to drop because they had almost cleared the land of decent timber to feed the furnaces of the boiling houses, as the returning Muslims would sadly discover. However, the Europeans had learned much from their occupation, and they could replicate the system of plantations and refineries wherever they liked.[9]

Christian sugar production also spread to Crete and Cyprus, by now an established stop-off point for Crusaders on their way to aid the Christian fight for the Holy Land. The cultivation and processing of sugar required a substantial labour force and masses of equipment for cultivation, crushing, boiling, refining and shipping – this was not a venture for the modest businessman. It required a considerable amount of investment, and it was only the likes of the wealthy Hospitallers and Knights Templar or Venetian merchants who had the resources or could take out the massive loans needed to purchase the capital and pay the workforce.[10]

The Islamic sugar industry hung on, producing sugar south of Baghdad. However, this stalled suddenly with the invasion of the Turks in the mid-thirteenth century. It shook what was left of their sugar industry to its core when they captured a caravan of 600 camels laden with sugar.[11] The Turks overpowered the region and 'the last Abbasid Khalif … was executed after the capture of Baghdad in 1258 by Hulagu, the grandson of Jenghiz [Genghis] Khan, and with the disruption of the Persian Empire also disappeared the sugar industry.'[12] Some Syrian plantations managed to carry on, but when the Near East was badly hit by the Black Death in the fourteenth century the numbers dwindled to just a handful. The industry's fate was finally sealed when the more efficient Christian sugar moved onto Madeira, the Canary Islands and the New World.

Christian Europe was now the primary producer of sugar around the globe, and the methods they used 'anticipate[d] the plantations of the Caribbean [and] the template was now set for all future sugar production.' It also needed an army of skilled workers such as blacksmiths to produce tools, and coopers to make packing crates and hogsheads.[13] Because of the timber shortages, the sugar industry was forced further west and south, but there were very few places left to exploit, and this is when the industry turned its attention to its Western fringes: Madeira, the Canary Islands, São Thomé and Western Africa. The pioneers in this respect were the Portuguese.

Supplying an ever-increasing demand for sugar required a great deal of commercial, technical and social organisation. Together, these three aspects of the industry formed the sugar *ingenio* – a combination of plantation, mill and refinery.[14] Their interactions were highly complex, but the well-seasoned men coordinating and running the show made it a system that was easy to transfer to new areas. It is considered the world's first capitalist venture and it was European aristocracy and merchants who happily stumped up the cash to get the cogs whirring.[15]

Capitalism requires efficiency and economy of scale, and to address this the final stage of refining was moved to the European mainland. This broke the cycle of using waste from the refining process to fertilise the cane fields, and it did not take long until the consequences began to be seen as soils were stripped of their nutrients. Of course, timber was burnt in the boiling houses, but the wood was not locally sourced, it had to be shipped in from elsewhere because Madeira had been cleared of its own timber to fuel other *ingenios* on the timber-starved Mediterranean. Indeed, Madeira was so heavily forested that a significant amount of cash was raised by selling timber to the mainland, and the profits used to invest in the capital needed for the Madeiran plantations.[16] When it turned out that sugar could be grown almost all year round on Madeira, the first large-scale sugarcane monoculture was planted. It was quite the task to transport the equipment required over such a distance, but the first sugar mill and waterwheel was successfully installed in 1436, financed by Genoese merchants.[17] In 1446 Madeiran sugar landed in England via the docks at Bristol and by the 1460s the Portuguese had the monopoly on European production.[18] Madeira would go on to produce over 2000 tons per annum between 1505 and 1509[19], but the sugar pioneers were living beyond their means – there was no more indigenous timber, and because they were farming a monoculture, they had become totally reliant on food imports. Furthermore, the lack of forest on the island led to extensive soil erosion and production began to fall.

Their hopes of repeating this success in the Canary Islands were dashed by a bitter war between the Portuguese and the Castilians, with the former losing control of the islands. They must have felt relieved, and somewhat smug, when in 1491 plagues of caterpillars ravaged their lost islands, enabling the Portuguese to keep the upper hand.[20] Nevertheless, the Spanish did manage to produce some sugar and adopted the Portuguese model. They could never match their rivals, but they did have a trick up their sleeve: they had been given the right to colonise the New World by Pope Alexander VI in the treaty of Saragossa in 1529. Colonists landed in the West Indies, growing sugarcane on Hispaniola and then Cuba.

The Spanish did retain a foothold in the Old World after they acquired the sugar plantations left behind when they forcibly ejected the Muslims from Spain in 1502. However, it could not compete with the large-scale Portuguese industry and it began to falter; Spain was just too temperate and seasonal, the sugarcane growing only two-thirds of the year. Amazingly, a few Valencian sugar plantations did manage to carry on production until the 1750s though their fate was eventually sealed when a particularly cold winter killed the entire rootstock.[21] By now, the industry needed sustained high yields to satisfy demand and only the tropics and subtropics could satiate those needs. However, the issue of fuel shortages quickly surfaced: 7kg of sugarcane juice needs 5kg of water boiled from it to produce 2kg of crystalline sugar.[22] The vast amounts needed were either shipped over from newly occupied Brazil or sourced from North Africa and the deforested Mediterranean at great cost, so despite the scale of sugar produced, prices remained high. This allowed the Spanish plantations to remain in production as long as they did because they had access to cheap Northern European timber and benefited from exporting short distances. What Valencia lost in yield, it gained back in low fuel and transport costs.[23]

Sugarcane was in its perfect habitat in subtropical Madeira and grew relentlessly, keeping the furnaces burning twenty-four hours a day and giving no respite. The set up was simple and straightforward: free men worked the technical operations of the *ingenios*, overseeing and coordinating every stage, including the doling out of punishment. The Portuguese regime was draconian, and one supposes that it had to be because of the constant effort needed to keep the plantations and refineries going. At first, the island's indigenous people did the heavy labour, but when they died from overwork the Portuguese were left with a labour vacuum. With demand from Europe forcing the industry to drop its prices, plantation owners found they couldn't use freemen if they wanted their profits to remain healthy, so they addressed the issue by importing slave labour sourced from the fringes of Western Europe. One notorious example of this occurred in 1493 when 2,000 Portuguese-Jewish children aged between two and ten years old were shipped to São Thomé solely to work on the *ingenios*. These children were orphaned because their parents had been executed by the Inquisition for refusing to adopt the Christian faith. Only 600 survived the first year.[24]

As the Portuguese explored the coast of Africa, the continent's north and west became part of Europe's fringes, and it was only a matter of time before the people of Western Africa would come in contact with them. The first black slaves were traded by the Portuguese who, under the tutelage of Prince Henry 'the Navigator' of Portugal, appreciated the importance of being the first to lay claim to new and exotic tropical and subtropical colonies. But it wasn't just sugar they had on their minds; they set up colonies on the African coast at São Thomé, Fernando Po and Angola in search of gold and spices[25], and it is here that the unfortunate association between the slave trade and the African peoples was forged.

In 1441 an inexperienced but ambitious captain named Antam Gonçalvez sailed his ship down the west coast of Africa to find some exotic spoils in the hope that they would 'curry favour' with the prince.[26] On his 'adventures' he kidnapped men of both Asian and African descent, thinking them perfect gifts for the prince and his court. As it turned out, they were all Muslims, and they managed to reason with him that being men of God, they were too noble to be paraded about the Portuguese court and live out the rest of their lives in servitude. However, they knew of 'Sons of Ham' in the continent's interior who would be much more suitable. Ham was Noah's second son, who was cursed by Noah himself to live a life of servitude after seeing his father's naked (and drunk) body. This seems a little harsh, especially when Noah extended the curse to all of Ham's descendants. An agreement was reached between Gonçalvez and the men whose freedom they would exchange for the 'Sons of Ham', and they aided in the organisation and capture of 223 Africans who were promptly shipped out from Guinea to Portugal. Happy with their first cargo, the Portuguese Crown allowed one ship to sail to Guinea each year and bring back 150 slaves.[27]

There wasn't an immediate switch to African slavery at this time, nor were Africans sent to the Madeiran *ingenios* in any significant number, but the number of black slaves soon started to increase, and by the end of the 1440s over 1,000 were being traded per annum to work in domestic service or urban occupations in Portugal.[28] Indeed, this steady trade meant the Algarve population was ten per cent African by the mid-sixteenth century, and had begun to integrate into Portuguese

A nineteenth century representation of sailors returning to the Spanish mainland with sugar from the Canary Islands in early sixteenth century, by Piet Verhaert. (WQUlrich/Wikimedia Commons)

society, so much so that the slavery of Africans was on the wane. However, the rapid expansion of the sugar industry was to change all that, as Africans were sent exclusively to the sugar colonies to help cope with demand. The Portuguese chose Africans simply because they were the closest to hand and therefore most efficient to transport.

Madeira produced 1000 tons of refined sugar per year in the latter half of the fifteenth century, but the soil became exhausted by this aggressive farming and production started declining, possibly as early as 1430.[29] Madeiran and Canary Island sugar had had its day, and the baton of the sugar industry was passed onto the New World. The Spanish had already colonised the Greater Antilles in the West Indies, and the Portuguese had landed on Brazil, going against the terms of the Treaty of Saragossa. Here, they made enough profit selling timber to the Old World to make the capital investments required to set up their own *ingenios*, producing more sugar than they ever had on Madeira. As for Madeira, the island went from major sugar producer on the fringes of the Old World to a mere stepping-stone to the New.[30]

Chapter 3

Pioneers of the New World: The Spanish and Portuguese Sugar Industry

Without sugar, there might only have been a minor slave trade; with sugar, the slave trade drove European commerce and development.

Peter Macinnis[1]

After a 'protracted journey westwards' in 1492 Christopher Columbus saw land for the first time and mistook the group of islands he initially landed on to be off the coast of India, hence their name, the West Indies.[2] With their discovery he created a route for Spanish colonisation, trade and opportunity that would go on to connect the South American mainland. This was his first voyage, but we are more interested in his second a year later.

Columbus was a Genoese merchant who had dealt in Madeiran sugar,[3] but when the industry started to falter he, like many others, turned his attention to the Spanish Canary Islands. He attempted to set up *ingenios*, but was so notorious for his tyrannical manner that others were reluctant to work with him. As a result, he failed to get any *ingenios* successfully up and running on the island. Nevertheless, it was here that he met his mistress, Beatriz Enríquez de Arana, the daughter of one of the most prosperous plantation owners on the islands. It was a successful pairing and being just as driven as her lover, Beatriz convinced him to take a large number of sugarcane cuttings on his second voyage, suspecting that they would grow well there. He didn't need much convincing, and 'in that simple act' says Peter Macinnis, 'he probably did more than anybody else to shape the Americas today

[and] many of the events that moulded the New World had their roots in [those] cane fields.'[4]

The second trip was a voyage of colonisation, and when he left the Canaries in 1493 for the island of Hispaniola, the second-largest in the Greater Antilles, he took with him domesticated animals, a cache of seeds of several essential food crops, and 12,000 settlers. These settlers were expected to work the land and nurture a new civilisation from this stock of plants and animals.[5] They were also expected to grow sugarcane.

There is something naïvely brave and hopeful about these new settlers, eager and ready to create a brand new world for themselves. But disaster would fall upon not only these colonists, but also the unwitting Taino, the indigenous people of the island of Hispaniola. On his first voyage, Columbus had been enthusiastically welcomed by these people, but on his second their fate had already been sealed because he carried with him a writ from Ferdinand II, King of Spain. It was addressed to all of the indigenous people of the New World and contained details of the Spanish Crown's intentions and their legal and holy right of ownership of this New World. In their eyes, their impending conquest was their right: Pope Alexander VI had split the non-Christian world into two, gifting Africa and India to Portugal and leaving the New World to the Spanish.[6] The letter declared that, 'the late Pope gave these islands and mainland of the oceans and the contents hereof to the above-mentioned King … as

is certified in writing and you may see the documents if you should desire,' but if anyone stood in their way, they were explicit in how they were to occupy it: '[w]e shall enslave your persons, wives and sons, sell you or dispose of you as the King sees fit.' Not only that, but they washed their hands of all responsibility: 'And we

Portrait of a Man, Said to be Christopher Columbus 1519. He 'probably did more than anybody else to shape the Americas today' (Metropolitan Museum of Art)

shall declare you guilty of resulting deaths and injuries, exempting Their Highnesses of such guilt as well as ourselves and the gentlemen who accompany us.'[7] In committing this to paper they had given themselves full legal permission to not only do whatever they liked, but also firmly made clear which party would be responsible for the consequences of any future resistance. The Taino were bamboozled, to say the least. They had no concept of land ownership, and did not expect any cruelty from these white invaders.

Columbus later described the Taino as being 'of a very keen intelligence,' yet 'wondrous timid'. They had no weaponry, 'nor [were] they capable of using them', and the Spanish had no problem overpowering them.[8] These peaceful people represent the antithesis of the Europeans' burgeoning and merciless capitalism: they lived in synergy with their surroundings, didn't exploit their resources, and farmed a variety of crops.

Several distinct peoples lived in the West Indies including the peaceful Arawaks, but most notorious were the Caribs, a warrior tribe that originated from Brazil but could be found scattered over the Indies on Trinidad, Guadeloupe, Martinique and Dominica. Like the Taino, they lived in tune with nature, but unlike the Taino they were fierce warriors who spent much of their time either raiding other tribes or terrorising Spanish settlements. During their raids they would regularly kidnap high status individuals, but most concerning was the fact that they were cannibals and they took great pleasure in mocking the Spanish, saying that they gave them stomach ache, and that their meat was tough; they preferred the French who were much more tender. In reality, the Caribs believed eating another human to be a most sacred and mystical act, which instilled the consumer with the victims' 'strength, courage and skills.'[9] The Caribs clearly thought enough of them to be worth eating, though one doubts there was cold comfort to be found in that fact. That said, one has to wonder whether some of these cannibalistic acts were carried out with relish, as this retelling of an incident in 1666 involving the ex-governor of Antigua suggests:

> A party of Caribs landed, and cruelly treated the defenceless inhabitants. At length they proceeded to the house of the ex-governor, Colonel Carden, who treated them very kindly, and administered to their want. Upon their leaving, they

requested their entertainer to accompany them to the beach, who instantly complied; but the Caribs, more treacherous than the wild beasts that haunt the desert, had no sooner reached the place where their canoes were stationed, than they fell upon their kind host, cruelly murdered him, and broiled his head, which they afterwards carried with them to Dominica. [Un]satisfied with this horrible piece of barbarity … they returned to Colonel Carden's house, seized his wife and children, and after telling them of the fate of their kind relative, hurried them away into a captivity worse than death.[10]

Despite their aggression, the Caribs eventually succumbed to disease and persecution like all of the West Indies' indigenous peoples. However, some did survive on a Dominican reserve created there by the British after they took the island from the French.[11]

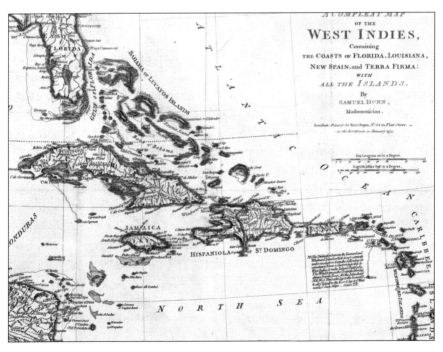

Detail from 'A compleat map of the West Indies' (1774), the tiny islands of the Lesser Antilles dwarfed by the greater islands, Cuba and Hispaniola. (Library of Congress)

The Spanish settlers landed at Santa Domingo and set about colonising the island of Hispaniola, cultivating their crops and creating their New World. Columbus may never have got a sugar plantation off the ground in the Old World, but he could here, where he had no one to answer to and had full reign over the island and its colonists. At first, people were encouraged, and no doubt relieved, that staples such as wheat grew readily.[12] But Columbus and most of the settlers had their attention not on farming staples but on the acquisition of gold which was plentiful on the islands. They started by forcing the natives to give up any gold dust and nuggets in their possession and 'according to their own Historians, [drove] them to Slavery in Mines, where the greatest part of them perished.'[13]

Their new land was handed out piecemeal to the colonists, taking no account whatsoever of whether there were native settlements present or not. Allowed to remain on their lands as slaves, the Taino quickly succumbed to Western diseases: tuberculosis, whooping cough, influenza, pleurisy, measles, typhus, cholera, bubonic plague and, worst of all, smallpox, from which ninety per cent of the Taino died.[14] The Spanish wrongly identified these deaths as being caused not by virulent disease but by feebleness and an inability to apply themselves to hard work, and Columbus's cruel regime made sure the natives were set to work immediately. Before the arrival of the Spanish, there were between three and eight million Taino, in 1514 there were around 20,000, and by 1520, only 200 individuals remained. Decimated by disease and worked to death, they managed to hang on in small numbers for a few decades before finally becoming extinct around 1560.[15]

It didn't take long before the colonists also started dying as it became all too clear that the land grants given to the settlers by Columbus were not nearly enough to sustain them. There followed a period of intense hardship as the malnourished colonists tried in vain to produce enough food to sustain themselves. It was a case of too little, too late. Columbus's regime had focused too much on the acquisition of gold than the formation a productive and settled colony. First there was 'chaos and misery', and then there was revolt.

In these dark years the only thing exported to Spain was news, and none of it was good. When the Spanish Crown heard of the colony's situation, it sent Knight Commander Francisco de Bobadilla to investigate. When he arrived at Santa Dominica in 1500 he was greeted by the sight of the swaying corpses of seven hanged Spanish rebels.[16] Upon alighting he discovered a further seventeen shackled settlers with death sentences hanging over them. Columbus was sent back to Spain in chains and the Knight Commander took it upon himself to oversee the colony.[17]

The colony turned itself around under his management, and sugarcane, as well as food staples, were grown more successfully,[18] but the focus remained on the acquisition of gold. A Taino by the name of Hatüey was overheard explaining to his kin that it was 'gold and jewels' that the Spanish worshipped, not their Christian God, observing: 'For these they fight and kill; for these they persecute us and … they tell us, these tyrants, that they adore a God of peace and equality, and yet they usurp our land and make us their slaves. They speak to us of an immortal soul and of their eternal rewards and punishments, and yet they rob our belongings, seduce our women, violate our daughters. Incapable to matching us in valour, these cowards cover themselves with iron that our weapons cannot break.'[19]

In 1503 the first black slaves were imported from the Canary Islands, not to work the cane fields but to replace the Taino in the gold mines. It took a Spanish surgeon, Gonzalo de Vellosa, to encourage the colonists to focus on sugarcane when he noticed the hike in sugar prices in Europe caused by the timber shortages, and organised for the immigration of sugar masters from the Canaries and the import of cutting-edge vertical mills.[20] It is incredible that there was anything to come of the chaos wreaked by Columbus's tyrannical management at all. The next year, with gaps in the workforce supplemented by black slaves from the gold mines, the first commercially grown West Indian sugar was produced and sent to the king as a gift: a rather paltry six sugar loaves. One expects he wasn't too crestfallen because they were supplemented with large amounts of gold.[21]

The gold mining industry was a flash in the pan, as the colonists quickly mined the majority of deposits. After its demise focus quickly and firmly moved to sugar – white gold – with new colonists bringing over fully trained workers from Madeira and the Canaries: kettlemen to boil down the cane juice into a viscous syrup; purgers to purify and crystallise the sugar; and sugar masters to oversee the entire process. In these early days of sugarcane cultivation oxen were used to plough fields, newly created from 'considerable deforestation'; considerable because each *ingenio* was using around 740kg of wood per day.[22] As we have already seen, *ingenios* need investment; and at first, the Spanish Crown provided it and offered various incentives. They waived taxes on sugar-making equipment, reduced tithes on sugar, and handed out loans and royal grants. There was such a switch to sugar that the island economy quickly became dependent upon it and some remarkable engineering feats were achieved: one *ingenio* had a water mill powered by 'a dam seventy meters long, one of the largest of its time.' However, *ingenio* owners left to their own devices with their grants and generous loans became complacent, taking their time building them and exaggerating their debts so they could receive more grants from the Crown's seemingly infinite coffers.[23]

Meanwhile, Columbus had avoided jail and used his natural doggedness to improve his position at court, both commercially and socially; his grandson had 'strategically married' the king's grandniece and he had acquired the investments needed to reignite his sugar plantation. He returned to Hispaniola in 1520 to create the grandest plantation yet seen, made up of four horse-powered and twenty water mills.[24] The gravitational pull of this super-plantation attracted others and invigorated the remaining planters.

However, the colonists found themselves with a shortage of slave labour, so to compensate for the death of the majority of the Taino, planters scoured the other 'useless islands' of the Bahamas and the Lesser Antilles, capturing 15,000 individuals. These 'imported workers along with the [remaining] native inhabitants, served as the basis for the early growth of the industry and continued to predominate into the middle of the 1520s, far outnumbering the few Africans who began to appear as workers.'

Of course, it wasn't long before these enslaved migrants succumbed, and more Africans were imported to replace them. By the 1540s some 15,000 were being delivered to the Spanish colonies each year. As a result, the colonies' economics had to change because an African slave cost four times that of a West Indian, and consequently many businesses either folded or were bought out by owners of larger plantations. To avoid losing their livelihoods, some turned back to using Indians, while others attempted to diversify by ditching sugar altogether and turned to the production of animal hides. They went about this new industry with as little forethought as they had sugar, and animals were 'killed indiscriminately', their carcasses fed to pigs, thus creating a meat shortage on the island. Not only that, but the value of the currency dropped, and the little sugar that was produced could not compete with the low prices the

Portuguese in Brazil were offering.[25] On the South American mainland Brazilian plantations could spread through the vast rainforests that were feeding the fiery furnaces in their boiling houses, reaching Paraguay and sweeping along the Pacific coast as far north as Mexico, and with that 'the early achievements in Santo Domingo and the rest of the Caribbean were outstripped by the developments on the mainland.'[26]

***

A minority of people condemned the enslavement and treatment of the native people of the West Indies in this early period, especially members of the Church, who criticised the system of granting land containing Taino communities, and they called the colonists out on their greed and inhumanity. It was merely a way of allowing themselves to 'legally' extract gold nuggets without guilt. In 1511 Anton Montesino, a Dominican friar, saw the way the Indians were being treated and preached his concern of the 'cruel and horrible servitude' that they had been forced into, asking 'why do you keep them so oppressed and exhausted without giving them enough to eat or curing them of sickness they incur from the excessive labour you give them, and they die, or rather, you kill them.'[27]

Most famous – or perhaps infamous – of these early humanitarians was Bartolomé de las Casas, who became known as 'Protector of the Indians'. As a younger man, he had owned an *ingenio* on Cuba and produced his own slave-grown sugar. A pious man, he considered himself compassionate and treated his slaves well, until it dawned on him that compassionate slavery was in fact a contradiction in terms.[28] He gave up his plantation and devoted his life to arguing the case against the West Indian people's enslavement. He had seen his slaves, and those of others, quickly succumb to illness and perish, and had observed how they were slaughtered by the Spanish if they mustered the strength to attempt a revolt. When he left Cuba for Hispaniola he witnessed the same mistreatment and could see that the Indians' destruction was inevitable if nothing changed. He wrote later that '[t]heir culture and dignity was robbed from them and they were taunted and humiliated for their religious beliefs and polygamous family structure.' If they committed a 'minor' offence they were punished by having their ears cut off as an example. For more severe crimes, they were set upon by hunting dogs – large mastiff crossbreeds – that 'ripped out their throats or eviscerated them'. Cruel innovations such as these stuck and became standard methods of punishment and correction on all of the West Indian and Northern American sugar plantations right up to the emancipation of the slaves in the nineteenth century.[29] Cruelty was also seen as a good thing for slaves and slave owners alike, for it supposedly made better servants of them. Many were sold onto Europeans, with Columbus himself shipping over 500 to sell at a Seville slave market.[30]

Las Casas estimated that 15 million Indians from several tribes across the whole of the Americas died through colonisation either directly or indirectly.[31] He saw how unjust it all was, and upon hearing him talk, many plantation owners agreed and that it should stop. He went a step too far, however, when he suggested that if they were truly penitent, they should give up their lands and return them to the Indians. Initially this provoked anger, but then the planters came back with a different solution: they would free their Indian slaves as long as they could replace them with black slaves. Blinded by his desperation to free the Indians, Casas agreed, telling them that it was best all round because the Africans on Madeira were so well adapted to their lives on the plantations. Las Casas thought they would thrive in this environment and the Indians, who simply did not have the constitution for this sort of work, could get back to living in peace with nature once more.[32]

So it was decided: 4000 would be imported from Spain, and in doing so, las Casas had facilitated the wholesale 'enslavement of the Africans, [by] giving to humanity with one hand what he took away with another,' instantly mopping up all the available African slaves in Spain. As a result, Portuguese traders brought Africans straight from Africa.[33] With this large influx, the population density of the island increased substantially, and a second swathe of novel communicable diseases cloaked the plantations, affecting Europeans and Indians alike: malaria, yellow fever, dengue fever, hookworm and schistosomiasis.[34] Africans now outnumbered Europeans, and to keep control they were immediately and cruelly overpowered, their fates as chattels now sealed.

It seems inconceivable today that las Casas would not have extended precisely the same logic of the mistreatment of Indian slaves to that of the Africans. Later, he realised his error, writing: 'before there were *ingenios*, we used to think in this island, that, if a negro were not hanged, he would never die, because we had never seen one die of illness, and we were sure that, like oranges, they had found their habitat this island being more natural to them than Guinea. But after they were put to work in the *ingenios*, on account of the excessive labour they had to endure, and the drinks they take made from cane syrup, death and pestilence was the result, and many of them died.'

He admitted that the same argument he used in opposition to the slavery of the Indians applied equally to the people of Africa.[35] Las Casas eventually become Bishop of Chaipas in Mexico, but he resigned the bishopric to campaign against slavery of all types until his death in 1566.[36] However, his championing of the suitability of African slavery over Indian, rather than denouncing all slavery, left an indelible stain on his character. Not only that, but despite all his efforts the exploitation of the Indians did not end. How naïve he had been.

***

The Treaty of Saragossa may have given the Spanish the right to colonise the New World, but in the faraway world of the Americas little regard was paid toward treaty lines, and the Spanish found themselves having to fight off the English and Danish on the sugar islands.[37] Taking full advantage of these distracting scuffles, the Portuguese quietly took Brazil and claimed it for themselves just as sugar production on their island of Madeira was on the wane. As soon as there was enough land cleared, they began growing sugarcane and sought out gold, just like the Spanish. Unlike the Spanish, they hit the ground running by immediately bringing in Portuguese sugar masters (many of them trained black slaves) who had worked the Madeiran *ingenios*.[38] And they did not mess about with the first cargoes of Brazilian sugar beginning to arrive in Europe as early 1519. It didn't take long before the Portuguese Crown saw the trade's potential and gave the colonists financial backing, which in turn attracted more experienced workers.[39]

Accounts by Cuthbert Pudsey, an Englishman who accompanied the Dutch during their invasion of Portuguese Brazil, give us a unique insight into life on these Brazilian sugar plantations in the early seventeenth century. He tells us of their sugar industry and its complexity: 'they Invent mylnes to grinde their sugar reede … foonderes to cast their kettles, masons to make furnaces, carpenters to make chests,' and that the kettles sat on frames, 'in which sugar to purge & refine.' He tells us that the focal point of the plantation was the sugar mill: 'every mylne is as a Common wealth within itself and the lord of the mylne Justicer and Judge within himselfe.'[40]

To allow the sugar industry to thrive the planters needed a labour force, and they used a combination of skilled and unskilled free labour supplemented with slave labour to produce it. They turfed out the Caribs and Aldeas peoples from their villages, razed their settlements and set them to work growing sugar cane and mining gold.[41] Pudsey describes them: 'the woomen are handsoome, well favored, and goe naked, and nevertheless, although this be a wilde divelish people, yet doe they punnish very stricktly any one, that is found in adultery.'[42] Despite their 'wilde' ways they were the 'primary labour force in the sugar economy and remained so until the first decades of the seventeenth century.'[43]

The epidemiological consequences of European colonisation were the same as on Hispaniola: an almost total annihilation of the indigenous people by measles and smallpox that caused many survivors to flee deep into the forests, thus passing disease onto remote undiscovered tribes. And just like on Hispaniola, a shipment of black slaves landed to replace them. Again, black slaves cost much more than Indian slaves, but the Portuguese saw it as a cost-effective business approach; they were stronger, less likely to run away (after all, where would they run to?) and less likely to succumb to disease. Many of these black slaves gained skills on the job, and there would be 'a general tendency … to replace … white artisans with either slaves or former slaves who had gained their freedom.' For example, in 1574 *Ingenio São Jorge* had just seven or eight African slaves who made up seven per cent of the workforce. By 1591 this had increased to thirty-seven per cent, and by 1639 one hundred per cent of the workforce was made up of African slaves. It differs from the Spanish strategy in that the Portuguese brought in many skilled workers who had learned their craft on Madeira.[44]

Portuguese Brazil was also the perfect habitat for growing sugarcane. There were huge swathes of *massapé*, a dark, rich and unique clay soil that was the perfect substrate for this most valuable crop, and 'the portigezes, havinge found the trewe tryall of the land, [found it] excellent for sugar.' It was so good that fresh setts only needed 'to be planted once in seaven years.'[45] A report on Brazil's sugar industry stated: 'The most excellent fruit and drug of sugar grows all over the province in such abundance that it can supply not only the Kingdom [of Portugal] but all the provinces of Europe.'[46] The industry transformed Brazil as it flourished: in the 1570s there were sixty *ingenios*, in 1585 this had risen to 120, and by the 1630s there were 346. This exponential growth was fuelled by demand from Europe and the excellent prices Brazilian sugar could offer. To power the industry at this new scale, the slave trade had to react and intensify to levels never before seen just to meet demand.[47] The Portuguese responded, improving their slavery portfolio by claiming Angola on the east coast of Africa in 1575 and developing a trade in black slaves that would tear 2.8 million Africans from their native lands to the Americas, the overwhelming majority going to Brazil.[48] And with that, the Portuguese gained their monopoly in the trade of both sugar and slaves.

In the 1600s the Portuguese honed their skills in mass sugar production and by the following decade they were shipping 10,000 tons of sugar per year, and up to 20,000 tons per year in the following decade. Pudsey remarked: 'it is an Infynitt of sugar one of these mylnes will make in a summer season.'[49] Efficiency increased by the revolutionary three-roller vertical mill which removed the requirement of a second cane pressing.[50] Its construction was essentially 'two great Pyllars, which are made rounde, bound abowte with Iron, mayde to coome close to each other, but not to touch, and betwixt these pyllars they use to feede with reede by two or three slaves which pass and repass the reede,'[51] and they achieved such good prices because the sugar arrived already refined, graded and gleaming white.

As Spanish and Portuguese sugar took the African Atlantic islands and then the New World, the Dutch carved out a lucrative niche as traders of slaves, sugar and other exotic goods and set up the Dutch West India Company in 1621. However, the company was resentful that the Portuguese had managed to bypass their trading infrastructure altogether, exporting sugar and importing slaves themselves. The Dutch arrived in Brazil in 1626, riddled with scurvy after a seven-month voyage. Despite this, they were in sufficient numbers to successfully capture Salvador and Bahia, destroying several mills in the process.[52] They occupied areas of Brazil for the best part of twenty-five years, but the Dutch were a nation of traders, not manufacturers and it showed, so while they made an attempt at making their sugar, they had no aptitude for the management of the *ingenios* and relied on the expertise of the Portuguese whom they held under militia control. This disruption led to a sudden increase in sugar prices. In 1630 Brazil supplied London with eighty per cent of its sugar, but by 1670 it had dropped by half. This fall should have been a mere blip,

A slave is punished by his overseer on a Brazilian plantation. Note in the background, a slave tied to a tree is receiving a flogging by a black slave driver. It was fairly common to force slaves to punish their peers. (Jean-Basptiste Debret c.1830)

but during this time the English had been working with the few Dutch who had gained some skill and knowledge in the Brazilian *ingenios* and were producing substantial amounts of sugar much closer to Europe.[53]

This caused yet another significant shift in the sugar trade which meant that there had to be an equivalent shift in the slave trade. As a result, Brazil received fewer slaves and was subject to a substantial increase in prices. At the same time there was a drop in sugar prices associated with the waxing Anglo-Caribbean industry and so Brazil also had to drop its prices.[54] The Brazilian plantations struggled to compete and stopped making a profit, but they had followed the pattern of burning bright and creating vast wealth before petering out just as the industry, driven by fickle capitalism, was picked up somewhere else. The English had taken some of the West Indian islands and applied the Portuguese model with a level of exploitation, violence and oppression that dwarfed anything yet seen. The darkest history of sugar belongs to England, its colonies and empire. Yes, Britain would be the first to abolish slavery, but not before it had set up the largest, most complex and cruellest trade in, and treatment of, African slaves.

Chapter 4

Life on the Sugar Colonies

> Circumstances had given the Spaniards and the Portuguese
> a substantial start in the race. But soon crowding on their
> heels came exiles and adventurers from England.
>
> *V.T. Harlow*[1]

If the Portuguese in Brazil drove the sugar industry in the sixteenth century, then the English most certainly picked up the reins in the seventeenth. Already a great consumer of sugar, it was just a matter of time before it would achieve a stake in the industry. With some trial and error, they made a vast amount of white gold, but it was only achieved with ruthlessness and brutality on a scale never before seen. If you were expecting that the liberal and gentlemanly English would make things a bit more civilised then you'd be very wrong. England's century was one of great riches and even greater cruelty.

The story of how the English managed to achieve this begins in 1592 when infamous buccaneer Captain Sir John Hawkins 'acquired' some black slaves while on a voyage to Africa to procure goods such as ivory and gold with which to trade. Before we go on, it should be pointed out there were a lot of euphemisms being used at the time for the despicable acts done by supposedly civilised gentlemen, so when I say 'procure' what I really mean is 'steal', and a 'buccaneer' is a pirate, as is an 'adventurer'. Adventurers such as Hawkins were important because they established novel trade routes around and between Africa and the Americas, away from mainland Europe's beady eye.

Piracy was big business and the English excelled at it. In the 1570s Sir Frances Drake had managed to steal £40,000 worth of gold, silver and pearls from the Spanish, and sacked Santo Domingo.[2] Based on these early successes, 'Queen Elizabeth in the 30th year of her reign, erected a Company for the better carrying on of the Trade [to the Coast of Africa], and making Discoveries in Africa,'[3] and in the last two decades of the sixteenth century, and until 1604, English piracy was responsible for acquiring £100,000 worth of booty per annum.[4]

Pirates could not be too picky when they attacked trade ships laden with goods, because they only found out what those goods were when they boarded. This was how Hawkins came to procure 300 African slaves from the Portuguese, which he later exchanged for repairs and upkeep to his ship on Hispaniola. This makes Hawkins the first Englishman to trade black slaves. This did not make him part of the slave trade proper, just an opportunistic thief, albeit one with a title and backing from the English Crown. All he cared about really was that they could be traded for something else more useful. Once on Santo Domingo, Hawkins saw the gold and sugar plantations and dutifully reported all of this to the English Crown. When he returned to the West Indies, he brought with him six ships, two of which belonged to Queen Elizabeth herself. He filled his boots, and amongst the swag was the first West Indian sugar to arrive on English soil.[5]

In the 1560s the only nation to legally own any of the West Indies was the Spanish, but these islands were on the fringes of their newly extended empire and they only laid down substantial colonies on the Greater Antilles (Cuba, Hispaniola, Jamaica and Puerto Rico).[6] The Lesser Antilles were important to the Spanish for the cultivation of a few staples, and as a useful stopping-off point for ships sailing from Seville to the colonies. During the tensions of the Anglo-Spanish War (1585-1604), their absolute ownership was taken away when the English laid claim to several islands of the Lesser Antilles. Later, St Christopher was taken from the Spanish in 1624 in a rare display of collusion between the English and the French and was considered England's mother colony. At the time, the Dutch held nearby St Martin and regularly supported the two nations during Spanish attacks. The three nations also worked together to protect themselves from the fearsome Caribs[7] whom the colonists killed in '[g]reat numbers including their King.'[8] The English then went on to take other islands in the archipelago: Barbados, Nevis and Antigua, as well as parts of the southern and central American coast.

All of this buccaneering, fighting and theft went on 'beyond the line': far enough away from mainland Europe for 'a general flouting of European social conventions [where] they robbed and massacred … more freely than the rules of civility permitted in European combat.' Their investors

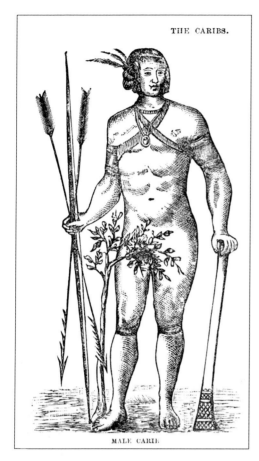

THE CARIBS.

MALE CARIB

An 1888 wood engraving of a male Carib, a formidable people who often killed and cannibalised their prisoners. They were the inspiration for the character Man Friday in Daniel Defoe's 1719 novel *Robinson Crusoe*. (Library of Congress)

back in England were happy to turn a blind eye as long as they got a good return on their investments. The French took Martinique, Cayenne and the Guyana coast in addition to St Christopher. Then, in 1655, in what is described as an 'example of the aggressive self-confidence of the *nouveau riche*, the English took Jamaica,' in the heart of the Caribbean. Though excellent for adventuring buccaneers, Jamaica did not significantly contribute to the sugar industry of the British plantations in their formative years. Much later, the English would go on to take the islands of Grenada, Dominica and St Vincent during the Seven Years War (1756-1763).[9] As the English and French picked up islands, the Dutch took the trade routes; the Treaty of Saragossa was no longer worth the vellum it was written on, and Spain and Portugal were forced to recognise begrudgingly that other nations now had stakes the in New World and Africa.

These early colonists' lives and attitudes were very different from the New England and Chesapeake pioneers. Judging by their behaviour, it is hard to believe that they were all part of the same series of migrations populating the English Americas. The mainlanders lived relatively austere lives within their means, in a place with a seasonal climate much more similar to that of England. However, the West Indian colonists 'lived fast, spent recklessly, played desperately and died young.' Prior to their migration, the English had 'heard ample tales about the gold and pearls that had been found in these isles and stories of Spanish cruelty, English robbery, and Indian and Negro slavery. They associated the Indies with incredible wealth and amazing savagery. Everything was larger than life.'

They were expecting to find an El Dorado that was never there – though they lived the life regardless. These stories attracted 'mettlesome gamblers' who could see the method by which they could make their fortunes, and so rapidly turned the islands into 'sugar-making machines', and throughout the seventeenth and eighteenth centuries used hundreds of thousands of slaves to make it happen.[10] This was entirely different from those mainlanders who were steadily and piously developing their towns to live out their lives in permanence in their New England.

During the seventeenth and early eighteenth centuries the colonies received many English visitors; traders, naturalists, anthropologists and missionaries, as well as the well-to-do on extended, meandering holidays, came to the islands, and they wrote detailed accounts of all aspects of daily life. The great historian V.T. Harlow's detailed history of the early colonisers and wonderful collection of edited manuscripts, letters and journals from the period are captured in *Colonising Expeditions to the West Indies and Guiana, 1623-1667*. Hans Sloane, the future founder of the British Museum, himself an investor in the slave and sugar trade, made detailed observations in the introduction to his 1707 book *A voyage to the islands Madera, Barbados, Nieves, S. Christophers and Jamaica*. Richard S. Dunn's wonderfully written history, *Sugar and Slaves: The Rise of the Planter Class in the English West Indies, 1624-1713* (1972) is a comprehensive synthesis of a century's journals and letters, and his account of life on the English sugar plantations is indispensable. The most important primary source is Richard Ligon's *A True & Exact History Of the Island of Barbados* (1657). Upon deciding that England during the English Civil War wasn't the safest place to be, Ligon upped sticks in 1647 and remained on Barbados for three years.[11] His accounts are detailed, comprehensive and vividly describe workers' conditions and the relationships between planter, servant, African and Indian. Aside from these manuscripts, we have almost no information on the social history of the slaves of the seventeenth century because the slaves left behind no written evidence of their own. Therefore, the only accounts of their lives and personalities come from those white Christian Englishmen who are often naïve, racist, patronising and chauvinistic. However, they seem blissfully unaware that their attitudes and prejudices were in any way wrong.

The first English colonists arrived on the West Indies on the *William and John* in 1627. On board were sixty English settlers and six black slaves who had been taken, in typical fashion, from an unwitting Portuguese ship *en route*.[12] The prospectors expected to find their fortunes on these islands in gold, minerals, dyewoods or pearls just as other nations had on the Atlantic islands and on the South American mainland. Unfortunately, they didn't find any of those; what they *did* find was that they were stuck out on a limb on the edge of a minor archipelago thousands of miles from home in an oppressively humid 'perpetual blazing summer'. Forced to 'moderate their expectations', they turned their attention to cash crops such as tobacco and cocoa,[13] but 'looking about them for some more lucrative employment, the settlers determined to imitate the Dutch sugar planters of Brazil ... Unfortunately, ignorance in the art of sugar making rendered their early efforts abortive. It was only after two or three years of failure that the proper methods of planting, grinding, and boiling were learnt from the Dutch ... The hardship and anxiety attending this period may well be imagined. But Roundhead and Royalist alike worked with patience – experimenting, learning and finally achieving success.'[14]

They persisted, and within just a few growing seasons it was evident that sugarcane was 'to be the main Plant, to improve the value of the whole Iland: And forbent all [of the settlers'] endeavours to advance their knowledge in the planting and making [of] Sugar.'[15] It certainly had them coming into contact with a lot more gold than they ever would by mining or plundering it from the Spanish. One major contributing factor to their success was that the islands of the Lesser Antilles were closer to Africa than either the Spanish or Portuguese colonies, which meant better access to slave ships.

A great deal was achieved during these initial years of hardship. This can be attributed to the fact that the two warring factions of Roundheads and Royalists cast aside their political differences. Indeed, when Cromwell later demanded allegiance from the Barbados planters 'the island government stood firm, announcing their unalterable determination to remain neutral.'[16]

The soil and climate were perfect for growing sugarcane. However, what was perfect for the cane was quite the opposite for the English, whose constitution was more used to chilly drizzle and a couple of weeks of sun in June. Here it was sweltering. Add to that the dangerous and irritating flora and fauna associated with such environments, and it became all too hard to bear, or it would have been were it not for the expectation of a great fortune coming their way. Indeed, by 1640s sugarcane was considered such a cash crop that tobacco was dropped altogether in favour of a sugarcane monoculture.

In the early years of colonisation the English were very much dependent upon Dutch traders 'with their inexpensive ships and superior banking system … By availing themselves of the easy terms which were offered, the planters were able to buy [goods] from them [and] provide them with food.'[17] It was a simple set up, and as soon as one had sugar to trade one had access to all sorts of staples and fancy goods.[18] But it wasn't long before that familiarly began to breed contempt. The English soon became unhappy with the fact that the Dutch had done rather too much of a good job in establishing their monopoly over trade routes, and they attempted to compete. A 'bitter rivalry [developed] between the English "Company of Royal Adventurers trading to Africa" and the Dutch, who had done their utmost by threats and violence to exclude the English from the slave trade.'[19] Eventually, in the 1670s the English achieved their own monopoly in both trade and cultivation with the creation of the Royal African Company, establishing the infamous triangular trade route: taking sugar from the colonies to English docks, loading up with food, fancy goods and equipment before sailing on to West Central Africa to capture and export slaves to the English sugar islands.

The English settlements were not – and could not – be a replication of their lives in England. Even so, they brought with them English clothes, shipped over their English furniture and built English-style homes to put them in. Almost everything was imported:

> The Commodities these Ships bring to this Iland: are, Servants and Slaves, both men and women; Horses, Cattle, Assinigoes [donkeys], Camells, Utensills for boyling Sugar, Coppers, Taches, Goudges, and Sockets; all manner of working tooles for Trades-men, as, Carpenters, Joyners, Smiths, Masons, Mill-wrights, Wheel-wrights, Tinkers, Coopers, &c. Iron, Steel, Lead, Brasse, Pewter, Cloth of all kinds, both Linnen and wollen Stuffs, Hatts, Hose,

> Shoos, Gloves, Swords, knives, Locks, Keys, &c. Victualls
> of all kinds, that will endure the Sea, in so long a voyage.
> Olives, Capers, Anchovies, salted Flesh and Fish, pickled
> Maquerelles and Herrings, Wines of all sorts, and the boon
> Beer, d'Angleterre.[20]

Barbados even had to import timber from the 1680s, such was the scale of the deforestation in the English sugar colonies.[21]

The English also brought with them their social structure and their prejudices. Maintaining the distinctions between classes meant everyone knew their place, and as a consequence it was clear that those at the bottom had little chance of moving up the ladder, and those a few rungs up knew very well the significant likelihood of slipping down. At the very top were the big planters, then the small planters, tradesmen, then indentured servants and finally the black slaves. The big planters lived ostentatiously in their showy clothes, periwigs, frockcoats and multi-layered petticoats, all totally unsuitable for the climate.[22] They quickly rejected the tropical staples and dined on pies, boiled and roasted meats and drank beer. Sometimes their showiness became gratuitous; wealthy planters who owned many slaves often dressed their favourites in the finest livery and had them carrying out 'ceremonial tasks' in their grand houses.[23]

To keep up appearances many planters lived on a financial knife-edge, often mortgaging the following year's sugar crop to pay for that year's luxuries. The average worth of an estate on Barbados at the end of the seventeenth century was £2,000, but this average hides the fact there was a very uneven distribution of wealth, and most planters lived in 'grinding poverty'.[24] Many of the islands' poorest were made up of the scholarly: schoolmasters, booksellers and the clergy. A few did die with decent estates, but only those who had had a stake in a plantation.[25]

Of the English colonists, indentured servants found themselves at the bottom of the social pile. These servants were not the well-respected butlers and liverymen one might imagine in the upper classes' grand houses of the time, but the dregs and unfortunates of society. Initially, they were made up by the peasant class who, upon arriving, didn't know where they fitted or did not have the funds or skills to start a plantation of their own. Sugar plantations require labour, so a place for them was quickly established. As the plantations grew in number and size, these peasants were needed more and more.

Things changed during the Civil War (1642–1651), when instead of receiving peasant migrants, the colonies began to receive prisoners of war. Such was the success of this system that after the war an act was passed in England in 1652 allowing magistrates to send criminals to the colonies and serve their sentence in servitude.[26] These servants were treated with disdain and viewed largely as worthless troublemakers. This indentured labour system conveniently solved the problem of overcrowding in English prisons, but disease and exhaustion kept the turnover of these convicts high, and soon the English courts found it difficult to keep up with demand from the colonies. To solve this problem, judges began to sentence individuals to a stint of servitude on trumped-up charges, just to help keep the plantations fully-stocked.[27]

The courts were not the only source of indentured labour: mysterious people dubbed 'the Spirits' helped to maintain a healthy black market trade in white servants. There are several cases of them taking drunks, and even drugging unsuspecting unfortunates to 'spirit' them away on ships bound for the sugar islands complete with forged papers.[28] However the servants were sourced, 'they [were] put to very hard labour, ill lodging, and their dyet [was] very sleight.'[29] Richard Ligon observed: 'if they be not strong men, this ill lodging will put them into a sicknesse: if they complain, they are beaten by the Overseer: if they resist, their time is doubled. I have seen an Overseer beat a Servant with a cane about the head, till the blood has followed, for a fault that is not worth the speaking of; and yet he must have patience, or worse will follow. Truly, I have seen such cruelty there done to Servants, as I did not think one Christian could have done to another.'[30]

All rights were taken away from them, and any subsequence offence – serious or petty – could add several years to their period of servitude. They were not allowed to engage in any type of commerce and they had few or no possessions. The punishments they received were corporal, though extremely severe. Only very rarely were capital punishments used; these were reserved for black slaves. These white servants were not chattels like the African slaves. It was 'the Custome for a Christian servant to serve foure years, and then enjoy his freedom,' and they fully expected to leave the horrors of the place, unlike 'the Negros and Indians [who] are Slaves to their owners to perpetuity.'[31]

Of all of the sugar islands, Barbados was the most societally developed because it was the coolest and least humid of the islands, though it was not without its hazardous weather: 'The Winter onely consisteth of great raignes; it beginneth aboute Agust, and lasteth till Christmas, in which time wee have often Land flood, which fall into Severall gullies, that many lose their Lives. Not three Weekes since above a dozen were drowned, as alsoe some horses and Asugos [donkeys] Lauden with Suggar, a Gentleman that waited on my Lord was drowned not ¼ of a mile from our dwelling, and one other of our family hardly escaped with his life.'[32] It had no mountains or rivers, but was covered in dense forest that would be almost wholly cleared within forty years to make space for sugarcane: 'Before the colonists came, the island was thickly covered with primeval forest, in which large herds of wild hogs roamed at large. But now the woods have gone, and the traveller's gaze is met by planters' houses and negro cabins dotted among the sugar canes, and by the handsome port of Bridgetown.'[33]

'A topographicall description and admeasurement of the yland of Barbados in the West Indyaes' Richard Ligon's map showing the position of the larger plantations on the island at the turn of the eighteenth century. The map also shows other regions and the activities associated with them, including areas hiding escaped slaves. (Jessica Lee)

Jamaica had rich valleys, regular heavy rainfall and daily morning fog which made it difficult to traverse, requiring one to travel by horse. The conditions for photosynthesis, however, were perfect, making the land verdant and the life it supported, fecund. The colonists found it 'a very strange thing to see' how quickly the old Spanish houses had already become 'quite overgrown' by the roots of tall trees.[34] As they felled those trees, they discovered that some were aggressive:

> The fellers, as they cut them down, are very carefull of their eyes … for if any of the sap flie into their eyes, they become blinde for a month. A Negre had two Horses to walke … and the Horses beginning to fight, the Negre was afeard; and let them go; and they running into the wood together, struck at one another, and their heeles hitting some young trees of this kind, struck the poysonous juice into one anothers eyes … and they were both led home stone blind, and continued so a month, all the hair and skin pilling off their faces … And as this tree's poyson is in her sap … and 'tis said to be one of those poysons, wherewith the Indian Caniballs invenome their Arrowes.[35]

The sheer amount of plant life produced a diverse ecosystem, including a large number of vermin and irritating insects. Everyone was tormented by insects, though the gnats and mosquitoes were particularly annoying, making a feast of everyone as soon as they arrived: 'you have such aboundance of smale knatts by the sea shoare towards the sunn goinge down yet bite so as noe rest can be had,'[36] and were 'of so small a sise, and so thin and aereall, [one could only discern them] by the noise of their wings, which is like a small bugle horn, at a great distance: Where they sting, there will rise a little knob, as big as a pease, and last so a whole day; the mark will not be gone in twenty four hours.'[37] To rid the room of mosquitoes at night they were forced to sleep in hammocks set over fire,[38] and those that were too stubborn to give up their beds sat their legs in water to deter 'Cockroches, a creature of the bignesse and shape of a Beetle … He appears in the evening when 'tis dark, and will, when he pleases, flie to your bed, when he findes you sleeping, and bite your skin, till he fetch blood, if you do not wake; and if you take a Candle to search for him, he shifts away and hides himself … The Negres, who have thick skins, and by reason of their hard labour, sleep soundly at night, are bitten so … their skins are rac't, as if it were done with a currie-comb.'[39]

Even the ants gained a fearsome reputation. According to Hans Sloane, 'Ants are said to have killed the Spanish Children by eating their Eyes when they were left in their Cradles.'[40] And if that wasn't enough, there were the 'Scorpions, of which, some of them … as big as Ratts.'[41] Worst of all were chiggers – mites that bury themselves under the toenails, causing horrible foot ulcers and infected lesions, and Richard Ligon got first hand (or perhaps, foot) experience of them:

> This vermine will get thorough your Stocken, and in a pore of your skinne, in some part of your feet, commonly under the nayl of your toes, and there make a habitation to lay his offspring, as bigge as a small Tare … which will cause you to go very lame … The Indian women have the best skill to take them out, which they do by putting in, a small poynted Pinne, or Needle, at the hole where he came in, and winding the poynt about the bagge loosen him from the flesh, and so take him out. He is of a blewish colour, and is seene through the skinne, but the Negroes whose skinns are of that colour (or neer it) are in ill case, for they cannot finde where they are; by which meanes they are many of them very lame: some of these Chegoes [chiggers] are poysonous, and after they are taken out, the Orifice in which they lay, will fester and rankle for a fortnight after they are gone. I have had tenne taken out of my feet in a morning.[42]

Therefore, a decent pair of shoes was essential, and plantation owners made sure their white servants had them,[43] though this goodwill was not extended to their slaves.

The oppressive humidity and high temperature could not be escaped: daytime temperatures were consistently over 30°C. The humid air quickly rusted anything made of iron: 'This moysture of the ayre, causes all our knives, etweese [tweezers], keyes, necdles, swords, and ammunition, to rust; and that in an instant for take your knife to the grindstone, and grind away all the rust; which done, wipe it dry, and put it up into your sheath, and so into your pocket, and in a very little time, draw it out, and you shall find it beginning to rust all over.'[44]

The English colonists could have chosen areas of the island that were breezier, but they chose to avoid the coast because of the constant threat of hurricanes and Carib attacks. Their houses could have had better ventilation too, but at the time it was believed that breathing outside air at night was bad for health, so they opted instead to hide away in stuffy sheltered spots.[45]

Storms and hurricanes were 'quick and terrific,'[46] and many lives and buildings were lost to them. The worst hurricane of the seventeenth century was on Barbados in 1675. It took just three hours to kill 200 people, destroy 1000 houses, three churches and almost all of the mills. In hurricane season people took to living in caves and even strapped themselves to trees. The English were very suspicious of the Caribs' uncanny skills in predicting encroaching hurricanes; when they attempted to forewarn the English, instead of heeding good advice they assumed they must have been liaising with the devil to acquire such knowledge, concluding that it was their witchcraft that was forcing God to send such storms in the first place.[47] Aside from the extreme weather there were 'terrifying earthquakes' that were all 'too frequent'.[48] One on Nevis caused an entire town to slide into the sea, and another destroyed Jamaica's main port, drowning and burying hundreds alive.[49] However, 'despite Indian attacks, starvation, internal feuds and civil war, and the danger of destruction by Spaniards, Dutch, and French, these small communities steadily grew in prosperity.'[50]

***

When the colonists first landed on the West Indies they ate local produce, but they preferred standard British fare: bread, beef, beer and cider. However, they could not be self-sufficient with respect to bread and beer because neither suited the climate: wheat and barley would not grow well; the humidity and warmth turned flour rancid and bread mouldy, and they were both a magnet for insect pests; and low alcohol drinks like cider and ale quickly spoiled 'in this strange climate.'[51] Despite all this, they would not lower themselves to eating tropical foods, which were only fit – in their opinion – for the savage Indians, so they put up with weevils in the flour and turned their noses up at perfectly edible and plentiful cassava bread complaining that 'Cassavi makes bread of noe tast. It is tough, & very hard when it is dry, & looks white like chalk.'[52]

Slaves were given 'meagre rations' of bland, starchy tropical and European foods such as 'corn, plantains, sweet potatoes, peas and beans.'[53] Those slaves who were allowed to cultivate their own crops found it a real slog because their harvest time coincided with the sugar harvest, and it was not always possible to muster the energy to work on their plots as well. It is ironic that many slaves had a more varied diet than their masters, though tiny portions kept them hungry and therefore their spirits low, reducing the chances of revolt. The bulk of their diet was made up of 'loblolly', a bland porridge of mashed overcooked maize meal made 'by pounding it in a large Morter, and boyling it in water, to the thicknesse of Frumentie [wheat porridge]; and so put in a Tray such a quantity, as wil serve a messe of seven or eight people, give it them cold, and scarce afford them salt with it. This we call Lob-lollie. But the Negres, when they come to be fed with this, are much discontented, and crie out, O! O! no more Lob-lob.'[54]

When it came to meat, the English preferred beef. Unfortunately, cattle did not take to life in the tropics and produced low-quality meat, so beef had to be imported cured in barrels. By contrast, pigs took to the tropics very successfully, their flesh becoming 'the most generall meat, and indeed the best the Iland affords.' A great deal of fish was imported, and planters dined on cured salmon, while slaves were given poor quality salt cod and haddock, or pickled herring and mackerel from New England and Newfoundland.[55] Slaves and servants were only given fresh meat when 'cattle dyed by mischance by any disease: the servants eat the bodies, and the Negroes the skinnes, head, and entrails,'[56] though they were allowed to catch and eat wild animals: 'Racoon … is eaten. Rats are likewise sold by the dozen, and when they have been bread amongst the Sugar Canes, are thought by some discerning people very delicious Victuals. Snakes or Serpants and *Cossi* (a sort of Worms) are eaten by the Indians and Negros.'[57]

This is in stark contrast to a meal that Ligon attended in one planter's house where a single course was made up of:

> a Potato pudding, a dish of Scots Collips of a legge of
> Porke, as good as any in the world, a fricacy of the same,
> a dish of boyl'd Chickens, a shoulder of a young Goate …
> a Kid with a pudding in his belly, a sucking pig … with the
> pognant sauce of the brains … a shoulder of mutton which

is there a rare dish, a Pasty of the side of a young Goate … a loyne of Veale, to which there wants no sauce being so well furnisht with Oranges, Lymons, and Lymes, three young Turkies in a dish, two Capons, of which sort I have seen some extreame large and very fat, two henns with egges in a dish, four Ducklings, eight Turtle doves, and three Rabbets and for cold bak't meats, two Muscovie Ducks larded, and season'd well with pepper and salt.[58]

***

The English kept their slaves at arm's length, at least in the first few decades of the seventeenth century: they were not allowed to enter planters' homes, and they would not allow them to convert to Christianity. Ligon befriended an African slave and enquired if Christianisation could be made possible, but was told that 'being once a Christian, he could no more account him a Slave, and so lose the hold they had of them as Slaves, by making them Christians; and by that means should open such a gap, as all the Planters in the Iland would curse him. So I was struck mute, and poor Sambo kept out of the Church; as ingenious, as honest, and as good a natur'd poor soul, as ever wore black.'[59]

Worried that they would civilise these heathens too much, it was decided it would be more appropriate to take the opposite approach and treat them like pack animals, dehumanised and required only for work.[60] One supposes they slept easier at night after dishing out the horrors of the day, safe in the knowledge that these men, women and children were not that different from cattle or horses.[61] The Portuguese and Spanish took a different view. They saw slaves as humans – albeit a primitive sort – who therefore had to be Christianised. These fundamentally different attitudes led to different behaviour. The Spanish and Portuguese had obligations to their slaves now that they were fellow Christians: for example, all of God's men could enjoy days of rest on Sundays and Holy Days, so one can argue that these slaves' lives were less harsh than those of slaves on the English colonies. However, having a new religion and way of life thrust upon them had a detrimental cultural effect because many of their languages, beliefs and customs died. Ironically, on the English colonies where they were not viewed as human beings, any Christian obligations could be waived and therefore the slaves were able to hang onto many of their beliefs and customs.[62] Left to their own devices, they sang and danced, and created a patois that their owners could not understand. Hans Sloane tells us, '[t]he Indians and Negros have no manner of Religion by what I could observe of them. 'Tis true they have several Ceremonies, as Dances, Playing &c. but these for the most part are so far from being Acts of Adorations of a God, that they are for the most part mixt with a great deal of Bawdry and Lewdness.'[63]

'A Negro Festival drawn from Nature in the Island of St Vincent' 1801. On the larger islands, festivals such as these were quickly made illegal, but were allowed to continue on the smaller, more lenient islands. (National Maritime Museum)

They were inventive and creative: 'They have several sorts of Instruments in imitation of Lutes, made of small Gourds fitted with Necks, strung with Horse hairs' and rattles tied to their ankles.'[64] In keeping with typical seventeenth century thinking, the English interpreted it as witchcraft and devil worship and restricted it. The planters banned the use of drums, paranoid that slaves were communicating with each other between plantations, so much so that it became law that no slave master 'shall permit or suffer his or their Negro … at any time hereafter to beat Drums, blow Horns, or use any other loud Instruments, and shall not cause his Negro-Houses once every week to be diligently searched, and such Instruments, if any be found, cause to be burned.'

If any masters were seen to be allowing a 'publick Meeting or Feasting of strange Negroes [they] shall forfeit Fifty Shillings Sterling for every offence.'[65] Many mistook their songs and dancing as an indication of their contentment, but this could not have been further from the truth; their songs reflected their sorrow. The slaves sang because they *wanted* to be happy, not because they *were* happy. For them, it was escapism, fleeting moments in time where they could escape their torment, a behaviour also displayed by convicts sentenced to lard labour.[66]

Song was allowed when it helped keep up tempo and spirits during repetitive tasks, often aided by a nip of rum to help warm the muscles.[67] Singing together also produced solidarity, but this had to be tempered by the overseers; too much could lead to unrest, yet too little caused efficiency to drop. On the more draconian large plantations, little or no time was allowed for slaves to let off steam, and so they had to sneak away to the plantations' borders to play music, socialise and dance secretly.[68]

The English planters of the West Indies were the first Englishmen to practise slavery on a vast scale, and they took to it like ducks to water. Portugal and Spain both took a while to come round to the wholesale adoption of black slaves, but the English had seen how important slaves were in Dutch Brazil, so they imported them in great numbers. Remember, too, that there were black slaves on the first English colonists' boats, picked up with a load of other booty *en route* to the islands, so there was never a time when there were no African slaves were on the English plantations. On Barbados in 1627 there were ten slaves; by 1642 there were 500; three years later there were 1,000, and by 1660 there were 20,000 slaves on the English sugar colonies.[69]

The colonists' policy of dehumanisation worked very well, and consequently the English regime was to be 'one of the harshest systems of servitude in Western history.' However, '[e]ven the most authoritarian master, supported by the most oppressive laws, was to some extent limited by the will of his slaves, who had the power to appeal, flatter, humiliate, disobey, sabotage or rebel.'[70] The severity of their foul treatment changed throughout the seventeenth century as the black slave population grew and quickly overtook Europeans in number. By 1730 African slaves outnumbered whites four to one.[71] As the population grew, the work became more gruelling and their treatment worse as the English got to grips with oppressing a forever-expanding slave population.

Richard Ligon was particularly interested in the slave population and made this comparison between the Africans and Indians:

> [The Indians] are very active men, and apt to learne any thing, sooner then the Negroes; and as different from them in shape, almost as in colour; the men very broad shoulder'd, deep breasted, with large heads and their faces almost three square, broad about the eyes and temples, and sharpe at the chinne, their skins some of them brown, some a bright Bay, they are much craftier, and subtiler then the Negroes; and in their nature falser; but in their bodies more active, their women have very small breasts, and have more of the shape of the Europeans then the Negroes, their haire black and long, a great part where of hangs downe upon their backs, as low as their hanches, with a large lock hanging over either brest, which seldome or never curles.[72]

Male African slaves were regarded as 'beasts of burden',[73] and the women were objectified, as this description by Richard Ligon illustrates: 'The young Maides have ordinarily very large breasts, which stand strutting out so hard and firm, as no leaping, jumping, or stirring, will cause them to shake any more, then the brawnes of their armes.'[74]

The Africans' polygamous family structures remained broadly intact for some time. Males insisted upon having multiple wives and many children were born. Pregnant women were exempt from lashings until the baby was born, but the women were worked just as hard during pregnancy 'and hence suffer[ed] many an abortion; which some managers are unfeeling enough to express their joy.'[75] When their child was born, they were allowed two weeks to rest and bond with their child before returning to the plantation: 'In a fortnight, this woman is at worke with her Pickaninny at her back, as merry a soule as any is there: If the overseer be discreet, shee is suffer'd to rest her feete a little more then ordinary; but if not, shee is compelled to doe as others doe.'[76]

Hans Sloane despaired of their postnatal physique: 'The Mother when she suckles her young, having no Cloths to keep her Breasts from falling down, they hang very lank ever after, like those of Goats.'[77] Slaves were not allowed to name their children; babies were named by overseers. Sometimes they would give them African or English names, but more often they would degrade them with names such as 'Monkey, Baboon, Hard Times, Trouble, Oxford [and] Cambridge.' However, the most popular name was 'Sambo.' And with these names, they were placed 'in limbo somewhere between the dumb beasts and rational men.'[78]

Inevitably, there was a significant amount of interracial sex, both forced and consensual. It will probably come as no surprise that it was the consensual sex with which the English had a problem. In 1644, standard punishments surrounding fornication were set, and they tell us a lot about the differences between slaves, servants and freemen. For example, if a free white man or woman was found to have had sex with a black slave, they were fined. If it was a white servant, their punishment was to have their bond extended, black slaves found guilty of fornication with whites were branded with hot irons and whipped. However, slave masters would often sleep with slave women, keeping the prettiest ones in their homes as domestic servants to facilitate access. Many of these men were young bachelors or newly married with young families, away from home for the first time. Although disallowed, a blind eye was usually turned, but if a slave master or overseer were found to be having sexual relations with a white servant, they were typically dismissed of their duties.[79]

Many mixed-race 'mulatto' children were loved by their white parents: a Jamaican planter named William Bonner fathered four children with one of his slaves, and when he died he freed their mother and gave each child one hundred acres of land.[80] That all four children were born to the same mother and that she was freed suggests there was a stable family unit, and that Bonner knew of his responsibilities, though he obviously did not feel responsible enough to manumit the mother *before* he died. Unfortunately, most mullato children were not born of these circumstances, and simply became slaves.[81]

As the decades went on, especially from the early eighteenth century, owners started freeing their slaves when they retired. Thomas Wordall, a Barbados councillor, freed all slaves over thirty-four years of age and had them baptised. But don't be fooled, these gestures were not without cynicism: slaves had been worked so hard that by their mid-thirties they were physically exhausted and freeing them meant their ex-owners were no longer obliged to clothe and feed them. Richard S. Dunn points out that freed slaves and mullatoes 'were not allowed to vote, hold office, have profitable jobs or much land,'[82] and so ended up stuck on an island they despised and continued to work the plantations for a pittance. There was no escape.

Chapter 5

Making Sugar

The discipline of a sugar plantation is as exact as that of a regiment: at four o'clock in the morning the plantation bell rings to call the slaves to the field. Their work is to manure, dig, and hoe, plow the ground, to plant, weed and cut the cane, to bring it to the mill, to have the juices expressed and boiled into sugar.

James Ramsay[1]

A white European in the New World had several career options ahead of him: the romantic life of the buccaneer lured many, and many chose to farm one of several exciting exotic cash crops such as ginger, citrus fruits, pimento chillies, tobacco, indigo and cacao. But those who wanted to make *serious* money went into the sugar business where the potential profits were better than any other New World crop or commodity.

The English had had the benefit of receiving enough investment from the motherland to create the infrastructure needed to become the world leader in the sugar trade, but planters had their work cut out: they had to clear and develop land, purchase livestock, and import food for their labourers, servants, slaves and livestock. They also had to import building materials, tools, hardware and specialist equipment.[2] And when everything had been purchased, the whole affair had to be organised and implemented with skilled precision. A plantation was a well-oiled machine, and it was a machine of many parts. Planting times had to be staggered so that the millers and boilers could be worked at their optimum output. The men and women of the associated trades such as sawyers, coopers, carpenters and blacksmiths had to anticipate supply and demand of their products. It is easy to see how running a plantation was certainly no mean feat, and comparing it to the standards of the day, work was efficient and well-organised.

England was proud of its productive sugar islands, but successful planters had to take a completely different attitude towards land cultivation and management back home, the main difference being of course that to make the enormous profits that they and their investors expected, the brutal work was carried out by slaves and indentured servants. This meant that the Englishmen in these colonies had to handle their workforce very differently to their countrymen back home. A fortune could be made as long as one had appropriate initial investment, focus, skill, drive, and to no small degree, ruthlessness and luck.[3] Storms and disease could raze entire towns and plantations, but carelessness could cause equal damage. The sugar business was also highly unpredictable; profits wildly fluctuated due to acts of God and the constantly changing sugar prices and costs of slaves. Boom years could be followed by sudden drops in production and so planters needed to know about financial planning and debt management. They had to be tenacious too, for they were dependent upon merchants who provided them with the credit to buy slaves and brought with them new equipment, clothing, and fancy goods. Then there was the Crown, which provided naval and military support and protection from other nations in the Atlantic colonies.

Above all else, though, they were reliant upon a steady supply of African slaves who were transported and traded by the Royal African Company during England's peak sugar-producing years.[4] Sugar production doubled, and even trebled, on some of the larger plantations: in 1650 Barbados exported 7,000 tons of sugar, and by 1700 the colonies exported 25,000 tons, overtaking Brazil's sugar production by 3,000 tons.[5] Unfortunately, this was reflected in the slave trade. At its peak in the eighteenth century the West Indies imported 74,000 slaves per annum, more than all of the other European nations put together.[6] Meanwhile, the Portuguese and Spanish colonies were just about breaking even, relying on the production of spirits from by-products to creep back into the black. The English policy of receiving free trade sugar from the colonies and then selling the excess to Europe was such an effective model that by 1700 Barbados alone was shipping 143 tons of sugar per annum and 200 ships were needed to transport it away.[7]

***

A typical planter in the seventeenth and early eighteenth centuries required two mills and around eighty acres of land to plant and harvest enough sugarcane to yield around eight tons of sugar per year.[8] According to Richard Ligon, 'an acre or good Canes will yield 4000 pound [1800 kilograms] weight of Sugar, and none will yield lesse then 2000 weight [900 kilograms].'[9] The planters needed a boiling house, curing house, storehouse, and distillery to produce spirits: rum on the English colonies and *cachaça* on the Portuguese. He also had to clothe, feed, house and supervise his labour force which was typically made up of sixty-four per cent field hands, ten per cent factory workers, fourteen per cent domestic staff and twelve per cent specialist overseers, drivers and tradesmen.[10] Not all of the labour force made sugar directly; every plantation was a microcosm of industry, with skilled carpenters, coopers and potters carving their niches. The skills of the smith were perhaps the most highly valued, producing 'Howes of all sises, but chiefly small ones to be used with one hand, for with them, the small Negres weed the ground: Plains, Gages, and Augurs [drill bits] of all sises; hand-Bills, for the Negres to cut the Canes; drawing-Knives, for Joyners ... Upon Iron, Steel, and small Iron pots, for the Negres.'[11]

Key to running a productive plantation on a day-to-day basis were the overseers and slave drivers, who typically would 'go out with severall Gangs, some tenne, some twenty, more or lesse, according to the ability of the overseer hee so imployes; and these are to go out upon severall Imployments, as he gives them directions, some to weed; some to plant, some to fall wood, some to cleave it, some to saw it into boards, some to fetch home, some to cut Canes, others to attend the Ingenio, Boyling-house, Still-house, and Cureing-house.'[12]

There was a basic rule of thumb for plantations all across the New World, and that was that there should be around one field labourer for every acre (0.4ha) of land: that's one person to do what would have been the work of both animal and machine were they on a farm in England. This may seem to you wholly inefficient; we have already seen that in the early days on Spanish Hispaniola oxen were used to plough the cane fields,[13] but the Brazilians had the rich *massapé* to deal with, which was too slippery for ploughs and therefore had to be dug by hand. The English had no such excuse; their reason for doing it was because of their fear of revolt and rebellion, especially during free time, so they made sure there was no free time to be had and kept their slaves busy with slow, degrading and monotonous work all year round. Equipping slaves for working the fields this way was cheap; fifty slaves could be kitted out with hand axe, hoe and handbill for £5.[14] This unnecessarily strenuous work was designed to break spirits and produce slaves who may have been both demoralised and inefficient, but were *under control*: 'underfed to break his resistance, [he] was given childish tasks to numb his intelligence,' producing the 'docile, stultified and infantile' 'Sambo' personality.[15]

Careful timing and organising of planting and harvesting was required if the work was to be spread out as much as possible without pause.[16] Typically, sugarcane grows in the wet months between June and November and takes fourteen to eighteen months to ripen. It is harvested in the driest months, usually January, when the sucrose content is highest. To accommodate this uneven cycle, fields were divided into ten-acre sections, each with slightly staggered planting times, all of which was done by slaves and their meagre set of tools. To plant, they were organised into groups of around thirty, making trenches and planting sets across two acres (0.8ha) every day during the growing months from October to December.[17] 'Negros with Hoes, make … deeper holes, at … farther distances according to the thing to be planted, and another coming after … plants the Root, and covers it with Earth, and so if a good Season has preceded it seldom misses to thrive, and is kept clear of Weeds till it be of its self to choak them.'[18]

There now were four months of weeding the fields, which was typically done by the women and was 'stooping and painfull worke,'[19] but '[i]f this husbandry be not used when the Canes are young, it will be too late to finde a remedy; for, when they are grown to a height, the blades will become rough and sharp in the sides, and so cut the skins of the Negres, as the blood will follow; for their bodies, leggs, and feet, being uncloathed and bare, cannot enter the Canes without smart and losse of blood, which they will not endure.'[20]

To achieve such dense growth, the fields were heavily manured with up to thirty cartloads of dung per acre (seventy-five cartloads per hectare).[21] The sugarcane was at risk from pests and vermin, and the worst of all were the rats, 'the main enemies to their profit … which do infinite harm in the Iland, by gnawing the Canes, which presently after will rot, and become unservicable in the work of Sugar. And that they may do this justice the more severely, they begin to make their fire at the outsides of that land of Canes they mean to burn, and so drive them to the middle, where at last the fire comes, and burnes them all.'[22] But though they may have lost one crop, the roots usually survived their ordeal and regrew, and all was not lost.[23] Between June and November the staggered cane crops would reach a maximum height of 2.5m, where they slowly ripened, turning from a 'pure grass green [to] a deep Popinjay.'[24]

As harvest time approached, the sugar masters took to the fields to assess the ripeness of the canes and from there would work out the best way to process them quickly because 'only he had the skills to see the machinations of the integrated processes of cultivation, milling, cooking [and] purging.' Once harvesting began, the work days were long and arduous. In Brazil the mills turned from four o'clock in the afternoon until ten o'clock the next morning, before sitting in wait until the afternoon when the new day's cane harvest came in. On the English islands, they worked from six o'clock in the morning until midnight in two or three shifts. At peak times, the working days could be as long as twenty hours. A working week was six days long but could be extended to seven days when required.[25]

Canes were always cut by hand by the strongest men and women, their outer leaves stripped, and then bundled into oxcarts by a second wave of gangs and taken to the *ingenio*.[26] 'The manner of cutting them is with little hand bills about six inches from the ground; at which time they divide the tops, from the Canes, which they do with the same bills, at one stroake; and then holding the Canes by the upper end: they strip off all the blades that grow by the sides of the Canes, which tops and blades, are bound up in faggots, and put into Carts.'[27] The work was gruelling and was only achieved by extreme force from the drivers, or the threat of it. As the great sugar historian James Walvin points out, it was 'not an artistic fancy that when outsiders sketched or painted slaves at work in the sugar fields, they invariably portrayed master and drivers, in the saddle, whip in hand, ready to goad the labour to work harder.'[28]

From this first harvesting, a second crop, known as a *rattoon,* could be grown from the root stock which took between nine and ten months to mature. On the Brazilian *ingenios* the harvest would last until the rainy season, which made the treacherous '*massapé* impossible to traverse'. Here, the slaves' daily quota was expressed in 'hands', a system that made it easy for them to keep track of their gruelling task. It went like this: twelve canes made a sheaf, ten sheaves made a finger, and five fingers made a hand. When they had harvested seven hands, they had

Slaves of both sexes cut sugarcanes on the island of Antigua, 1823. (British Library)

met their quota; a total of 4200 canes per day.[29] Their work was regularly inspected and '[i]f the overseer thinks their bundles too small, or if they come too late with them, they are punished with a number of stripes from four to ten. Some masters, under a fit of carefulness for their cattle, have gone as far as fifty stripes, which effectually disable the culprit for weeks.'[30]

Planting had been made mind-numbingly difficult, and now the same idea was being applied to the harvest. On Brazil the mills turned between 270 and 300 days of the year, stopping only on Sundays, and only after the Church had insisted that even slaves (now Christianised) had to have their day of rest. The plantation owners argued that they could not stop the mills for anything – not even God Himself – because the canes had to be pressed and the juice boiled within a day. On the English islands, the season was shorter, 120 to 180 days per year.[31]

Upon delivery at the mill, the canes were unloaded onto a large platform called a 'Barbycu' which was 'done about with a double rayle, to keep the Canes from falling out'. It was important that they were processed promptly, 'for if they should be more then two dayes old, the juyce will grow lower, and then they will not be fit to worke, for

A horse powered three-roller mill in the mid-eighteenth century. The centre cog was positioned sightly in front of the other two so that sugarcanes could be fed through and crushed, achieving around fifty per cent extraction. (Kersti Nebelsiek)

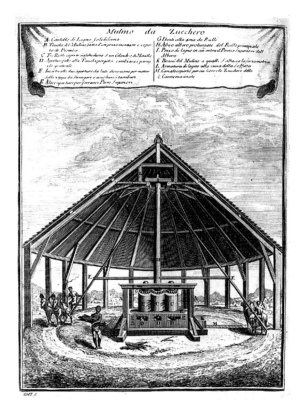

their soureness will infect the rest.' First, the canes had to be crushed in the three-roller mill; the rollers cogged so that the centre roller stuck out of kilter, crushing the cane twice. For a small plantation, animal-powered mills were standard, but in the larger plantations *ingenios* powered by water and wind were common. Ligon explains the process:

> the Horses and Cattle … go about, and by their force turne (by the sweeps) the middle roller; which being Cog'd to the other two, at both ends, turne them about … [A] Negre puts in the Canes of one side, and the rollers draw them through to the other side, where another Negre stands, and receives them; and returnes them back on the other side of the middle roller, which drawes the other way. So that having part twice through, that is forth and back, it is conceived all the juyce is prest out.[32]

The principle may have been straightforward, but the work required of the slaves was immense. An animal-powered mill could process thirty cartloads of cane a day, enough to produce half a ton of finished product. It was even more exhausting than working the cane fields, so much so that the Portuguese saying 'as sleepy as an *ingenio* slave' was borne of its notoriety. The mills ran on momentum and could not be easily stopped once they had begun turning, and there were frequent accidents. If a slave caught their arm in a roller, as they did frequently, it would be swiftly cut off at the shoulder by a fellow worker or overseer using a sharpened machete kept by the side of the machine. Cane-milling was considered women's work on Brazilian plantations, and inventories are peppered with entries for female slaves with one arm.[33] This is seventeenth-century health and safety, and the same system was used across all the New World sugar plantations. Edward Littleton viscerally and succinctly described such an event in his anti-abolitionist pamphlet *The Groans of the Plantations*: 'If a Mill-feeder be catch't by the finger his whole body is drawn in, and he is squeez'd to pieces.'[34] Today, there would, of course, be some kind of emergency stop lever, but in seventeenth- and eighteenth-century plantations the mills stopped for nothing. Those who survived the ordeal were not cast aside; slaves are expensive after all, so planters had to get their money's worth from their capital investment, employing them as watchers or overseers, and a constant reminder to the others working the mill of the consequences of taking one's eye momentarily off the ball.

After crushing, the freshly-milled brown cane juice was next

[poured into] a receiver, as big as a large Tray; into which the liquor falls, and stayes not there, but runs under ground in a pipe or gutter of lead Cover'd over close, which… carries it into the Cistern, which is fixt neer the staires, as you go down from the Mill-house to the boyling house. But it must not remaine in that Cisterne above one day, lest it grow sower; from thence it is to passe through a gutter, (fixt to the wall) to the Clarifying Copper, as there is occasion to use it, and as the work goes on, and as it Clarifies in the first Copper, and the skumme rises, it is conveyed away by a passage, or gutter for that purpoise; as also of the second Copper, both which skimmings, are not esteem'd worth the labour of stilling; because the skum is dirtie and grosse.[35]

The boiling house was considered the most important part of the plantation, not just because it was where the sugar was clarified and purified. It contained the most expensive equipment too. Inside was a series of five wide, shallow copper pans sat in a frame of brick and plaster of Paris, arranged in decreasing size from 820 *l* down to 136 *l*.[36] The pans were precious, not just because copper was an expensive metal in itself, but because they had to be imported from Britain at great expense.[37] Overseeing the process of purification was the boiler, the most important of all the sugar workers. The 'liquor is remov'd, as it is refin'd, from one Copper to another, and the more Coppers it passeth through, the finer and purer it is.' As the pans became smaller, the syrup became more viscous, and the heat applied greater. It required much skill, experience and judgement, and it had to be done in hellish and suffocating working conditions: 'And so the work [went] on, from Munday morning at one a clock, till Saturday night, (at which time the fire in the Furnaces are put out) all houres of the day and night, with fresh supplies of Men [i.e., slaves], Horses, and Cattle.'[38]

A French *ingenio* in 1591. Note the water-powered mill, boiling kettles and, in the foreground, sugar loaves ready for export. (British Museum)

The furnaces burnt their limitless timber with such ferocity that they acquired the name 'wide open mouths' by the slaves. The English plantations and Portuguese *ingenios* used wood exclusively to feed them, rather than the waste cane husks and leaves (called bagasse). Why should they bother with that when timber was so plentiful?[39] The temperatures were so hot that overseers had to watch their boilers particularly closely in case they looked like they were about to faint or lose concentration. Edward Littleton describes just how dangerous it was working in the boiling house: 'If a Boyler get any part into the scalding Sugar, it sticks like Glew, or Birdlime, and 'tis hard to save either Limb or Life.'[40]

By the time the liquor reached the fourth copper pan, it had become a thick, dark brown syrup and was ready to go on to the next stage of production; crystallising and purifying (sometimes called curing, kerning or purging). First, the syrup was mixed with oil and either wood ash or lime, and then turned into either brown muscovado sugar or white sugar.[41] For muscovado sugar, the dark, viscous syrup was poured into clay pots, rather like flowerpots, which contained a hole through which the molasses could drain. They were left around twelve hours in a hot room to dry-cure, before being transferred to a cooler room where:

> the Molosses drops out, but so slowly, as hardly to vent it selfe in a month, in which time, the sugar ought to be well cure'd before they knock the pot hard against the ground, [so] the Sugar comes whole out, as a bullet out of a mold; and when it is out, you may perceive three sorts of colours in the pot, the tops somewhat brownish, and of a frothy light substance; the bottom of a much darker colour, but heavy, grosse, moist, and full of molosses; both which they cut away, and to be boyl'd again … The middle part, which is more then two thirds of the whole pot, and looks of a bright colour, drie and sweet, they lay by it selfe, and send it down daily upon the backs, of Assinigoes [donkeys] and Camells, in leather baggs, with a tarr'd cloth over, to their Store-houses at the Bridge.[42]

For white sugar the thick syrup was cured in pots sealed with a thick wet clay top which worked as a reservoir for water. As the molasses drained from the bottom, a pressure gradient formed that drew the water from the wet clay, purifying it, hence the term 'purging'. This latter method was preferred by the Portuguese and the French, and it was this pure sugar, which required no further refining, that gave them their competitive edge. However, it was not typically adopted by the English, who had to pay higher duty on refined sugars. It made better business sense for them to send muscovado sugar on to Europe for further processing, though they sometimes sneaked some white sugar into Europe mislabelled as 'muscovado'.[43] The unrefined sugar was then packed into wooden casks weighing between 200 and 300kg, and each was then registered and marked with its weight and quality grade, and was stamped with the producer's trademark before being 'ship't away for England or any other parts of the World, where the best market is.'[44] In a good year, and if due care was taken in producing the sugar with little waste, 'One Acre of Canes [could] yield sometimes four thousand [pounds] of sugar,' equivalent to 4.5 tons per hectare.[45]

Every plantation had a distillery for rum-making and associated equipment and workers. It was the most common and by far the most popular alcoholic drink on the sugar islands. '[S]kimmings of the three lesser Coppers [are taken] down to the Still-house, where of the strong Spirit is made, which they call kill-devill,[46] as well as "Cane-juice not fit to make Sugar."'[47] Molasses, which had traditionally been given to cattle and slaves as a source of ready calories,[48] became an extra income stream; indeed, for Brazil it was the only way plantations became viable businesses once the English sugar machine had gotten in full swing.[49] Like all stages of manufacture on the islands, it could be extremely hazardous:

> After it has remained in the Cisterns, which my plot shewes you in the Still house, till it be a little soure, (for till then, the Spirits will not rise in the Still) the first Spirit that comes off, is a small Liquor, which we call Low-Wines, which Liquor we put into the Still, and draw it off again) and of that comes so strong a Spirit, as a candle being brought to a neer distance, to the bung of a Hogshead or But, where it is kept, the Spirits will flie to it, and taking hold of it, bring the fire down to the vessell, and let all a fire, which immediately breakes the vessell, and becomes a flame; burning all about it that is combustible matter. We lost an excellent Negre by such an accident, who bringing a Jar of this Spirit, from the Still-house, to the Drink-room, in the night, not knowing the

force of the liquor he carried, brought the candle somewhat neerer than he ought, that he might the better see how to put it into the Funnell, which conveyed it into the Butt. But the Spirit bein stirr'd by that motion, flew out, and got hold of the flame of the Candle, and so set all on fire, and burnt the poor Negre to death, who was an excellent servant. And if he had in the instant of firing, clapt his hand upon the bung, all had been saved; but he that knew not that cure, lost the whole vessell of Spirits, and his life to boot. So that upon this misadventure, a strict command was given, that none of those Spirits should be brought to the Drink-room ever after in the night, nor no fire or candle ever to come in there.[50]

Said Cuthbert Pudsey of the Brazilian *ingenios*, 'they use their slaves very strictly in making them work immeasurably, and the worse they use them, the more useful they find them, such were their dispositions, as by experience they find kind usage perverts their manners.'[51] It was a widely held belief in all New World plantations that Africans preferred to be treated in this way, such was their constitution, and that slavery 'took [them] away from a continent given over to murderous warfare to "a much happier state of life"' in comparative comfort.[52] Though the English never went so far as to consider African slaves as beasts, they were thought of as bestial, as one West Indian planter named Edward Long made very clear, 'I do not think an orang-outang husband would be any dishonour to a Hottentot female.'[53]

Once their fortune had been sufficiently made, most planters got out of the hell-hole they had created and moved back to England as swiftly as possible. Their plantations, managed by inexperienced caretakers, became unproductive and terribly overgrown. Hardest hit were the poor slaves who were utterly dependent upon their masters. 'I heartily pity the poor slaves, the mules and the stock,' commented one observer.[54] And it was the English who were most cruel, for it was they who had made it law that Africans should have so few rights. Their regime was wicked, vicious and extreme, but it also worked, and their system of power was transposed and enthusiastically implemented on the other sugar islands and then in the mainland American colonies. Indeed, all the cruelty, violence and genocide that was to follow in North America was based on English sugar-slave management.

Chapter 6

Fear of Freedom

The price of tyranny is eternal vigilance.

Richard S. Dunn[1]

By the seventeenth century the English planters were purchasing thousands of black slaves every year. Conscious of how reliant they had become upon forced labour, it prompted them to confront the issue of what a slave actually was and how they should be treated. They were no longer just prisoners of war like those in the Near East, and they were no longer there to supplement the workforce like they had been on the plantations on Madeira; now they *were* the workforce, and they were here to stay. The planters knew very well that if it were not for these slaves there would be no sugar industry, at least as they knew it. This realisation did not make them more humane, it only made them recognise the importance of slaves in terms of work done. The English were dealing with a slave population the size of which the world had never seen. As a result, slavery had to change, and with so many slaves to control they required a set of rules, that way they could have a united front and a slave population that knew its place.

Terrified of revolt, the English planters on Barbados set about writing into law the power they held over their slaves. To justify it they made it clear that because Africans had no civility they lacked humanity, preferring – and in some cases deserving – a life of servitude. Violence was seen as a positive form of control and correction. As far as the planters were concerned, Africans were barely human, and using this logic it was only by behaving inhumanely toward them that the planters could maintain the upper hand. If any planters felt that this was in any way wrong, they should not worry; Africans preferred this treatment. In fact, it was the only language they understood such was their previous life in West Africa.

These concepts were written into the 'Act for the Governing of Negros' which was presented at the Barbados Assembly in 1661 and later updated in 1688. With its implementation, the English took away almost all rights of enslaved Africans on the basis that they were different to whites on a fundamental level: 'the said Negroes … brought unto the People of this Island for that purpose, are of Barbarous, Wild, and Savage Natures, and such as renders them wholly unqualified to be governed by the Laws, Customs, and Practices of our Nations.'[2] Once employed, the act gave the planters total control over their slaves and therefore almost full reign to treat their slaves as they saw fit. As long as the result was an oppressed and subdued black population who could never contemplate freedom as an option they would never attempt to attain it. The Barbados acts are short and comprehensive, and quickly became the blueprint for the future treatment of slaves, not just on Barbados but also on the other English sugar islands, North Carolina and Antigua.[3]

Their point made clear that the slaves were simple and savage. The act set about dehumanising them to the point that planters and drivers felt they could behave cruelly without feeling the associated guilt one would usually feel after treating another human so poorly. They did admit they were fellow humans, but 'humans without the knowledge of God in the world.'[4] The act stated that 'the Negroes and Slaves [should] be well provided for, and guarded from the Cruelties and Insolences of themselves or other ill-tempered People or Owners from the hands of overbearing and violent owners.'[5] But this statement did not exist because they felt their duty of care should extend to these fellow humans they were abusing; their duty of care extended to a precious capital investment that they wanted to protect: 'if any Man shall of Wantonness, or only of Bloody-mindedness, or Cruel Intention, wilfully kill a Negro or other Slave of his own, he shall pay into the Publick Treasury Fifteen Pounds Sterling; but if he shall so kill another Man's, he shall pay to the Owner of the Negro, double the Value, and into the Publick Treasury, Twenty-five Pounds Sterling.'[6]

The act's purpose was to ensure masters knew their rights and obligations, and what the consequences would be if rights were not upheld or obligations unfulfilled.[7] Indentured servants also had fewer rights, but by virtue of their Christianity they at least retained some.

The acts did insist that the slaves were clothed, and they were provided only with very basic garments. They went naked until they reached puberty and after that were given clothes made from blue canvas. Males wore drawers and loincloths and sometimes shirts, and women wore loincloths, smocks and shirts. They rarely received hats or shoes. It cost just £35 per year to clothe one hundred slaves.[8] There was nothing in the act with respect to the amount of food they received or the quality of their dwellings. White servants on the other hand were given food and clothing allowances, they could sue if their master mistreated them, and masters were fined should they fail to properly care for servants if they fell ill. Should a servant die at their hands, they ran the risk of being tried for murder. However, masters could punish a black slave in any way they saw fit.[9]

The severity of the punishment doled out to servants and slaves differed greatly too. The act declared that for white servants most crimes were punished by lengthening their servitude: two years for theft, three for running away and seven for 'entertaining a fugitive slave.' For black slaves, punishments included being whipped, fire-branded – sometimes all over the body – or having their noses slit.[10] Writing a century later after the act was implemented, freed slave and abolition campaigner Olaudah Equiano recounted: '[that it was] very common in several of the islands, particularly in St. Kitts, for the slaves to be branded with the initial letters of their master's name, and a load of heavy iron hooks hung about their necks. Indeed on the most trifling of occasions they were loaded with chains, and often other instruments of torture were added. The iron muzzle, thumb-screws, &c … I have seen a negro beaten till some of his bones were broken, for only letting a pot boil over.'[11]

Another popular 'correction' for males was to castrate them, though it was not prescribed in the act, perhaps because it was too cruel even for the members of the assembly.[12] For slaves, it was a capital crime to steal anything worth more than a shilling, to rape, assault or to commit arson. It was also now the duty of the slave master to act as policeman and judge, and they were advised to suppress their 'humanitarian instincts'.[13] For the theft of goods under the value of twelvepence, the guilty party '[shall be] publickly and severely whipped, not exceeding Forty Lashes'. For a second offence they had 'their noses slit, and [then] branded in the Forehead with a Hot Iron, that the Mark thereof may remain,' and if a slave 'shall be found guilty a third time of any of the Offences [they] shall be adjudged to suffer Death.'[14]

More serious crimes were held in a court with 'Two Justices and … Three Free-holders, [who heard] and examine[d] all Evidences, Proofs and Testimonies [and gave] Sentence of Death upon them accordingly.'[15] To ensure more petty crimes, such as food theft, were kept to a minimum, the slaves' quarters were searched regularly. In the second version of the act it was recognised that sometimes slaves were driven to crime when their care was not sufficient. In this case, the blame fell at the planters' feet: 'Masters and Owners … who do not make sufficient Conscience of providing what is necessary for their Negroes or other Slaves, or allowing them to plant or provide for themselves; for which Cause such Negroes or other Slaves are necessitated to commit crimes contrary to the Law [the Owner should then] pay the Damage to the Party injured out of the Value of the said Negro or other Slave.'[16]

Their only real concession to slaves' freedom was to allow them to visit other plantations and hold markets on Sundays, but the rules around it were stringent. Slaves were not allowed to leave a plantation without a ticket from their master proving they been permitted: 'And if any Master … shall find any Negro or other Slave in their Plantation at any time without a Ticket, or Business from his said Master, and doth not apprehend them, or endeavour so to do; and have apprehended them, shall not punish them with a moderate Whipping.'[17] If you are wondering, fifty lashes was considered a 'moderate whipping'.[18]

Sloane tells us that those guilty of lesser crimes 'are usually whipt by the Overseers with Lance-Wood Switches, till they be bloody … being first tied up by their Hands in the Mill-Houses … some put on their Skins Pepper and Salt to make them smart; at other times Masters will drop melted Wax on their Skin … These Punishments are sometimes merited by the Blacks, who are a very perverse Generation of People, and though they appear harsh, yet are not scarce equal to some of their Crimes.'[19]

All of these punishments were borne of the English penal system. Keith Thomas points out that: 'Standard punishments in the early modern period including hanging (i.e., slow strangulation), branding, pillorying, flogging, amputation of hands and ears and slitting of noses … Traitors were hanged, taken down still alive, castrated, disembowelled and quartered … A French visitor in the reign of Mary I was predictably appalled by the English practice of indiscriminately killing criminals for offences that in France would have merited no more than a whipping.'[20]

Iron mask, collar, leg shackles and spurs used to restrict slaves. Iron masks were often fitted with tongue depressors, preventing swallowing, including saliva; collars had long spurs so that they could not rest, lie down or sleep. From 1807 book *The Penitential Tyrant* by Thomas Branagan. (Library of Congress)

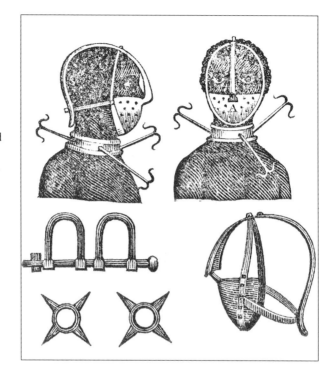

In short, the English were particularly cruel, and they extended this cruelty to their slaves. The difference being that these men, women and children were not murderers or traitors, but the innocent and the vulnerable. Olaudah Equiano wrote that the 'overseers are for the most part persons of the worst character of any denomination of men in the West Indies,' calling them 'human butchers'.[21]

With all of this violence and death, the slaves had to deal with their dead regularly. 'When any of them die,' says Richard Ligon, 'they dig a grave, and at evening they bury him, clapping and wringing their hands, and making a dolefull sound with their voyces.'[22] Their graves were surrounded by bunches of slowly burning aromatic herbs, and they placed offerings, such as rum or sugar, in the graves to sustain the dead as they travelled to their homelands to be born again, 'and have their youth renewed. And lodging this opinion in their hearts, they make it an ordinary practice, upon any great fright, or threatning of their Masters, to hang them selves.'[23] The slaves believed that to reach their destination their bodies had to be intact, a fact that masters shockingly exploited. If ever the draw of their homeland became too strong and there were suicides, masters made sure their slaves' souls could not reach the afterlife:

> Collonell Walrond having lost three or foure of his best Negres this way, and in a very little time, caused one of their heads to be cut off, and set upon a pole a dozen foot high; and having done that, caused all his Negres to come forth, and march round about this head, and bid them look on it, whether this were not the head of such an one that hang'd himself. Which they acknowledging, he then told them, That they were in a main errour, in thinking they went into their own Countries, after they were dead; for, this mans head was here, as they all were witnesses of; and how was it possible, the body could go [to the afterlife] without a head. Being convinc'd by this sad, yet lively spectacle, they changed their opinions; and after that, no more hanged themselves.[24]

Only three years after implementing the 1661 act, the Jamaican planters decided that they would take on the Barbados model. Slave trials had become costly and time-consuming, so devolving power to owners to both try and punish made sense. The act was modified and made slightly more lenient; slaves were far less numerous and more expensive here than on Barbados, so there were fewer capital crimes. Instead, they opted for the dishing out of more corporal punishments. The most significant change was to allow slaves to convert to Christianity, but how they dealt with the moral incongruence of treating other Children of God the way they did was an astounding feat of hypocrisy on their part. On the smaller islands of Antigua and the Leeward Islands, where the slave population was even smaller, the act was adopted with even more leniency. Make no mistake, 'more leniency' was still extremely brutal: thefts were punished by a whipping rather than death, and if a slave stole meat, he or she had an ear cut off. Planters had to provide a hectare of land for every twenty slaves so they could grow their own provisions. One surprisingly forward-thinking introduction was that freed slaves had the right to become an apprentice and own some land.[25]

In the 1670s the slave population continued to grow, and these changes slowly spread to the larger islands. Many slaves were given the right to learn a craft away from the plantations. For the first time a significant (though small) proportion of the slave population worked in a trade with the islands' coopers, carpenters and smiths. This decision was not made because planters thought that slaves needed this stimulation for their own well-being, but because it made better business sense: the monthly wage of a tradesman could pay for the upkeep of a slave for the whole year.[26] Worried that these new rights would encourage revolt, policing levels were cranked up should any slave, having been given an inch, attempt to take a mile.

There was a major policy change on the Leeward Islands when planters 'redefined' slaves as real estate rather than as personal property like livestock. Now they belonged to a plantation rather than a plantation owner. This meant that they could not be sold at auction and 'deprive an estate of its productive capacity. [T]he death of a planter sometimes resulted in the ruin of his estate when … minor heirs needlessly disposed of slaves.'[27] New owners often found themselves unable to get their new plantation up and running because they did not have the capital to invest in slaves. As a result, their business went under before they even got started. In order to avoid vacant, unproductive plantations, the revision provided an incentive for budding and seasoned planters alike to invest, thereby preventing the stagnation of the industry. It also made the slaves serfs, which, while benefitting the English, made no real difference to their lives on the island.[28]

One of the worst crimes a slave could commit was running away, and that constituted a trial by court-martial. Any fugitives hiding in the woods were hunted down and caught dead or alive. A favourite way of hunting them down was with hounds 'to guide us to the runaway Negres, who … harbour themselves in Woods and Caves, living upon pillage for many months together.'[29] If they were brought back dead, the planter would be appropriately compensated:

> it shall and may be lawful for any Justice of the Peace, Constable, or Captain … to raise and arm any number of Men, not exceeding Twenty, to apprehend and take them either alive or dead. And for every Negro or other Slave that they shall take alive, having run away above Six Months from his Master, they shall receive Fifty Shillings Sterling; for every [one] having run away above Twelve Months,

Five Pounds from the Master or Commanders of the said Negro or other Slave; if killed in taking, they shall receive Fifty Shillings Sterling from the Publick.[30]

The most serious crime of all was rebellion. The planters lived in fear of it, and it is the reason why they made such great efforts to hunt down absconded slaves so efficiently. If caught alive, the slaves were put in 'Iron Rings of great weight on their Ankles, or Pottocks about their necks, which are the Iron Rings with two long Necks rivetted to them, or a Spur in the Mouth.'[31] Under no account should escaped slaves be given the opportunity to collude away from the eyes of their masters, so 'if any Negroes … shall make Mutiny or Insurrection, or rise in Rebellion against this Place or People, or make Preparation of Arms' they would be punished by death or 'other pains'. The owner of the slaves was, of course, compensated up to 'the Sum of Five and twenty Pounds Sterling for any One Negro.'[32] According to Hans Sloane, they punished them by 'burning them, by nailing them down on the ground with crooked Sticks on every limb, and then applying the Fire by degrees from the Feet and Hands, burning them gradually up to the Head, whereby their pains are extravagant. For Crimes of a lesser nature Gelding, or chopping off half of the foot with an Ax.'[33]

There were seven incidents of mutiny on Barbados between 1640 and 1713, but there could have been many more as most of them were nipped in the bud. They were so few in number because successful uprisings required careful planning, great forethought, and above all, secrecy. Richard S. Dunn points out that 'black rebels could not simply seize a few guns, kill a few whites, burn a plantation or two, and disappear into the woods.'[34] Many others were stopped because loyal slaves disclosed the plans to their masters, which may seem selfish, but in protecting their owners they were protecting themselves. They knew what would happen to those found guilty, so stopping things before they got started surely led to less carnage, chaos, and, when the revolt subsided – as they always did – fewer gruesome, agonising deaths.[35]

In the 1670s the risk of revolt increased because there were no longer any free white labourers, having been 'ousted' by the tropical climate and replaced 'by the negro,'[36] who were worked harder than ever before. With a slave population sufficiently subdued, many masters became overfamiliar and overconfident with their slaves, leading to carelessness.

In 1675 some planters even gave slaves firearms and allowed them to become part of the islands' militia. In that same year, and with their guard down, Jamaica had one of its most significant 'frights'. Loyal slaves once again informed their owners of the plot. The ringleaders were caught, and the revolt was quashed just in the nick of time. Those captured were tortured for more information about the plot, though not all of them confessed their secrets: 'If you Roast me today, you cannot Roast me tomorrow,' announced one brave slave. In the end, they were sentenced to death by court-martial: six were burned alive and eleven beheaded. Some had their lives spared to be made an example of to any others who might get similar ideas. A revolt on Antigua saw fifty slaves take arms, hide and systematically raid the plantations until the island's militia found their camp. Most were killed, but the ringleader had a leg amputated and his tongue cut out so he could never plot or run away again. Giving slaves firearms and the powers of the militia may seem foolhardy, but this system worked on the tiny Leeward Islands where there were no forests in which to hide. Here they fought well with the English against the French, though it was not through loyalty or some form of Stockholm Syndrome; they knew that if the French were victorious they would take them and thrust them into their servitude, which was likely to be much worse than their lives on this relatively lenient island.[37]

Revolts were a real problem on Jamaica because it did have large, wooded areas in which the slaves could hide. In 1678 the slaves on a plantation owned by Captain Edmund Duck rose against their masters, killing Duck's wife, Martha, in the process. Most were caught immediately, but around thirty escaped. As news spread to neighbouring plantations, more slaves rose against their owners. Most were rounded up and executed. A description of one of the executions is truly shocking: 'His legges and arms was first brocken in peeces with stakes, after which he was fasten'd upon his back to the Ground – a fire was first made to his feete and burn'd uppe by degrees; I heard him speake several words when the fire consum'd all his lower parts as far as his Navill. The fire was upon his breast (he was burning neere three houres) before he dy'd.'[38]

All of these uprisings were, of course, proof positive that Africans did not prefer servitude over freedom, though none of the planters ever seemed to acknowledge that.

The most infamous of slave insurrections occurred not on the English colonies but the French colony of St Domingue. Just as in England,

France had acquired a sweet tooth and by the late eighteenth century sugar was firmly cemented in the basic diet of the middle and upper classes, with Parisians by far the greatest consumers. The secret of France's success in the sugar business was not due to consumption on home ground, but to the re-exportation of three-quarters of it to Germany and Holland. By the 1770s France was becoming the major sugar producer, and St Domingue – known as the Pearl of the Antilles – was its largest. The colony was situated on the western side of Hispaniola, shared with the Spanish who occupied the eastern side in their colony of Santo Domingo. Over the following four decades England and France would vie for dominance in the trade, and a period of peace between the two counties allowed both of their businesses to grow and prosper relativity unabated. By 1789 St Domingue contained half a million black slaves, 24,000 mulattoes and 30,000 white planters, and had produced just under 80,000 tons of sugar.[39] Planters of both nations didn't take peace for granted; there was a constant cloud of worry hanging in the air because of the political animosity between the two nations. They knew that political spats and wars would inevitably disrupt their shipping routes. That the French would take over from the English as the major producer is remarkable because their industries were set up in fundamentally different ways. There was one overriding similarity – the extensive use of slave labour – but, unlike the English, the French planters never formed a cohesive union like the English. Instead, the French competed against each other and therefore lacked the political influence that English planters enjoyed. There was a similar situation amongst France's sugar refiners who continuously undercut each other while paying high taxes imposed by the French Crown. So while a large amount of sugar was produced, they did not make enormous profits like the English.[40]

The Storming of the Bastille and the Declaration of Man in 1789 was a defining moment in French history. The French Revolution changed the rights of the common man in France, but this did not extend to the slaves in the colonies, though it did generate some moral debate on the rights of slaves. Eventually, these ideas percolated down to the French colonies, and soon the slaves themselves heard tales of revolution and the moral debate surrounding it. Feeling empowered by the news, the slaves decided that the time was right for an uprising. Three brothers named Jacques, Vincent and Victor Ogé and a free mulatto man called Chavane attempted to create one but were stopped in their tracks after planters were informed of their plans. Not wanting this attempt at an uprising to inspire any future notions, two were hanged and two were broken on the wheel – a favourite form of execution on the French colonies – and died in agony for their crimes. Victor somehow managed to escape and was never heard from again.[41]

As a result of this unrest, the French Assembly granted the slaves the right to sit in colony assemblies. The planters were not happy about this, but agreed, and the news quickly restored calm to the colony. The planters waited for peace to descend, then repealed. Anger spread quickly among the slave population. Hearing this news led to the largest, and most significant, of all slave uprisings. It had been plotted on the north side of the colony, but unlike previous failed uprisings it was successfully kept secret, and thousands were in on it. The plantations were isolated and scattered, but communication between them was facilitated by the most trusted African on the colony, a freed slave named Toussaint Louverture who had carved a niche in the community delivering mail and messages. He was the son of a chieftain, was educated, and probably considered by the French planters a cut above his fellow Africans. Louverture sent secret messages throughout the colony swiftly, orchestrating something the French planters could not – a coordinated and supportive front. The slaves hid in the forests and worked together to systematically attack planters, killing managers and drivers, and burning the bagasse sheds.[42] News of the uprising eventually reached France and in 1792, three commissioners arrived with 6,000 men. But when they landed and saw that the assembly's original decree had not been honoured, they sided with the slaves and fought off the planters who had stubbornly and violently refused to give up the old regime. The slaves of St Domingue were now free, self-liberated and part of the Republic of France.[43]

The English were so terrified that their slaves would hear of this and get their own ideas of revolt that they hatched a plan to invade St Domingue. Their plan was to kill two birds with one stone: first, they would take over the colony (or failing that, cause enough bother) to demonstrate that it was they who were the dominant force in the Caribbean, quashing any thought of revolt on their colonies. Second, they could finally get their satisfaction for France aiding the American colonies in the War of Independence, a fact that still stuck in their craw. Hundreds of troops from mainland Britain were sent to the island, but

An 1805 English engraving entitled *Revenge taken by the Black Army for the cruelties practised on them by the French*. The Haitians were seen by the English as heroes and depicted as such, in fine livery as they exacted their revenge. French illustrations were very different, depicting the slaves as brutish, wearing only loincloths and using clubs as weapons. (Library of Congress)

Louverture knew exactly what to do: wait. He knew they would quickly succumb to yellow fever, and sure enough, by the time they had scoped the island and worked out their offensive strategy, the British began to drop like flies. Louverture told the British that if they retreated he would spare neighbouring Jamaica, and off they went with their tails between their legs.[44]

In 1801 Louverture declared himself governor-general of the colony and asserted his own independent constitution. Napoleon, being the official owner of the colony, was not best pleased with this brazen disrespect and sent one of his top brass, General Charles Leclerc, to restore balance,[45] a development the English very much approved of. Upon arrival, the general took the same seemingly sensible strategy as the British and kept his men undercover in the middle of the day, where most succumbed – again – to yellow fever. However, this time he did manage to get the upper hand after declaring a false amnesty, capturing the self-proclaimed governor-general and taking him back to Europe for sentencing by Napoleon himself. Louverture died on 7 April 1803 of 'pneumonia and apoplexy' in a freezing cell high in the Alps without sufficient firewood, clothing or food.[46] Stories of the uprising captured the British public's imagination, with the freed slaves viewed as heroes, and there was an expression of great sadness when news of Toussaint's death was heard.[47] This empathy for the slaves on the sugar colonies came as a great annoyance to the planters who really did not want any attention drawn to the conditions in which they kept their slaves.

The French decided that the only way to restore order on the colony, was to reinstate the old system of slavery. However, former slave Jean-Jacques Dessalines had already picked up where Louverture left off. He was very different to his predecessor; he was illiterate and unpredictable, but he was also an excellent strategist, and when General Leclerc succumbed to yellow fever in October 1802 Dessalines wasted no time in retaking the colony. In retaliation, Napoleon sent another

Portrait of the greatest hero of the Haitian Revolution, Toussaint Louverture (1743-1803). He died, at the request of Napoleon, in a freezing cold cell high in the French Alps. (Europeana)

77

bigwig, General Donatien-Marie-Joseph de Vimeur, Viscount of Rochambeau and veteran of the American War of Independence, who arrived on the colony confident of success. Starting as he meant to go on, he announced his intentions to Dessalines: 'when I take you, I will not shoot you like a soldier, or hang you like a white man; I will whip you to death like a slave.'

But this campaign would also be a disaster: first, the packs of Cuban hunting dogs he had brought with him did not discriminate, killing black and white alike. Then his men died of disease, and after thirteen months on the colony Rochambeau succumbed to fever himself.[48] All in all, 100,000 Haitians and 50,000 French died. Upon hearing the news of these developments, Napoleon decided to withdraw and left them to their own devices. Dessalines issued a proclamation of independence from France and renamed it Haiti, its original Arawak name, meaning 'Island of Mountains'. Not only that, but Napoleon also sold most of the remaining New World French colonies to the newly formed United States of America for the sum of $15 million in what was known as the Louisiana Purchase. As Peter Macinnes observes, 'the foundations of the modern North America were laid in the mismanaged French sugar colonies of the Caribbean, and in the French willingness to pass up on Liberty, Equality and Fraternity, when those ideas stood between them and making sugar profits.'[49]

Having washed his hands of the colony, Napoleon was faced with the issue of a potential sugar shortage, not only that but, annoyingly, the British sugar islands were back in full swing, top dogs in the sugar trade once more. Down, but not out, he set about waging an economic war with the British, promptly unleashing a fleet of ships to block their islands' sugar exports. Not taking this lying down, the British adopted a tit-for-tat strategy and blocked the French vessels in a stalemate that led to a further drop in European sugar imports.

With sugar now intrinsic to daily life, Napoleon became worried that there would be discontent if it had to be rationed. So he decided that he would transform the French sugar industry by switching from tropical sugarcane to temperate sugar beet. Sucrose had already been shown to be the substance that made sugar beet sweet, and German chemists had demonstrated in the 1740s that it could be purified. If sugar could be produced in a temperate climate, and if the process could be streamlined for mass manufacture on an industrial scale, Europe would have a domestic sugar supply that would totally undermine the

British. Napoleon poured one million francs into an incentive scheme for farmers to grow sugar beet and granted a hundred scholarships to budding chemists to develop and refine further the process of producing white sugar from beet. Understandably, the British were worried that this would devastate their sugar trade and offered huge sums of money to the developers to abandon their projects. Napoleon's investments paid off: by 1812 forty factories had refined 1500 metric tons of sugar from over 100,000 metric tons of sugar beet. But with Napoleon's defeat at Waterloo in 1815 the blockades were removed and cheap slave-grown sugar could pour lavishly once more into Europe. Sugar made by free men could never compete with cheap slave-made sugar, and the sugar beet industry collapsed just like that.[50]

The Haitian republic, meanwhile, dragged on. Instead of rebuilding the colony's infrastructure, the black and mullato people bickered over who should have dominance; and pro-slave Europeans embargoed any sugar they did manage to produce.[51] Dessalines was eventually assassinated in 1804 and the colony split into two warring factions. Not only that, but the French also refused to recognise it as an independent republic, insisting that if they wanted their freedom, they would have to pay for it, and the price tag was 150 million Francs, a sum that took a century to pay off. But the Haitian Revolution would have far-reaching consequences – it would accelerate the abolishment of the slave trade and instil a degree of self-pride never before seen in a slave population. In Europe, it began to crystallise ideas surrounding universal freedom and the morality of colonialism, and progressive ideas that had been floating around for a while were suddenly catalysed.

Britain and its sugar colonies were left with a predicament; the post-Waterloo peace they were enjoying allowed production to increase, which, in turn, caused sugar prices to plummet again. Ordinarily, this would not have been an issue, for they were well prepared to work their slaves harder to make their profits, but with slaves empowered by the events on Haiti, and the British people viewing the Haitian revolutionaries as heroes, slavery was being threatened and questioned more and more. If these people who were discussing the merits of abolishing the trade were in any way successful, it could spell the end for the sugar industry as they knew it, and they were not prepared to allow that to happen.

Chapter 7

The Slave Trade

Death thins the cargoes in various modes; suicide destroys
the many, and many are thrown overboard at the close of the
voyage.

F. Harrison Rankin[1]

The Atlantic slave trade formed part of a 'trade triangle' between
Europe, Africa and the American colonies. It wrenched Africans from
their homelands and exchanged them in the sugar colonies for cash or
sugar. These were promptly shipped to Europe where the ships picked
up British staples and fancy goods for the colonies, then left for Africa
to collect more slaves before returning to the West Indies. The gruelling
passage between Africa and the Americas was known as the 'the Middle
Passage', and though most Europeans were unaware of its existence, it
would, in time, become symbolic of all of the 'horrors of transatlantic
slavery'.[2] The squalid, wretched conditions for those on board the ships
became notorious in the latter half of the eighteenth century when they
were reported in pamphlets written by slave reformers and abolitionists.
In the 200 years between the 1660s and 1860s ninety per cent of slaves
went either to the Caribbean or Brazil (just seven per cent went to
mainland North America), and the vast majority of those worked the
sugar plantations.

In 1788 the British Parliament attempted to improve things by
introducing Dolben's Act, which reduced the density of slaves to a
maximum of eight per ton of ship (a rather clumsy measure) and insisted
that a surgeon was present on every ship to care for the slaves and record
deaths. As a result, their quarters were kept cleaner, slaves were screened
for disease before embarking the ship and sick ones sent back to shore.
As an incentive to keep following the new legislation, the captain and
surgeon were given a cash payment if deaths were kept below two per

cent.[3] This may seem high, but deaths on ships were expected and unavoidable as both crew and cargo were hit by inevitable onboard epidemics.[4] Mortality rates, though, should be taken with a pinch of salt, because it's very likely that deaths were underreported, especially in the eighteenth century when traders were obliged to monitor mortality and keep death rates low.[5]

In the first few decades of the English sugar trade, planters organised the import of slaves, but as the sugar business grew rapidly, it quickly became a task handed out to third parties. The Dutch West India Company was one such third party, which, until the 1590s, had been trading in sugar, gold, ivory and other exotic goods from Africa and the Americas. It became wealthy very quickly, as did its European investors, and always keen to add more commodities to its trade portfolios, it inevitably toyed with the idea of trading African slaves. The company could see how lucrative it could be, but the concept of trading humans did not sit well with them, so it discussed the merits and drawbacks of the trade with theologians, who concluded that such a trade was immoral. This left the way open to independent traders, including other Dutch traders, to export Africans to the colonies unimpeded. However, once the profits that could be made were apparent they jettisoned their morals and made a rapid U-turn. Not only that, they went for it wholesale, displacing even the mighty Portuguese from their slaving centres.[6]

This turn of events displeased the English Crown. If anyone was going to get a monopoly on trading to the English it would be the English. There had been great interest in colonial trade ever since John Hawkins's voyages, but this would be the first time the English Crown became heavily involved in the slave trade specifically, with royal companies set up by James VI/I and Charles I trading in slaves, 'and by the 1620s, black slaves were to be seen in ports in England such as Bristol and London.'[7] The first few companies would be short lived. However, after the abolition of the monarchy, Lord Protector Oliver Cromwell saw how the sugar and slave trade were really two sides of the same coin and encouraged development of both in tandem. Many English planters identified as Roundheads well into the Restoration (they were apolitical, it seems, only when it suited them). In reality, living away from England meant that their political thinking greatly lagged behind that of the motherland, so as England reconciled its Crown and Parliament, the planters steadfastly refused to accept it.

In an attempt to quell their obstinance and force them to toe the line, Charles II ordered the banishment of smaller Roundhead planters from the islands and heavily fined larger and more powerful ones. In some cases they were physically punished, their skin branded or their tongues 'bored out with hot irons'.[8] This behaviour did not help matters, so the king made the seemingly sensible decision to appoint Francis Lord Willoughby as governor of the sugar islands. On paper, Willoughby was a good choice: an ex-Roundhead who had changed allegiance to the Crown and who could appreciate both sides of the issue. He was sympathetic, 'urged moderation' and, upon arrival, even reversed the banishments hoping there could be peace and agreement. However, unbeknownst to Willoughby, some prominent Roundhead planters had successfully lobbied Parliament, convincing some members that the governor was a Royalist who would run a regime of theft and betrayal.

Willoughby arrived on Barbados around the same time as this fake news, and there was a Royalist versus Roundhead stand-off. With his superior forces, Willoughby overcame the Roundhead militia and claimed 'colonial autonomy'. Then, during the celebration feast, three Commonwealth ships sent from England arrived in the dead of night, their mission to take out the supposedly treacherous Royalist Willoughby and restore law and order. The ships were anchored and sent swimmer scouts to collect intelligence. They were small in number but gained the upper hand by chipping away at Willoughby's defences and slowly closing in, killing one hundred Royalists and taking another eighty as prisoners in the process. Parliamentarians won the day in this most vexatious manufactured civil war, but being true English gentlemen (and therefore respecters of class and hierarchy) they allowed Lord Willoughby to stay and keep his land. However, he soon left the islands, his character ruined, and 'was never heard of again'.[9] Back in England, it was decided that perhaps the best idea would be to post Parliamentarian governors in the future.[10]

Things calmed down enough for the English Crown to set up the Company of Royal Adventures, a name evocative of bravery and patriotism, whose purpose was to provide the English plantations in the Americas with 'a competent and constant supply of Negro-servants … at a moderate Rate'. The company gave itself the target of exporting 3,000 Africans 'so as the Planter shall have no just cause to complain of any want.' It had quite the portfolio of backers too, declaring 'The

KINGS Most Excellent MAJESTY, The QUEENS MAJESTY, His Royal Highness the DUKE of York [the future James II & VI], His Highness [first cousin of the King] PRINCE RUPERT.' Once the bigwigs had their feet under the table, the opportunity to invest became available to everyone as long as they could stump up the minimum amount of £5.[11] There were many large investors, including the likes of diarist Samuel Pepys and philosopher John Locke.[12] A great deal of the money was spent on improving infrastructure in Africa, building several ports and warehouses on riverbanks as deep into the interior as possible: 'The export trade in human beings, entirely originating in the whites, and maintained by them, is confined to the rivers … established slave-factories at the mount of nearly every stream which would allow the entrance of a vessel.'[13]

With this improved infrastructure they gained control of English trade and successfully met their target of '3000 Negroes'. This riled many planters who lobbied Parliament hoping that they would be able to trade themselves as they did in the old days prior to the company's formation.[14] The monopoly was not to last, with the company dissolving due to non-payment of planter debts, but real success came in 1672 when it relaunched as the Royal African Company. It had learnt from its mistakes and refined its system of lending to planters, managing to reach new heights by successfully delivering over 13,000 African slaves to the English colonies between 1685 and 1686.[15]

Planters were less than happy when the company artificially inflated the prices for slaves sold to the plantations deeper within the West Indies. Henry Drax, the owner of a huge Jamaican plantation that boasted a workforce of over 300 slaves, was very dissatisfied with the price hike, complaining of 'unreasonable rates'. He had good reason; slaves were traded at £24 on Jamaica compared to £17 on Barbados. The Royal Africa Company quickly changed their tune when the Jamaican planters voted with their wallets and began purchasing their workforce from clandestine traders, sneaking them onto the island via its rocky northern coastline. Drax smugly noted: 'The Royal Company now begin to supply us well, there being two Shipps with 700 Negroes in port.'[16]

This mass trade of slaves by the English to the English came at just the right time for planters who had been struggling to turn a profit and pay their freemen labourers after sugar prices had fallen by more than a third between the 1650s and 1680s. Though they cost roughly double that of a white servant, slaves made good economic sense as they never received a wage – unlike the freemen – and they didn't leave after five years like indentured servants.[17] Production increased, allowing the planters to get a handle on their shrinking profit margins, but the only way for planters to achieve this was to expand, either by merging with others or buying out smaller operations.

A total shift to slave labour with just one supplier may have helped the planters to creep back into the black, but it didn't last. With no competition, the company increased prices across the board and simultaneously reduced the quality of the care that slaves received. As a result, planters complained of receiving slaves 'wholly Unaccustomed to worke, which in shorte time Dye upon our hands to our Irreparable loss.'[18] This again pushed planters to purchase slaves from interlopers, and so, realising it was losing its monopoly, and just a decade after it formed, the Royal African Company begrudgingly allowed open trade.

***

An empire was being built on sugar and slavery. One factor that prevented most people from cottoning on to this basic link is that the slave trade was something that happened elsewhere. However, many English were very much aware of the slaves and their treatment, because they produced the trappings of slavery: iron collars, ball-and-chains, tongue depressors and thumbscrews for punishment. Aside from these macabre instruments, there were all the day-to-day materials any healthy business requires: parchment, stationery, ink. And let's not forget the myriad of fancy goods: fine clothes, rich food, French brandy, artisanal furniture, fine drapery and so on that the planters wanted to purchase. For example, in 1685 when the ship *Samuel* sailed from Jamaica to Bristol it brought with it a limited list of valuable colonial products – sugar, indigo and logwood – but upon leaving England it carried twenty-four different types of goods destined for the colonies.

The trade created jobs for workers directly, like shipbuilders, dockworkers, crew, accountants and insurance brokers, but also indirectly, such as the tailors, carpenters and other artisans. Indeed, folk of all classes across the entire British Isles benefitted, from the Crown and their investors right down to the factory worker employed in one of the many mills that produced textiles destined for the big houses of the colonies. And that's not to forget those who dealt in sugar itself – refiners, confectioners and grocers: 'The article for guns alone for the African trade ... employs between 4 and 5000 persons in Birmingham [and] Manchester exports annually to Africa, to the amount of 200,000 [pounds Sterling, and] employs 18,000 persons.'[19] Sugar enabled the consumption of bitter tea and coffee more readily and boosted their consumption and trade. This sprawling web of commerce is known as the sugar-slave complex.[20]

Infrastructure grew around the docks as more people made their living within the sugar-slave complex. Merchants built townhouses, having grown wealthy exchanging their desirables for huge amounts of sugar; they even sold the sugar back to the planters after it had been refined in England at hugely inflated prices. By the 1780s, 14,000 seamen were working 689 ships,[21] which the government regularly utilised whenever the British Navy needed some extra hands in the frequent and often prolonged wars and rows with other nations. The country was doing great, money was pouring in and many British people benefitted from the employment that the sugar-slave complex provided.

The major slave ports in Britain were London, Bristol and Liverpool. London had been a port since pre-Roman times and Bristol since the thirteenth century,[22] and therefore received British slave sugar as soon as it was produced commercially. As sugar production increased exponentially, so did the trade in slaves and the ships required to carry them. By the 1720s 150 British ships were involved in the trade and in that decade alone 100,000 Africans would pass through British docks.[23] For those who worked at, or close, to the ports the connection between sugar and slavery was tangible.

Until the mid-eighteenth century Liverpool had been an obscure little port with an international trade that started and stopped with Ireland, but as West Indian and African trade traffic mushroomed, it was transformed into a huge commercial dock. It was so successful it quickly became the 'slave trade capital of Britain'[24] with twenty per cent of all slaves traded by the British passing through it. The port became almost entirely dependent upon the slave trade; half of its sailors worked in it, and shipbuilders and shipwrights received huge contracts. For example, Liverpool shipbuilder Baker and Dawson owned eighteen slave ships worth £509,000 and was contracted to traffic at least 3000 slaves per year. Liverpool was king, sending over one hundred ships to Africa every year, and in the 1760s the turnover was so large that traders of Liverpool could proudly announce that they could sell slaves cheaper than either London or Bristol.[25] Liverpudlian investors purchased shares in these businesses and became very influential both locally and politically.

By the mid-seventeenth century Liverpool had gained a small but significant black population. Sometimes planters returned from the colonies with an entourage of slaves or sent their mixed-race children to receive an English education. It even found itself hosting a number of sons of African kings. But for the most part the population was made up of cast out, escaped or freed slaves who found themselves trying to scrape a living on the streets, competing with the white working-class for jobs. For this, they received a great deal of racist violence. The only exception to this rule seems to be the black seamen, who seemed to work well alongside their white colleagues who treated them as social equals.[26]

For the people of Liverpool, the slave trade brought wealth and employment. They were proud of what they achieved, and they put the people responsible on pedestals, or rather statues of them on pedestals. They named buildings after them and embellished them with sculptures; the Cunard Building remains adorned with reliefs and statues of slaves and indigenous Americans, and the Church of Our Lady and St Nicholas – situated by the docks – still displays a golden slave ship atop its spire. Streets are named after prominent investors

Detail of the 'Slave Relief' in the entrance to Martin's Bank in Liverpool. It was installed in the 1920s and was – and indeed remains – extremely controversial. (Neil Buttery)

in the trade, the best-known being Penny Lane of Beatle's fame, named after James Penny, a financier and vocal opponent of the abolition of the slave trade. There was pride in the fact that Liverpool had gone from being a provincial backwater to the key player in the slave and sugar trade that fuelled Britain's empire-building.

***

Slave traders drew their quarry from all around the North and West of Africa, but the vast majority of trade occurred around the Gulf of Guinea and surrounding lands, a 3,400-mile-long stretch of coastline from Senegal to Angola.[27] For the English, the 'chief mart on the coast of Africa for the sale of human beings' was Sierra Leone[28] and they sourced their cargo from the interior of West Central Africa. The peoples of this vast area were particularly sought after because the region had a climate very similar to that of the sugar plantations, and the inhabitants were thought to eat a diet similar to that of the West Indian slaves: yams, plantains, cassava and only a little meat.[29] Africans were not taken from a single locale; it was in a trader's best interest to cast his net wide even though it took much longer to collect enough individuals for the transatlantic voyage. There was a great diversity in languages spoken, so slaves sought far and wide had difficulty communicating. Doing things this way retained inter-tribe animosity and reduced the likelihood of cooperation and connivance.[30] Slave traders were choosy and carefully selected their slaves; they were an expensive investment after all, and they had a reputation to uphold. Young males were the most sought-after, while women were less desirable but important in domestic slavery and to keep sex ratios balanced. Boys and girls from the age of around twelve were considered, but disregarded if younger, as were adults over forty years of age, and anyone obviously weak or sick was also rejected.[31]

In its early days, the Royal Africa Company paid just £3 per slave and sold them on for as much as £17 on the sugar islands. By the early eighteenth century the selling price of a male slave had risen to between £25 and £30. Higher prices forced traders to take carer greater care of their cargo; for comparison, in the seventeenth century the company shipped 60,783 slaves to the English West Indies, but only 46,396 were delivered. This equates to a loss – i.e., a death toll – of almost a quarter, but by the 1730s the mortality rate dropped to ten per cent.[32]

An eighteenth century map of the Gulf of Guinea, where the vast majority of African slaves were sourced. (New York Public Library)

European slave traders and their crews rarely ventured deep into the interior of West Central Africa themselves. Instead, they requested them for purchase from African chiefs. One particularly successful chief named Dalla Mohammedoo, leader of the Bullom tribe situated on the Sierra Leone coast, turned much of his land into a slave depot and grew very rich trading slaves to the English.[33] European traders would bring wares such as sugar and fancy goods to tempt the chiefs into making a deal. Once a deal was struck, the kidnappers would capture individuals from neighbouring warring tribes, or go further into the continent: '[if] he prevails, and takes prisoners, he gratifies his avarice by selling them.'[34] Some of those who were kidnapped came from so deep within the continent that they were unaware of the existence of white people.[35] Raiders focused most of their efforts on capturing individuals from the Benin region because of their 'hardiness, intelligence, integrity, and zeal,' as well as their 'vigour'.[36] But they also had another desirable characteristic that made them sought after; they farmed and worked their soil completely by hand using no 'beasts of husbandry,' using only 'hoes, axes, shovels and beaks, or pointed iron to dig with.'[37] This was perfect training for working the cane fields of the West Indian sugar islands.

Olaudah Equiano describes the circumstances that led to his and his sister's capture in his 1793 memoir. His tribe was situated in the Eboe region of Benin. On one occasion '[o]nly me and my dear sister were left to mind the house, two men and a woman got over our walls, and in a moment seized us both.' Their hands were bound, and they were thrust into sacks and separated. Olaudah 'cried and grieved continually' for his terrible ordeal and the loss of his sister. He was not taken to the coast to be sold on to European colonists, instead he was sold to another African tribe as a slave. Slaves were a very common sight in West Central African society, but it was of a very different nature to the slavery of the sugar Islands. According to Olaudah, 'they do no more work than other members of the community,' and although they were not free people, they were not worked anywhere near as hard as they were on the sugar plantations.[38]

He was bought and sold a few times again until, at one trading point, and purely by chance, he spotted his sister. The raiders saw that the children were siblings, and they allowed them to spend a little time together: 'As soon as she saw me she gave a loud shriek, and ran into my arms – I was quite overpowered: neither of us could speak, but … clung to each other … When these people knew we were brother and sister, they indulged us to be together; and the man, to whom I supposed we belonged, lay with us, he in the middle, while she and I held one another by the hands across his breast all night.'

Their reunion was not to last. The next day she was taken away. He grieved for his loss for the rest of his life: 'Though you were early forced from my arms, your image has always riveted in my heart, from which neither time nor fortune have been able to remove it.'[39] Olaudah also pined for his African childhood, explaining that although the people of his tribe had an outwardly warlike disposition, their leading characteristics were 'cheerfulness and affability'.[40]

This was very different to what Europeans, especially colonists, were told of the lives of Africans from this region. One piece of anti-abolitionist literature informs us that 'in Dahomey, the King is absolute master,' and a most 'savage and wanton' man who, after beheading his own subjects used their heads as 'Ornaments before his Palace Gates on festival Days, and on every public Occasion,' and that he strewed their bodies on the 'the Floors leading to his Appartments'. Not only that, the 'Area before his Bed-chamber, is paved with the Skulls of Prisoners taken in War, that he may daily enjoy the savage Gratification of literally trampling on the Heads of his Enemies.'[41]

Another trait attributed to the people of Africa is that they were 'haters of their own Children, and therefore,' Hans Sloane tells us, "tis believed that they fell and dispose of them to Strangers for Money, but this is not true.'[42] Their lives were quite the opposite, the vast majority living well in closely knit villages that were culturally rich, but planters readily believed the propaganda because it gave them reason to enslave them. As far as they were concerned, Africans preferred their despicable treatment on the sugar islands infinitely more than the treatment they received in their homeland. As the regular spates of suicide on the islands attest, it was not the case at all.

Captured slaves were brought to the African ports where they were exchanged between traders so that each ship contained a mixture of different ethnicities. This mixing may have prevented uprisings but it killed off their tribal cultures, and as a consequence they had to form new cultural alliances on the plantations, a factor that has only been appreciated in the last twenty-five years: '[The] African heritage of slaves cannot be ignored but the cultures of slave-based communities were essentially new and owed more to the conditions that Africans encountered in [the Americas] than to their upbringing in Africa.'[43]

One of the most important contributors to mortality was not the voyage itself but the 'purchasing strategies' of the traders prior to embarkation: how slaves were captured and treated upon capture; how far they had to travel from the interior of the continent to the waiting ships; and how long they had to sit and wait in ships' holds before they set sail.[44] Slaves could be kept for weeks or even months in the hold of a ship as they waited for traders to reach their quotas. This phase has not attracted much attention because mortality only had to be officially recorded from embarkation, creating a dearth of data. Equiano describes the conditions of the ship he was put on after he was sold to transatlantic slave traders: 'When I looked around the ship too, and saw a large furnace or copper boiling, and a multitude of black people of every description chained together, every one of their countenances expressing dejection and sorrow ... overpowered with horror and anguish, I fell motionless on the deck and fainted.'[45]

Mixing, followed by prolonged waiting times, encouraged the spread of the commensal (infectious) diseases that would cause many deaths.

For example, in 1859 the large slave ship *Orion* was intercepted by the British just two days after it had left port in the Congo,[46] yet 146 of the 874 slaves had already died, and the remainder were 'very emaciated'.[47] There were differences between nations: the French tended to use small, fast ships which took fewer slaves and therefore had shorter waiting times in dock and consequently left Africa with its slaves in better health, whereas the English (and later, British) slave ships tended to be large and slow and therefore took longer to fill and longer to make the voyage. The upshot of this was that Dolben's Act had no real measurable effect on mortality. Indeed, of all the factors that contributed to mortality on the slave ships, it was ship size and the speed by which ships traversed the Atlantic Ocean that seem to be the most significant.[48] The dominant thinking of the other slaving nations was that the most successful journeys were correlated with vessels that quickly crossed the Atlantic. The quicker the voyage, the more slaves survived, the more goods traded, and the more money made. Slavers of other nations knew this intuitively, yet the stubborn English carried on using their large ships and therefore trafficked – and caused the death of – the most individuals.[49]

Having no natural resistance to malaria or yellow fever, the crew were susceptible to disease, and it was during this time of loading and acquisition that they were most vulnerable. The long waits meant that slaves and crew had to endure the rainy seasons, the cascading water spreading disease efficiently through their quarters and holding areas. In 1833 a Captain Owen noted that 'the sickly seasons are September to October and from January to May when many of the inhabitants fall victim to dysentery, the most prevalent and fatal disease to which they are subject.'[50]

The traders formed prejudices about the people of the different African nations: those from the Gold and Slave Coasts, for example, were regarded as high quality,[51] whilst the Ibibio from the Bight of Biafra were sickly and lazy.[52] These prejudices originate from the fact that there was variation between tribes' natural immunity to novel infectious diseases.[53] Indeed, planters would often refuse slaves who had originated from these more impoverished areas. This was especially true for the peoples of Biafra, who were often malnourished before they were caught and consequently succumbed quickly to disease.[54] When slave traders sailed for the colonies, they arrived first at Barbados, the closest island, where planters got first refusal of slaves. Unless there was a shortage, those of an undesirable nationality would remain unsold until the slave ships reached the innermost islands or the mainland, where they would be typically sold to coffee planters who needed fewer slaves and were therefore visited last and had to 'make do' with the Biafra slaves who hadn't been selected by the sugar planters.[55]

Once the appropriate numbers of individuals had been captured, the voyage across the Atlantic could begin. The Royal Africa Company, and others who traded in human beings, kept meticulous records and accounts. For example, one set of accounts called the Du Bois dataset contains the details of over 4000 French slave voyages that transported some 1.25 million slaves from their homelands. The dataset reveals that there were on average 320 slaves on board each ship and accounts for just under an eighth of the total number of slaves traded by the French. The number of slaves on each ship began to climb from an average of 260 to 340 per ship during the latter decades of the eighteenth century.

However, looking at the averages can mask the extent of some of the atrocities: one ship, the *Antoinette*, landed in Rio de Janeiro with 900 slaves crammed inside, watched over by just ten crew members, and another had over 400 slaves die in a Middle Passage voyage that took over ten months.[56] Conditions inside ships' hulls were stiflingly hot and cramped: 'The stench of the hold was so intolerably loathsome, that is was dangerous to remain there for any time,' recounts Olaudah Equiano, 'but now that the whole ship's cargo was confined together, it became absolutely pestilential. [It] was so crowded that each had scarcely room to turn himself.' Soon the filthy suffocating conditions 'brought on a sickness amongst the slaves, of which many died, thus falling victims to the improvident avarice ... of their purchasers.'[57]

Mortality was a factor that was very difficult to predict, and the uncertainty increased the selling price of their cargo.[58] Epidemics came in waves: first, there were the fevers from malaria and yellow fever that peaked at around day fifteen; then, at around day thirty, a second wave of gastrointestinal infections spread through the ship.[59] Towards the end of the voyage, diseases associated with malnourishment such as scurvy crept in. F. Harrison Rankin gives an account of the conditions on the Spanish slave ship *La Pantica* captured by the British in the 1830s:

> The first hasty glance around caused a sudden sickness and faintness, followed by an indignation more intense than

discreet. Before us, lying in a heap, huddled together at the foot of the foremast, on the bare and filthy deck, lay several human beings in the last stage of emaciation–dying. The ship fore and aft was thronged with men, women, and children, all entirely naked, and disgusting with disease. The stench was nearly insupportable, cleanliness being impossible … The rainy season had commenced, and during the night rain had poured heavily down. Nearly a hundred slaves had been exposed to the weather on deck, and amongst them the heap of dying skeletons at the fore-mast.

He goes on: 'The height between the floor and ceiling was about twenty-two inches. The agony of the position of the crouching slaves may be imagined, especially that of men, whose heads and necks are bent down by the boarding above them … The body frequently stiffened into a permanent curve; and in the street of Freetown I have seen liberated slaves in every conceivable state of distortion.'[60]

As traders learnt to care for their slaves, conditions improved: the prevalence of smallpox and measles dropped greatly once traders started inoculating their cargo; their quarters were cleaned more often, causing a drop in dysentery rates; and limes were added to food provisions to prevent scurvy. Slave ships were also modified to increase the flow of fresh air through the deck, reducing stagnation: 'Additional portholes for air circulation were also an important below deck feature to keep slaves alive. Above the deck, special sails made slavers distinguishable by sight. These sails were used to push air below deck and increase air circulation.'[61]

Not all deaths were caused by disease. There was a small but significant number of accidental deaths and suicides as well as deaths caused by on-board uprisings.[62] Richard Ligon explains the circumstances around one revolt:

A Master of a ship, and a man accounted both able, stout, and honest, having transported goods of severall kinds, from England to a part of Africa, the River of Gambra [Gambia], and had there exchanged his Commodities for Negres, which was that he intended to make his voyage of, caused them all to be shipt, and did not, as the manner is, shakle one to another, and make them sure; but having an opinion of their honesty and faithfulnesse to him, as they had promised; and he being a credulous man, and himselfe good natur'd and mercifull, suffered them to go loose, and they being double the number of those in the ship, found their advantages, got weapons in their hands, and fell upon the Saylers, knocking them on the heads, and cutting their throats so fast, as the Master found they were all lost, out of any possibility of saving; and so went down into the Hold, and blew all up with himselfe; and this was before they got out of the River.[63]

Men often fared worse than women and children because they were stronger and were usually the instigators of rebellions. Wise traders took no chances, immediately separating them and incarcerating them in chains.[64] Suicides were prevented in some ships by installing netting that prevented the slaves from jumping overboard.[65] Mortality rates were carefully analysed after the introduction of Dolben's Act, and it was this incentive, rather than compassion for their quarry, that lowered the rate of death. This is reflected in the ways in which the slaves were treated. Olaudah Equiano recounts what happened when he refused food on the Middle Passage: 'one of them held me fast by the hands, and laid me across, I think, the windlass, and tied my feet, while the other flogged me severely. I had never experienced any thing of this kind before.'[66] They were also cruelly teased: 'Every circumstance I met with served only to render my state more painful, and heighten my apprehensions and my opinion of the cruelty of the whites. One day they had taken a number of fishes; and when they had killed and satisfied themselves with as many as they thought fit, to our astonishment who were on deck, rather than give us any of them to eat, as we expected, they tossed the remaining fish into the sea again.'

Some malnourished slaves tried to steal some of the catch, but 'they were discovered, and the attempt procured them some very severe floggings.'[67] The slaves were regularly let on board the deck to get some fresh air, exercise and respite from the foul conditions below. The crew knew that Africans danced, so 'song and dance were promoted' whether they wanted to take part or not – and they invariably did not. Therefore, 'the way the *song* and the *dance* were *promoted*, was by severe

A political cartoon entitled *The abolition of the slave trade Or the inhumanity of dealers in human flesh exemplified in Captn. Kimber's treatment of a young Negro girl of 15 for her virjen modesty* by Isaac Cruikshank 1792. A female slave is suspended on a ship. The captain – named John Kimber – has readied himself, whip in hand, to flog her as a group of female slaves look on in horror. (British Museum)

whipping.'[68] Equiano also made a point of the fact that the crew were often treated as inhumanely as the slaves: 'the white people looked and acted, as I thought, in so savage a manner; for I had never seen among any people such instances of brutal cruelty; and this not only shown towards us blacks, but also to some of the whites themselves. One white man in particular I saw, when we were permitted to be on deck, flogged so unmercifully with a large rope near the foremast, that he died in consequence of it; and they tossed him over the side as they would have done a brute.'[69]

The most shocking part of all this, and what really captured the imagination of the British during the abolitionists' campaign, was the over-packing of slaves on ships. Two ships in particular – the English *Brooks* and the French *La Vigilante* – were notorious for cramming in far too many slaves.[70] To spread the word of these horrors, drawings of the cramped quarters were printed and distributed by the abolitionist publisher James Phillips in the 1789 broadside *Description of a Slave Ship*. The illustrations are now infamous for representing the squalor and abuse of the slaves, and exposed the greed and callousness of their masters. The diagrams show the slaves lined up on tiny, thin palettes, unable to stand or even kneel. This was all true of course, but the diagrams were not correct; yes, there was overcrowding, but the diagrams clearly display it on almost every available inch of the ship. If the spaces reserved for cargo or supplies other than slaves had been left clear, the drawings might not have been so compelling. Dolben's Act insisted upon a maximum density of eight slaves per ton and may have eased minds, but slaves were usually crammed in relatively small sections of the ship and so the measure of slaves per ton was a poor estimate of slave density, and by extension slave mortality.

When the ships approached their destination they had to land successfully, which was perilous in itself. When Equiano landed at Monserrat the surf tossed the ships about so much that many suffered broken limbs or died 'mangled and torn'.[71] Those who did eventually

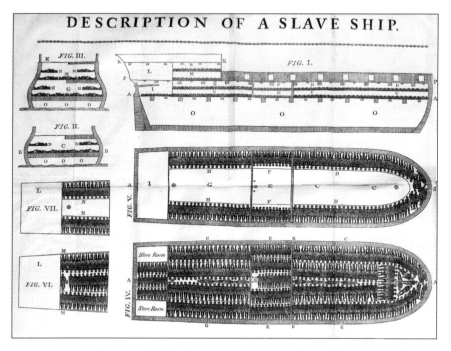

Description of a Slave Ship (1789) The now infamous pamphlet published by abolitionist James Phillips illustrating the tight packing of slaves inside the slave ship *Brooks*. (Sotheby's)

arrive at the colonies did so in a terribly weak condition, and a heavy toll taken upon their mental as well as their physical health, with some driven 'insane' by their ordeal.[72] They were given no respite after docking and were immediately readied for purchase. Richard Ligon describes the process on Barbados: 'When they are brought to us, the Planters buy them out of the Ship, where they find them stark naked, and therefore cannot be deceived in any outward infirmity. They choose them as they do Horses in a Market, the strongest, youthfullest, and most beautifull, yield the greatest prices. Thirty pound sterling is a price for the best man Negre; and twenty five, twenty six, or twenty seven pound for a Woman; the Children are at easier rates. And we buy them so, as the sexes may be equall.'[73]

Equiano describes his own experience: 'On a signal given, (as a beat of a drum), the buyers rush at once into the yard where the slaves are confined, and make choice of that parcel they like the best ... In this manner, without scruple, are relations and friends separated, most of them never to see each other again ... Why are parents to lose their children, brothers their sisters, or husbands their wives? Surely this

A slaver brands a captured African with his mark in Guinea, West Africa. (New York Public Library)

BRANDING A NEGRESS AT THE RIO PONGO
From a wood engraving in Canot's *Twenty Years of an African Slaver,*
New York, 1854

is a new refinement in cruelty [that] adds fresh horrors even to the wretchedness of slavery.' He goes on to say: 'I have often seen slaves … put into scales and weighed; and then sold for threepence to sixpence or ninepence a pound.'[74]

The scale of the slave trade was only really fully realised in the 1960s when Philip D. Curtin completed a ground-breaking census of the trade, where he estimated that the trade in African slaves displaced a total of 12 million individuals from their homelands. Just as shocking, he also managed to extract from the data that only 9.4 million arrived at their destination, meaning one in five perished *en route*. At its worst, the Middle Passage was killing 6-8,000 slaves per year.[75]

As they were bought and taken away to the plantations they would 'sing mournful songs', and when they arrived at the plantation, they were immediately fire-branded with their owner's mark. If anyone attempted to bolt – and many did – they were set upon by dogs. On the British islands they were taken to their final destination: a primitive hut made from bagasse and sticks where they were issued with a mat to sleep on, and sometimes a pot for cooking.[16] The horrors of their slavery were only just beginning.

Chapter 8

Abolition and Aftermath

> We may now consider this trade as having received its condemnation; that its sentence is sealed; that this Curse of mankind is seen by the House in its true light; and that the greatest stigma on our national character which ever yet existed, is about to be removed!
>
> *William Pitt, the Younger*[1]

Ever since their inception the sugar colonies received visitors who were appalled by the slavery they witnessed and called for the humane treatment of the slaves. The Quaker leader George Fox was one such person who, upon arriving on Barbados in 1671, quickly formed the opinion that slaves were men not just in his eyes but in the eyes of God, and therefore should be treated as such. He concluded that, as men of God, it was of paramount importance that they had their souls saved by converting them to Christianity.

He and his followers made several visits to the colonies and caused a lot of bother to the planters by distributing pamphlets encouraging masters to be kinder to their slaves. Not only that, he sidestepped the planters altogether and invited slaves to Quaker meetings so they could hear for themselves his progressive ideas. However, converting to Protestantism was not a simple case of a quick baptism; it required study which, in turn, required teaching slaves to read. In return for their meddling, Fox and his followers were harassed and persecuted until they gave up and left, accused of inciting the slaves to rebel. A few Quaker plantation owners were convinced enough to free a few slaves, but essentially his efforts came to naught. Christianisation was not an option in a land where slaves were kept at arm's length and dehumanised to prevent disorder and create compliance.

Independently from the Quakers, Robin Baxter published his work *A Christian Dictionary* in England in 1673, in which he described the slavery on the sugar colonies as a 'curse crime.'[2] He suggested buying slaves, converting them to Christianity and then selling them on to the colonies, souls saved. Again, nothing came of it because religion – or, rather, piety – was low on the planters' priority list. There was little religion to be found; on Barbados for example, there were just eleven ministers at the helm of a flock of 20,000 Christians.

Despite this pressure from Quakers and others, none went as far as suggesting slavery itself should be abolished, just that slaves had the right to be treated less harshly,[3] and we have to wait another century, and the Enlightenment, before ideas of abolition began to crystallise. One particular case brought the concept of abolition to the fore when Ordinance Clerk Granville Sharp, a self-taught lawyer, helped a slave achieve his freedom. Sharp had found Jonathon Strong on the streets of London in 1767 so severely beaten he was left almost blind. His master, David Lisle, cast him out, declaring him useless. However, having seen Strong in the street, Lisle had a change of mind and wanted him back to sell on to a slave trader for £30. This was all perfectly legal; Lisle was his owner, and even had the receipt to prove it. Sharp took the issue up with the mayor, and the case went to court, presided over by the mayor himself. Sharp won the case and Strong was freed, but there were no changes to the law (indeed, Lisle later attempted to sue the courts – his behaviour may have been immoral, but it was not illegal). And so, Sharpe spent the next five years studying law and ownership and how this related to slavery. Then in 1772, in what would be a defining case for the abolitionist movement, Sharp represented escaped slave James Somerset. In court, Sharp argued that in England a slave must 'willingly bind himself to his master' and could not be coerced into a life of servitude. Strong was freed, and as a direct result of this key case there was a flurry of manumissions of slaves across England.

Hearing this news, the planters despaired, worried that freed black slaves were inserting themselves into English society and marrying white women. More court cases followed and with each one the British people began to get a clearer picture of what slavery actually entailed. Groups calling for the abolition of slavery were formed and quickly acquired loyal followings. The first societies were made up mainly of freed slaves, but were led by alternative Christian groups like the Quakers and Methodists, and it is within these groups that the idea of slavery being 'intrinsically evil' began to develop. Sharp argued that the slaves needed help because the Bible – specifically Matthew 22:39 – instructed it: 'Thou shalt love thy neighbour as thyself', and that included slaves.

These progressive ideas did not filter down to the colonies in any significant way. Planters knew that knowledge was power, and they were certainly not going to have their slaves literate, Christianised and enlightened. They made sure they were kept in the dark; anything that created the merest whiff of unrest or revolt had to be stamped out, and they made sure that any visiting missionaries did not mix, and therefore meddle, with the slaves. Keeping missionaries separate from the slaves ensured they saw nothing untoward, and planters instructed their staff to spare the whip when the missionaries were present, or to at least wait until they were out of earshot.[4]

However, something far more worrying for the planters was on the horizon: the ideas surrounding free trade after the publication of Adam Smith's *The Wealth of Nations* in 1776. It became obvious that the British planters' monopoly was only good for the British planters. British sugar prices were inflated, in part by the planters themselves, but also by high duties and the cost of protection by the British military. British citizens had come to realise that cheap sugar was available to the rest of Europe but not to them. Smith also argued that free workers who were getting paid low wages would work harder and need less supervision. And then there was the emerging East India problem which was putting Smith's ideas to the test, rather successfully. India was now occupied by the British and producing cheap white sugar with free labourers, free from duties and without protection from pirates by the British Navy. As a consequence, the colonies were looking out of step now that ending slavery made economic and moral sense, and the planters did not like that one bit.[5]

***

In 1783 a non-denominational abolitionist group formed that would become The Society for the Abolition of the Slave Trade. Evangelical women made up a significant proportion of its members; the plight of the slaves, especially female slaves, struck a chord with them, and they were outraged by the stories of the sexual violence to which the female slaves were subject. What is more, they made the connection between the simple act of purchasing sugar for their families' tea tables with the horrors of slavery. The message was simple: buying sugar meant that *you* were part of the slave trade. So, even though women had no parliamentary power, they became very influential by making a somewhat intangible concept suddenly very clear.

Cementing this idea, Quaker William Fox quantified slaves' suffering in terms of sugar consumption and calculated that one pound of West Indian sugar was the equivalent to two ounces of human flesh. He didn't show his workings, so how he arrived at this value we do not know, but he succeeded in making the link between sugar and slavery even more evocative. At a time when the gulf between the rich and poor was particularly pronounced, the movement gained support from the working classes who had developed a real feeling that slaves on plantations and the unskilled workers of Britain were kindred spirits and even referred to themselves as white slaves.[6] Also in the ranks were missionaries, a cohort that made up for its small numbers by heavily lobbying Parliament.

In these early days of the abolition movement, freed slaves were the most committed members of the Society. Within this group three influential

men emerged who managed to make this very disparate assembly of people more cohesive and effective. Former slave Olaudah Equiano and his two friends, African brothers Ignatius and Cugoano Sancho, were tenacious and gregarious, and they managed to successfully improve communications by sharing their experiences and their philosophy. Equiano's 1783 memoir *The Interesting Narrative of the Life of Olaudah Equiano, or Gustavus Vassa, the African* is an excellent first-hand account of an African's

A portrait of Olaudah Equiano taken from his memoir *The Interesting Narrative of the Life of Olaudah Equiano, or Gustavus Vassa, the African* (1789). (British Library)

experience, from their home life to capture and eventually freedom via the hell of slavery.[7]

Because of its appeal to a great diversity of backgrounds, the Society's cause grew in popularity, its numbers swelled and attracted some of the most influential people in the country. Most notable perhaps was pot-maker to royalty Josiah Wedgwood, who created the Society's iconic seal of a kneeling slave with his arms outstretched looking up to the heavens asking, 'Am I Not a Man and a Brother?' As the Society gained momentum, efforts ramped up; members knocked door to door to spread the word to attract more new members. When speaking with the public, they also applied Adam Smith's ideas surrounding free trade to slavery and the sugar islands to garner more interest. Allowing the West Indies' monopoly on British sugar meant that families were paying through the nose for this blood-stained slave sugar.

Campaigners produced a vast number of pamphlets and books including the first-hand accounts of missionaries, ex-slaves and even ex-slavers, as well as real data to back up their claims. Their literature used striking diagrams and illustrations to communicate the horrors slaves had to endure, printing images of Liverpool shops selling handcuffs, thumbscrews and devices for prizing open the mouths of slaves who refused to eat.

There were also illustrations showing the terrible conditions inside slave ships, including – as we have seen – the cramming of slaves on the *Brooks*. Other ships had their

Tinted Wedgewood stoneware medallion (1786) carry the iconic illustration of the slave asking "Am I not a man and a brother". The legend would later be adapted by female abolitionists. (Brooklyn Museum)

horror stories too: in 1781 *The Zong*, a slave ship designed to hold 200 slaves but carrying 400, headed out from the African coast to the West Indies. Not long after embarkation the ship ran into some difficulties; first, the crew got lost, then just as the inevitable disease epidemics broke out, they found the ship was letting in water. The captain knew that if the slaves died of disease he would be liable for the loss of his cargo – after all, he was responsible for the conditions upon his own ship – but if they were killed by pirates, or the hand of God, it would be the underwriters who were liable. And so, in a shocking act of violent cynicism, he and his crew threw 132 of the sickliest slaves overboard, citing that he had to do it to prevent his damaged ship from sinking and to save the remaining cargo, slaves and crew.[8]

Accounts of incidents such as these captured the imagination of the public, but one of the most successful strategies was the telling of first-hand accounts of freed slaves like Equiano Olaudah. His memoir and gift for public speaking made all too clear the horrors the slaves encountered and how powerless they felt. His words are still very poignant today. There were others too, such as James Ramsay, an English pastor who had seen the treatment of the slaves himself. He wrote several texts, but his most influential was *An Essay on the Treatment and Conversion of African Slaves in the British Sugar Colonies* (1784). There were several aspects of slavery that the abolitionist groups focused on in their publications, but most important was the poor treatment of the slaves.

Slavers sling slaves overboard in this woodcut depicting the *Zong* massacre.

Ramsay summed up the issue very well: 'I recollect not a single clause in all our colony acts [that] save them from the capricious cruelty of an ignorant, unprincipled master, or a morose, unfeeling overseer. Nay a horse, a cow, or a sheep, it much better protected with us by the law, than a poor slave.'[9]

He points out how the English were especially cruel. On the French colonies, he tells us, if a French slave were to be 'rendered unserviceable, through age, hurts, or disease, be turned adrift by his master, he is to be placed in the public hospital, and to be maintained there at the expense of his master.'[10] This duty of care was not extended to the slaves on the English colonies. Equiano reinforced these claims: 'it was almost a constant practice with our clerks, and other whites, to commit violent depredations on the chastity of the female slaves,' and that '[t]ortures, murder, and every other imaginable barbarity and iniquity, are practised upon the poor slaves with impunity.'[11]

A political cartoon from 1791 titled *Barbarities of the West Indias* showing a cruel overseer plunge a slave into a kettleful of boiling sugar syrup to 'warm' them up. Says the overseer to the slave: "B-t your black Eyes! what you can't work because you're not well? - but I'll give you a warm bath, to cure your Ague, & a Curry-combing afterwards to put Spunk into you." Nailed to the wall in the background are a dismembered arm and amputated ears. (British Museum)

Equiano went a step further, making the point that slavery itself was fundamentally wrong, irrespective of treatment. Equiano spent some of his time in the cane fields, but also spent a considerable proportion of his enslavement working at the docks for his master, Mr King, whom he described as a man of good character who didn't flog his slaves: 'If any of his slaves behaved amiss, he did not beat them or use them ill.'[12] King taught him a whole range of skills and even gave him a managerial role in his business and paid him for his work. Despite all this, Equiano was not in control of his own life, and always looked for opportunities to escape it, and it is for that very reason – that loss of control – that made slavery intrinsically wrong.[13] Perhaps he thought this argument was not persuasive enough, adding the rather utilitarian economic point that free people 'worked harder, were healthier and stronger, and had a greater yield of sugar.'[14] He lamented that planters: 'stupefy them [the slaves] with stripes, and think it necessary to keep them in a state of ignorance; and yet you assert that they are incapable of learning; that their minds are such a barren soil or moor, that culture would be lost on them … are you not struck with shame and mortification, to see the partakers of your nature reduced so low?' Equiano appealed to the planters: 'by changing your conduct, and treating your slaves as men, every cause of fear would be banished. They would be faithful, honest intelligent and vigorous; and peace, prosperity, and happiness, would attend you.'[15]

***

The lobbying of Parliament eventually paid off when independent Yorkshire MP William Wilberforce joined the Society's ranks – suddenly there was potential for an Act of Parliament calling for abolition. They knew this was still a long way off, but it motivated the Society to make a political game plan so they could show a united front. This raised the issue of the practicalities of ending slavery: should it be ended totally and immediately, or dismantled slowly over a period of time? The gradualist approach was supported by Clark, Wedgwood and Wilberforce and it won out because it was reckoned to have the greatest chance of being accepted by both planters and Parliament. The first step, they argued, should be to abolish not slavery but the slave trade. Doing so would have two effects: first, the horrors of the

Middle Passage would end; and second, the planters, without access to a perpetual supply of fresh slaves, would be obliged to care for them more humanely. As part of this initial first step, it was suggested that the slaves should be Christianised. To aid its acceptance, they portrayed slaves as gentle savages who were crying out to be made into free, hard-working Christians. Slave women were described as timid and humble things who simply wanted to make a home and raise their children in wedlock.[16] By today's standards, this is all terribly patronising; that they might be pleading for a return to their own cultures and land probably never crossed their minds. But by projecting Christian values onto the slaves, the more the British could sympathise with a people who were culturally alien to them.

To counter these claims, anti-abolitionist groups such as the *West Indian Committee* were formed. They saw the assertions that were being made and tried to dismiss them. One pamphlet addressed the issue of slaves' treatment: 'To all impartial Strangers I appeal, whether the Inhabitants of the British Sugar Colonies are not the most benevolent, hospitable People in the World.'[17] To reinforce their point, the committee even commissioned a play called *The Benevolent Planters* that demonstrated to everyone the kindnesses planters showed to their not-at-all downtrodden chattels. Others thought it a simple issue of semantics, and the word 'slave' had acquired a bit of baggage: 'The vulgar are influenced by names and titles. Instead of SLAVES let the Negroes be called ASSISTANT-PLANTERS; and we shall not then hear such violent outcries against the slave trade by pious divines, tender-hearted poetesses and short-sighted politicians.'[18]

Another argument was that slavery was part of the human condition: 'Slavery [having] prevailed in most parts of the world at some point,' and that '[t]hroughout the Old Testament, indeed, Slavery is a state recognized as lawful and agreeable to the will of God.'[19] And if that argument didn't convince you, they also mentioned that they were already enslaved by their own people anyway: 'it is the lot of most of those that are brought to the Colonies, who, Generally speaking, were Slaves in their own Country, only to exchange a black Master for a White one.'[20] Not only that, they claimed that Africa had such a surfeit of slaves that it regularly culled them ('massacred as sacrifices to superstition' said one publication) and when the Portuguese arrived ready to trade their surplus slaves the people of Africa 'rejoiced'.[21]

Anti-abolitionists dealt with the notorious Middle Passage by describing it almost like some kind of cruise holiday: 'on the voyage from Africa to the West Indies, the Negroes are well fed, [have] comfortable lodges, and have every possible attention paid to their health, cleanliness, and convenience.'[22] The treatment had to be so because 'Negro property is an object of such value and importance to the proprietor, that he is disposed to cherish it by every prudent and humane method.'[23] This line of argument was developed to show that the black slaves had it much better than the British working poor who were 'obliged to exhale noxious effluvia, while Negro exhales an air, that to his tropical constitution is pure and healthy.' One chaplain wrote that he 'wished our labouring poor were half as well off as the Negroes: they have a little snug house and garden, and plenty of pigs and poultry.' He pressed on: '[e]very night of the year they have as much social enjoyment, as the lower class in England have at the season of Christmas gambols.'[24] Parliament was no longer taken in by this, especially when many planters had admitted to punishing their slaves and that planters viewed violence as a necessary element of life on the sugar colonies. 'It is a lamentable circumstance, that the dread of punishment is necessary to enforce the performance of duty.'[25]

The next anti-abolitionist argument was an economic one, and it had the potential to be somewhat more compelling. Abolition would ruin Britain for the simple reason that 'the British Sugar Colonies are a ... perpetual Fountain of Wealth to Great Britain.'[26] Remember too that the sugar-slave complex reached almost every part of Britain. In Liverpool alone the 'artificers and mechanics' received £100,000 annually from the sugar and slave trade.[27] And then there was the associated trade in African gold and ivory. Great Britain had become great off the back of the sugar and slave trade, whether you liked it or not, and abolishing slavery would spell an end to the comfortable life to which the British had become accustomed. Its importance to the British economy 'almost exceeds calculation' declared one pamphlet.[28] The damage to the country's economy would be so sharp and far-reaching that ending the slave trade meant creating a recession, with one anti-abolitionist going so far as to say that there would be 'widespread famine'.[29]

Wilberforce introduced the first bill for the abolition of the slave trade in 1789 where it was immediately defeated. He tried again year after year. Although interest, numbers, and enthusiasm in the Society waxed and waned, the core group – Wilberforce, Sharp and Wedgwood – kept lobbying, debating and producing anti-slavery literature. In 1804 interest picked up again, and by 1806 their rhetoric was accepted by the liberal Whig party. Suddenly the abolition of the slave trade became *the* election issue. The Whigs won, and their government promptly put the bill through Parliament the next year. It was to be its sixteenth airing in the Palace of Westminster, but this time politicians knew that the British public was overwhelmingly in favour of abolition. It passed through the House of Lords with forty-one votes for the bill versus twenty against, and then charged through the House of Commons with a landslide victory of 155 votes to five.[30]

In the streets people were voting with their wallets and purses by boycotting slave-made sugar, which forced grocers to source sugar produced by free people such as that of East India. This sent the West Indian sugar trade into crisis; they had already increased their prices because of the Haitian Revolution and the French blockades. This change in consumer habits of the British forced the West Indian planters to sell sugar at a price lower than the cost of production and planters reported that they could not get the credit from merchants to replace worn out equipment. Abolitionists were having none of it. As far as they were concerned the greedy planters were simply complaining because they were no longer making the huge profits they now expected. The planters were temporarily saved in 1808 when they successfully convinced Parliament that there was a grain shortage and therefore no surplus for distillers to make into spirits. The solution? Britain should buy up West Indian sugar for the distillers instead. This was not a sustainable strategy, but at least it provided a financial respite in which they could plead with Parliament to lower the crippling duty on their sugar exports; by 1812 Jamaican sugar was selling at one shilling per kilogram compared to 0.6 shillings per kilo for Cuban sugar, which was now available to the British. The benefits of free trade were now apparent to British consumers, and it looked like West Indian sugar was about to become a mere relic.[31]

To counter all of this, the anti-abolitionists set up the West India Interest to produce pro-slavery propaganda, though resorted quickly to smear campaigns, going as far as to claim that one member of the Society for the Abolition of the Slave Trade had gained his limp from beating and kicking one of his own slaves so hard it had left *him* with permanent injury. They also held Haiti up as an example of what would happen if the slaves were freed – destruction, death and a collapse of trade – but British citizens saw the Haitians as heroes, not terrorists. The only point that seemed to work in their favour was that freed slaves would not work as hard, or have the interest to keep production at the levels expected. However, the abolitionists made their counterclaim, citing one West Indian planter who actually paid his slaves to work, and how they were much happier and produced more sugar because of it.[32]

Abolition of the slave trade alone did not make the planters behave more kindly towards their precious slaves, and the slaves themselves were embittered that they were still a kept people; as a result, revolts were more frequent. Planters blamed the missionaries and other churchmen for planting the seeds of revolution, and many were imprisoned and their churches razed. The missionary John Smith was locked up because he wanted to teach slaves to read so that they could study the Bible and become civilised Protestants, inspiring them to demand their freedom. Upon hearing of their incarceration, the slaves of one of the larger plantations named Batchelor's Adventure rebelled, captured their masters and put them in stocks and taunted them. The revolt was quickly quashed by neighbouring planters. Some 250 slaves were killed during the incident and subsequent trial, and Smith remained imprisoned, eventually dying of malnourishment.[33]

Planters were now faced with a rapidly diminishing slave population, which they worked just as hard as before but could no longer replace with more slaves, at least by legal means. This led to an increase in the clandestine trade in 'black ivory' with Spain and France, and as a result both the West Indian islands and the African coast had to be constantly monitored by the British.[34] It wasn't to last though, because the mood was changing throughout the rest of Europe, with Spain agreeing to end its slave trade in 1811, and France following suit in 1815.

It was obvious that the next step had to be total emancipation; the gradualist strategy had caused more harm than good, and pressure was applied by abolitionists for this to happen immediately. Again, the women of these societies used their approach of highlighting the plight of female slaves, modifying Wedgwood's infamous seal to show a female slave asking the question: 'Am I not a WOMAN and a SISTER?' The new seal was put on hairpins and bracclets, and sewn onto bags and handkerchiefs, anywhere people would see them. This strategy was extremely effective, and it became apparent that the British public favoured total emancipation. News of this swiftly made its way to the West Indies, panicking the planters even more. In typical planter fashion, their knee-jerk reaction was to work the slaves harder and punish them more severely; they fully expected to have their slaves taken from them, so they got their money's worth before the inevitable day of emancipation. As a result there was a mass uprising of Jamaican slaves at Christmas in 1831; 200 slaves were killed during the uprising and once order had resumed a further 540 were hanged for their involvement. News of this heightened inhumanity reached British shores, which only made the abolitionists more focused upon their goal.[35]

***

On the 1 August 1834 the Emancipation Act was passed in England. Eight hundred thousand slaves should have gone free that day, but it did not happen. Instead, planters and Parliament had agreed that only children under six years of age would be manumitted. The remainder of the 'free' ex-slave population was obliged to work an 'apprenticeship' lasting four years for non-field workers and six for field workers. During these apprenticeships, the institutionalised African population would be taught how to be both free and civilised. More importantly, from the planters' point of view, it gave them time to work out how they would survive in a slaveless world.

Conditions of the Bill stated that the working week would be pared back to forty-one-and-a-half hours, and they would have twenty-six free days per year to work for pay or tend their own land. They were to be fed, clothed and housed and were to receive better medical care. Not only that, British officials would be sent to the islands to check adherence to these measures. The West India Interest were up in arms: if this was how slavery was going to end, the trade would collapse completely, and they pushed for compensation. Parliament agreed, controversially setting aside forty per cent of their annual budget – twenty million pounds – for planter compensation. There was public outcry over the deal, but it was accepted in Parliament as a necessary evil.[36]

The slaves were now free but living the life of a seventeenth-century white indentured servant. It was not manumission, and it did not produce the eager, productive workforce Adam Smith said it would. How could it? This was no freedom, and their labour remained unpaid. Unsurprisingly, the slaves were deeply unhappy and wanted true freedom. They went on strike, but the planters retaliated by slaughtering their livestock and felling their fruit trees. Work contracts were introduced that included brutal penalties if they did not fulfil them satisfactorily. They were given a week of hard labour if they missed two days' work and were abused and beaten no differently than before. In some ways the treatment was worse: pregnant women were now routinely flogged, often to the point of causing miscarriage; the planters had no incentive to keep the children alive because they would be born free and not under their care.[37] Olaudah Equiano said of the situation: 'I had thought only slavery dreadful; but the state of a free negro appeared to me now equally so at least, and in some respects even worse' going on to ask if they 'should prefer even the misery of slavery to such a mockery of freedom?'[38]

Owners of large plantations happily took their huge compensation payments and retired to their English mansions, but smaller planters felt dejected, destroyed by nosey, meddling missionaries. They could see their livelihoods evaporating before them as they were outcompeted by Cuban and British East Indian sugar. British capitalism had sold out West Indian sugar and as a consequence Anglo-Caribbean dominance was shaken to its core.[39]

The apprenticeship system was a miserable failure and was ditched in 1838. The Africans of the British sugar islands were finally free but were still stuck where they were without the means to transport themselves away. So they stayed and remained just as dependent upon white planters who forced them to sign work contracts that allowed the exploitation to continue. Missionaries did their best to offset this by providing humane contracts that paid real wages, establishing free villages of ex-slaves. Planters were forced into trying new methods – or at least methods new to them – such as the mediaeval horse-drawn plough and even tried developing new strains of sugarcane that would be easier to harvest and crush.[40]

Slavery, however, still existed on Cuban, French, Brazilian and US plantations. In the US the idea of total emancipation had spread quickly from Britain, and British abolitionist groups shared information with those of the United States, lending a helping hand in forming a more positive relationship between the two nations. Unfortunately, similar patterns occurred there too; planters simply paid less for more work and fewer obligations. And so, for many plantations in the New World, things remained essentially the same: Africans toiling and whites overseeing, organising, exploiting and doling out punishment.[41] Not only that, but slavery hung on in Cuba, keeping the Atlantic slave trade in reasonably good health. The United States, which did not enjoy a ready supply of cheap sugar, kept Cuban slave sugar in business until slavery was finally abolished there in 1886.[42]

***

The West Indian sugar planters were stuck in a post-slavery world. The cruel apprenticeship system had failed, and the number of black workers had drastically fallen, causing a drop in sugar production. Capitalism was taking its toll on the West Indian sugar industry. The planters needed labour, and it had to be cheap and plentiful; they could not see it any other way. The British Empire was now so proficient in building and managing sugar plantations that they sprang up in almost every tropical and sub-tropical colony within its sprawling borders, taking it not only to India but also South Africa, Mauritius, Fiji and Australia. These new plantations needed workers too of course, and the work fell to the indigenous peoples of these newly conquered territories. However, the West Indian planters did not have the luxury of exploiting the indigenous races; they had worked those to death already. Instead, they turned to the indigenous people of the empire to fill their labour vacuum.

India was one of the empire's longer-established territories, and so it turned first to the people of that country to provide 'free' indentured labour on the plantations. They successfully transported 1.5 million individuals between the 1830s and 1920s to territories old and new: a quarter of a million went to British Guiana and 150,000 to Trinidad, and later they were sent to Fiji, South Africa and Mauritius.[43] These Indians were nicknamed 'coolies', a term that quickly became derogatory. The first cohort to be sent to the West Indies left in 1838.[44] On paper this new system of indentureship appeared progressive and it could have worked well: planters received workers, upon whom they could depend and train up, for a five-year period. In return, workers got a guaranteed fixed period of work, plus a free trip home. Rates of pay, number of free days and holidays, accommodation fees, food rations – everything was agreed. But this was nothing like the reality, nor was it ever intended to be. Only the poorest and most desperate individuals were recruited; skilled workers would only ask for higher wages and better conditions, and many women signed up to escape the physical and sexual abuse they were suffering at home.[45] They sailed on cramped ships in terrible conditions; it was the Middle Passage all over again, but with higher mortality rates because of the voyage's extended distance. They disembarked ill, broken and skeletal. Upon alighting, they were allowed no time to settle in and were worked just as hard as the black slaves before them.

Planters used their old tricks of demoralisation, starvation and physical and sexual abuse. They bred animosity by mixing Hindus with Muslims to reduce the chances of collusion and revolt. It will probably come as no surprise that they did not receive the pay they were promised either; untrained new workers were not paid at all in their first year. Those who were paid got a fraction of the promised amount and were often charged exorbitant prices for the most basic of possessions: a fork, for example, cost three weeks' wages.[46] The planters also reneged on their promise of a free voyage home. The workers earned so little that they could not pay for their journey themselves and were therefore forced to sign up for a further five years indentured labour. When the French and Dutch saw the success of this system, they promptly adopted it too.

The West Indies then received 18,000 Chinese workers between 1853 and 1884. The contracted terms were essentially the same but differed in that this time they were not promised a free passage home and women were not allowed as workers but could live there as residents.[47] Planters quickly developed prejudices and made sure all races knew what those prejudices were: the Chinese were more industrious than Africans, and stronger than East Indians. They were praised for their quick wit and often worked the machinery and were given more 'thoughtful' tasks, yet they were also deemed sly and cruel. Black workers resented the Chinese and Indians because they accepted low wages, which robbed them of any leverage they possessed in their argument for better pay. The planters' plan was so successful in creating animosity that it is still rife between these communities to this day.[48]

Free cane cutters working on a Jamaican plantation, 1880s.

***

For the other sugar-producing colonies of the British Empire the source of labour came from the indigenous peoples, but because sugar needed to be produced in vast industrial quantities, migrant workers were shipped in from elsewhere in the empire to fill the gaps. As sugar historian Sidney Mintz points out, these people were hardly ever British or white, 'migrants from the more productive countries [of the Empire] would not be prepared to migrate for promised wages as low as those that could attract migrants from the less productive countries. But the exclusion of non-whites from the temperate world was the clear consequence of racist policies in such countries as Australia, New Zealand, Canada, and the United States.'[49]

The mix of indigenous immigrant labour promoted animosity, just like it had on the West Indian plantations: 'A new ethnic hierarchy had emerged – but so, too, had deep-seated enmity between the indigenous peoples and the descendants of the indentured workers. Sugarcane, once again, scattered the spores of animosity far and wide; it created social and ethnic divisions and hostility from the Caribbean to the remotest of the Pacific Ocean islands.'[50]

Every sugar colony had its own version of the same story. On Fiji the indigenous workforce was ousted in favour of Indian labour, and the living conditions were so grim – worse than on the British West Indies – that it had the highest suicide rate in all of the British sugar colonies.[51] Australia initially sourced its workforce from the kanaka people of Melanesia in a process known as 'blackbirding' in which kanakas were kidnapped and shipped overseas to work the cane fields. Their homeland was inhospitable and remote, and when any did return home with their few modest possessions – fishhooks and tobacco, for instance – the people were so impressed by these items, which made their difficult lives more bearable, that a system was developed whereby kanakas worked as indentured labourers. As they toiled, they accrued a few possessions in precious 'trade boxes' which they took back home at the end of their indenture – that is if they were not starved, beaten or worked to death like any other British Empire sugar worker. But then the Australians bucked the trend of thinking that only 'coloured races could work the sugarcane', and opened up their job market to Europe in a great 'whitening' of Australia. After 1916 it became policy that only whites were allowed to work the cane fields, but this change only happened because mechanisation had made the job less gruelling. It was so strictly adhered to that they even questioned whether they should consider Italians as white or 'coloured', because, though European, they had dark skin compared to the pasty British.[52]

When the British descended upon Natal (which now makes up part of South Africa) and set up plantations in the 1860s, the Africans were rightly dubious and avoided working them if they could. A system of

Indian indenture was set up as quickly as possible and British segregated all three races. In 1893 when young lawyer Mohandas Gandhi visited the province, he was shocked at the racism, segregation and treatment of his fellow Indians, and used his skills as a lawyer to end Indian indenture. Three-way racial segregation became two-way, and the British looked to Zululand and Mozambique to fill the gaps in the workforce. Far away from the prying eyes of the establishment, they even recruited children, often underage runaways hoping to make some decent money. The conditions and food were poor, and they worked them so hard that the planters were forced to improve conditions for the sake of their own businesses.[53]

The West Indian plantations responded to this by becoming vast – the tiny profit margins demanded it. In 1750 a large plantation was considered to be around 2000 acres, but by 1900 they had grown to 10,000 acres in size. By 1860 world sugar production was an astonishing 1.37 million tons and 'sugar was cultivated commercially on a huge scale, in all corners of the of the tropical and semi-tropical world.'[54] This was the advent of 'Big Sugar'.

Chapter 9

Sugar States

> The Louisiana sugar industry quickly established itself as a unique mix of old and new – old-fashioned, brutalised slave labour, kept at work by new machinery and modern management.
>
> *James Walvin*[1]

The United States' sweet tooth can be traced back to the days of English colonial rule, a time when there were 'strong economic bonds' between the English West Indian and North American colonies. The former provided sugar, molasses and rum, and exchanged it with the latter for clothing for slaves, salt fish and other foodstuffs, and timber. Because the vast majority of the sugar produced in the West Indies was unrefined, the American colonies needed their own refineries, the first being built in 1689. At this time, the North American mainland was really just an extension of England, and therefore sugar held a similar social standing as in Europe; only the wealthy could afford it, with the poorer members of society achieving their sugar fix in the form of molasses. [2]

However, this relationship was to break down in 1764 when the British government decided that the North American colonies were 'grossly undertaxed' and issued the Sugar Act, which placed a duty on the trade of sugar and sugar products between British colonies.[3] Not prepared to pay more for their sugar, the early Americans were forced to consider developing their sugar industry beyond just refining. The West Indian planters were up in arms; if the mainland colonies enforced a sugar embargo, or became self-reliant, it would spell disaster for them, so dependent were they on North American trade. Even a drop in trade was out of the question, not only because the lack of trade in essential goods would affect business, but they were also being asked to deny trade to friends and colleagues to whom they felt much closer than most of their contemporaries in Britain. The Jamaican Assembly even petitioned the British Parliament in the hope that they could renounce parliamentary sovereignty so they could be in charge of their own affairs, a move akin to that of the North American colonists who would, of course, later succeed in achieving their independence.[4]

The North American colonists experimented with growing sugarcane in Virginia, Georgia and South Carolina, but with minimal success.[5] All the Sugar Act succeeded in was fuelling further resentment between Britain and its colonies, and increasing smuggling.[6] Then, with the War of Independence in 1775, trade did almost stop. As a result the islands received just a fraction of goods from the American mainland and thousands of slaves died of malnutrition.[7] The drop in trade was compounded by the changes in consumerism brought about by free trade, and the West Indian plantations began to collapse. The British Navy withdrew many of its ships from the Atlantic, focusing instead upon newly-colonised territories such as Australia. The new Republicans found themselves without a source of cheap sugar, and so they turned their attention once more to home soil, but this time with rather more gusto. However, scant progress would be made until they acquired Louisiana from the French.

***

The French colony of Louisiana had flourished by the close of the Haitian Revolution and was producing up to forty-five tons of sugar per year, so when a somewhat deflated Napoleon Bonaparte sold it to the United States in 1803 for the sum of $15 million, it seemed he had cut his nose off to spite his face. The deal was almost too good to be true – as revolutionary war hero General Horatio Gates famously said to President Jefferson, 'Let the Land rejoice for [we] have bought Louisiana for a song.'

The United States instantly doubled its territories, and the sugar industry was picked up just where the French had left off. Naturally, this required a good steady supply of slave labour, which they sourced from the fifteen states of the 'Old South', setting up more Louisiana plantations and several in neighbouring state, Mississippi.[8] The slaves were put under the now-familiar cruel, inhumane regime. Here, the climate was a little cooler than that of the West Indies, meaning the growing season was shorter. As a consequence, the scale and intensity of work and production increased to unprecedented levels. There was a further pressure too; if the cane was not harvested on time, frost would infiltrate and kill the rootstocks. The slaves quickly succumbed to exhaustion, forcing the planters to look towards Africa for resupply, sourcing some legally from the Congo but also smuggling many from the Caribbean. The demand for slaves was huge: they needed more than ever to work the increasing number of plantations and replace those who were dying of exhaustion. The slaves also had to contend with insects, pests, disease and stifling humidity, toiling in often treacherous flooded fields. Their horrific lives 'became legendary, so much so that masters in other parts of the United States would threaten sale there to discipline their own recalcitrant slaves.' These high mortality rates in the southern States required the US's demand to rise to more than half a million individuals per year.[9]

It was during these early years of Louisiana's legendary productivity and cruelty that one of the largest and bloodiest slave revolts in the history of the United States occurred, when between 150 and 300 slaves escaped and descended upon the plantations of Orleans. 'During the insurrection the rebel force manifested military-like discipline and hierarchy and embraced slaves of different ethnicity, origin, colour, occupation, and status. African-born slaves and creole slaves, privileged slaves and field hands, mulattoes and blacks, leaders and soldiers, men and women marched toward New Orleans in rapid order with banners flying and drums beating.'[10]

They attacked the largest plantation first, then moved to the next, taking with them an ever-growing mob of freed slaves. The slaves were unsuccessful in taking the plantations, however, and the planters overpowered them swiftly with their superior weaponry. Escapees were rounded up quickly, the planters employing local indigenous Americans to track those hiding in the depths of the forests. Upon their return 'triumphant whites mutilated the corpses and carried the heads back … as trophies.' The barbarity was despicable: 'First [they] cut off their ears, hands and legs; then the head [was] severed … and stuck upon a pole passed through his mouth, and carried through the city by two of his black brethren.' Some slaves were reported to have been shot in the legs before being roasted alive. Only a few whites died, but over 100 slaves were killed either in battle or later by execution.[11]

The ringleader was a brave and determined mulatto slave named Charles. Unfortunately, we do not know what his heroic efforts were actually *for*; the planters cared only that he was guilty and no statement was taken. Was his objective to overthrow the white planters? Not a single slave who participated in the insurgence left any oral or written evidence of why it occurred. Though going by the secrecy and planning involved in the plot, one might hazard a guess his goal was revolution like that on Haiti.

There was major investment in the Louisiana plantations. In fact, sugarcane 'became the most heavily invested form of agriculture' in the country. In the following years there would be seventy-five mills all processing new strains of sugarcane that grew quickly and were resistant to frost.[12] Then in the 1830s, levels of production increased enormously once steam technology was applied to the industry.[13] This included the five-roller mill and vacuum pan in the 1830s, and the centrifuge in the 1850s, all of which made the extraction and purification process much more efficient. Not only that but the Americans produced all the equipment themselves, unlike the West Indian planters who imported their industrial equipment from Britain at great expense. The slaves were now tasked with feeding the new ultra-efficient steam-powered mills' 'insatiable capacity'.[14] Covered vacuum pans replaced the large open-air copper kettles, significantly increasing fuel efficiency. The pans were designed by a Paris-educated mullato freeman named Norbert Rillieux who, despite inventing this crucial piece of machinery, was still considered inferior to his white colleagues. He was never allowed to sleep in the 'Big House' with his white peers, having instead to sleep in the slaves' quarters.[15]

Also key to Louisiana's success was the fact that there were very few absentee planters. American planters were obsessive and knew everything about every aspect of the sugar business. They were 'technically precocious … and receptive to innovation,'[16] and they micromanaged all of their workers; the short growing window required them to do so. Everything had to be just right, and they were not going to entrust this most crucial stage to some hired overseer in the manner of the West Indian planters.[17]

The application of steam power to the sugar industry was a huge achievement, but it was too much for the slaves. Now they worked seven days a week, and *everyone* worked – men and women, young and old, healthy and sick. They were pushed 'past their biological limits, to toil on despite their hunger, debility, boredom, frustration and exhaustion.' If they collapsed or fainted, they were pulled up onto their feet, splashed in the face with water and instructed to carry on. The worst ordeal of all was during the grinding season when the 'fatigue [was] so great that nothing but the severest application of the lash [could] stimulate the human frame to endure it.' They worked eighteen to twenty-hour shifts, and many lost their lives and limbs – as so many had before them – feeding the ever-revolving roller-mills. Uprisings were few, the slaves having neither the will nor the energy. Instead, they resisted in subtler ways by sabotaging equipment, sometimes even dismantling it and selling the parts on to other plantations. It was still common for some to run away, but it was to escape their awful lives rather than plot the next big revolution. The difficulty of the work also skewed sex ratios, with the slave population being around eighty-five per cent male. The planters knew the importance of a balanced sex ratio, and indeed it is what they sought, but women and girls succumbed sooner than males. When women did conceive, their babies usually died by miscarriage or during childbirth, and the slaves were unable to 'sustain their own numbers'.[18] Those babies who survived their term were fed on their mothers' mineral-deficient milk and were the 'smallest documented for poor populations'.[19]

Business boomed upon adopting these new technologies, and by the 1840s there were over 1500 sugar estates and Louisiana sugar made up one-quarter of the world's sugar exports. In 1861 – the final year that cane sugar was harvested entirely by slave labour – 105 tons of sugar were produced by a population of 125,000 slaves.[20] The US put its Louisiana planters on a pedestal – they had achieved ultimate efficiency in their short and intense growing season with mechanical innovation and by openly sharing information. The misery and the death of the scores of thousands of enslaved individuals during that season were not considered in this assessment.

Outside of the plantations, slaves' lives were similar to those on the West Indian plantations: they slept in small, single-storey buildings on wooden planks, and were given tiny meat rations that were so disgusting they had to resort to catching wild animals to supplement their diet. One important difference was that they were given Sunday money. With their pittance, they bought themselves a few things, like

Sugarcane is loaded onto a cart on a Cuban sugar plantation c. 1910. (Library of Congress)

a kettle, plate or comb. The idea behind this new 'freedom' was that if the slaves earned a wage – even a tiny one – they would 'not view the sugar season or the plantations as their enemies, but rather a source of additional income.'[21] There was even some relief at Christmas when the slaves were allowed to cast aside their blue work clothes and exchange them for bright and flamboyant outfits. They feasted upon turkey and chicken, and some of the less austere planters even allowed them a drink in the Big House.

Religion too was used as a means of control. All slaves were Christianised and were taught by white masters who used the Bible to demonstrate to the slaves their inferiority, that they should know their place and that their servitude was God's will. This is not what the slaves wanted to hear, and while some may have accepted this, many could see it was plainly untrue: 'God don't think no different of the blacks and the whites. [We prayed] that a day would come when Niggers only be slaves of God.' If not that, then they prayed for 'shoes that fit our feet'. There were even weddings where planters officiated in mock marriage ceremonies, though the slaves did not know they had been duped.[22]

***

Louisiana's boom didn't last: it was brought to its knees after the American Civil War when President Abraham Lincoln's administration ended slavery of all kinds in the United States. Federal troops captured New Orleans in 1862, prompting many slaves to run away from the plantations knowing emancipation would soon follow. Lincoln signed the Emancipation Proclamation of 1863, but it took a further two years before all slaves were manumitted. Many stayed but refused to work under the US planters' regime, and as a result production fell by ninety-eight per cent. It ruined many, and those that did survive lost a huge amount; the large Patout Estate's sugar sales, for example, dropped by eighty-six per cent.[23]

The sugar industry was about to crash out of Louisiana completely, but demand was there for any planter who could adapt. In the 1860s and 1870s there was a flurry of invention as planters attempted to mechanise the process further with the Patout Estate being particularly successful, patenting machines that aided both planting and harvesting sugarcane, which was by now the only element of the industry still done by hand. Now the sheer volume of cane and juice that could be processed into sugar was so great that the already huge plantations had to fuse into mega-plantations just to supply the massive machinery with enough sugarcane to keep production constant.

In a post-slavery world black freemen and women did not want to return to the cane fields, but they did want a modicum of respect and control over their lives, such as choosing who they worked for and where they lived. They also wanted to find their families – many had been separated to work different plantations many miles from each other – and the new government supported them to do this. Gaps in the plantation workforces were filled by imported Chinese workers, who were closely followed by Irish, Dutch, French, Italian and Portuguese. However, when these European free people realised what their work contracts required of them, they immediately broke them. At the same time, liberal political leaders also encouraged free black people to negotiate and demand a living wage of $350 per year so they could improve themselves and rent and furnish their own homes. Planters were not happy with this, and they were not prepared to bow down to a people who should be their chattels: in their eyes, their white supremacy had been taken away and it had to be restored. In 1867 the first white supremacist society was formed: the Knights of the White Camelia intimidated free black men and threatened to kill any who attempted to vote.[24] Although they were short-lived, they were a great influence on the Ku Klux Klan.

Any progress made was to be undone when in 1877 the Republicans made an egregious bargain with the South. They asked for the southern states' votes in the upcoming election and in return, once elected, they would withdraw federal troops from the South. They won, and the violence and oppression of black people began in earnest once more. In 1883 white supremacists killed 100 black freemen on their way to vote, even though the majority of them surrendered. In Thibodaux in 1887 black sugar workers went on strike for better pay and conditions, but after three days of violence, resulting in dozens of freeman deaths, they were left with no choice but to return to the plantations. The old power balance was restored.[25]

***

The United States' sugar plantations did not recover, and from the moment planters knew emancipation was a dead cert they immediately turned their eyes to countries still producing slave-made sugar. Brazil was one option, but Cuba, only a few miles off the coast of Florida, was quickly earmarked as the perfect place with which to trade.

Cuba had already become a major sugar producer by the time Spain announced it was to abolish its slave trade by 1820. Cuban planters, knowing that the clock was suddenly ticking on the slave trade as they knew it, imported as many slaves as possible right up until the American Civil War, increasing the population as much as eight-fold in the process.[26] Spain, heavily dependent upon Cuba's sugar trade, turned a blind eye, and 'by 1830 Cuba emerged as the world's leading sugar producer [doubling] its output every 10 years until the 1860s.'[27] Cuba had become the home of Big Sugar.

Cuba was increasing production by importing industrial machinery manufactured in Britain. And all this time Britain lapped up the cheap slave-made sugar while simultaneously boasting to other Western nations about just how moral they were in having abolished the trade already.[28] The Cubans even managed to build a network of railway lines to replace the slow and lumbering beasts of burden, allowing them to delve deep into the island's forests. The steam-powered equipment gobbled up timber at an unprecedented rate, creating vast swathes of new land ready to be transformed into cane fields. They borrowed money, and the British happily invested, despite slavery being declared illegal in its own colonies.

New land required more hands to work it and the Cubans put their 200,000 slaves under a very similar regime to that of the Louisiana plantations. Like the US, the slaves responded by sabotaging equipment as well as refusing to work, or running away. 'The result,' as Elizabeth Abbot plainly puts it, 'was a seething workforce, inferior sugar, lower productivity and standards and a continual dearth of slaves.' The clandestine slave trade could not keep up with demand, and in the 1840s Cuba turned to indentured Chinese labour. Workers of other nationalities were lured in too, particularly those from Spain, Ireland and the Canary Islands, all of whom were treated just as brutally as the slaves. The Cubans – just like all other sugar planters – found it impossible to create a sugar industry that was not cruel, violent or coercive.[29]

By the 1870s Europe and Britain had begun to withdraw their business from the Americas to focus on trading in cheap European beet sugar and sugar made on its newer colonies. It was at this point the US jumped in and saved the day by filling Cuba's trade void, instantly taking the lion's share of Cuba's sugar exports. America heavily invested in the Cuban sugar industry, building several huge refineries on the American mainland and on Cuba itself. All in all, the United States invested $950 million, and when the US went to war with Spain in the closing years of the nineteenth century, the America annexed Cuba.[30] The island was no longer just under America's wing, it had become a vassal and

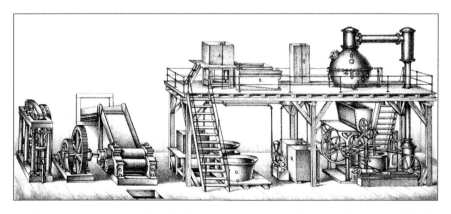

A fully mechanised sugar mill and boiling house, Pascal Iron Works, Philadelphia 1871. On the left is a roller mill fed by conveyor belt. A vacuum boiling kettle is shown top-right of the illustration. (Pascal Iron Works Illustrated Catalogues)

would remain so until the Second World War. Big Sugar now belonged to the United States of America.

With its successes in Cuba, it was only natural that the United States would look towards other potential territories that it could develop into sugar producers, and quickly identified Hawaii as a contender. Its climate had been proven suitable for sugarcane cultivation because it had already been grown there in the 1830s by missionaries who had used its cultivation as a means to convert Hawaii's indigenous people to Christianity. In the 1850s a reciprocity treaty between 'His Majesty the King of the Hawaiian Islands' and the 'Government of the United States' was drawn up, guaranteeing free trade of sugar to the US as well as a few 'trifling' items to the cash-poor Hawaiians.[31] Within a decade, the islands would produce 105,000 tons of sugar. Sugarcane became the main crop, and as a result Hawaii quickly became totally dependent upon the US. However, the American planters were disappointed with the indigenous workers because they 'lacked a capitalist work ethic and required constant surveillance.'[32] Their answer was to use indentured labour from China and Japan. By 1900 the Hawaiians found themselves a minority people in their own lands. Like Cuba, Hawaii was annexed during the American-Spanish War, but rather than becoming a vassal in 1898 its monarchy was overthrown and it became an American state in its own right. However, as a result of becoming a part of the USA at the turn of the twentieth century, both slavery and indentured labour were illegal, and the Japanese and Chinese were ousted in favour of cheap Filipino labour.[33]

When Fidel Castro rose to power in Cuba in 1959 he immediately increased the minimum wage for sugar workers. This inevitably led to an increase in the wholesale price of sugar. The US didn't like this one bit, and when it became obvious that Castro wasn't going budge on the issue, the US withdrew its financial support and sought sugar elsewhere. Cuba quickly filled its trade vacuum by supplying the Soviet Union with sugar, but the Americans had a problem; the islands of Hawaii could not fill the Unites States' sugar void, so it had to look inward to Florida.

Florida had had a little success in sugarcane cultivation in the 1930s, but after the USA cut ties with Cuba many exiled planters moved from Cuba to Florida. There was a huge amount of US investment, and the Everglades were quickly transformed from ecologically rich marshland to drained cultivatable land. By the mid-1960s it was producing a million tons of sugar per year.[34] This operation required a large workforce, and Florida's planters shipped in workers from the Caribbean and issued them with temporary visas. Far away from home and cut off from the outside world they were exploited on a vast scale, contractually bound and unable to complain because of threats of deportation. In the late twentieth century the exploitative system was exposed, and in 2000 the Florida planters were obliged to pay the workers a decent wage. There was no way they were going to do that, of course, and Big Sugar ditched manual labour and opted for mechanised cultivation and harvesting instead.

***

The twentieth century saw sugar grown everywhere and anywhere it was commercially viable to do so, and each time it was run by a management of exploitation and depredation, each one more callous than the last. Whenever workers gained more rights, planters found ways to either shift the goalposts and exploit them still further or avoid employing them altogether. Sugar, it seems, taints all who make it, and it is easy to forget that these evils were driven first by the insatiable appetites of the people of Europe and then the rest of the world.

The dark history of sugar was ultimately driven by those who ate it; individuals usually thousands of miles away from its place of cultivation and production. So to continue this dark history of sugar we now need to turn our attention to its consumption.

Chapter 10

Sugar Takes Hold in Court

A tothe is a sencyble bone, the whiche beynge in a lyvyng mans heade hath felynge, and so hath none other bone in mans body, and therefore the tothe-ache is an extreme peyne.

Andrew Boorde[1]

Richard II was and remains a king maligned. Foppish and self-indulgent, he revelled in monarchical opulence and epitomises the high living and high fashion associated with the Late Middle Ages. Richard's household was extensive and far-reaching, and his court was estimated to be 10,000 strong, 3000 of which were kitchen and food service staff.[2] Though possibly an over-generous estimate, it does suggest that he had many more people working under him than your typical mediaeval monarch (if there is such a thing) up until that date.

Richard was particularly fond of food and fine dining. He hunted wild game for the table – as many kings did – and he loved the pomp, ceremony and attention to detail of theatrical mediaeval feasting. To use modern parlance, he was a 'foodie'. There are two major culinary claims attributed to him: he invented the napkin, and he commissioned the first cookbook written in the English language. Written – or rather, dictated – by his master cooks, *Forme of Cury* was written around 1380 and is a scroll containing a comprehensive list of around 200 dishes with guidance on how to make them.[3] Many of those dishes contained sugar. It was copied by scribes so that duplicates could be sent to other households in the kingdom; the original manuscript, as far as we know, is long gone. There are several extant copies today, all slightly different to each other.

In mediaeval Western Europe sugar was considered a spice, and like the other spices that trickled into royal courts, it was not only deliciously exotic, but also a status symbol. There had been a little trade with the Islamic Empire prior to the Crusades, but it was very limited. The earliest mention of sugar in Britain comes from Anglo-Saxon England: when the great Anglo-Saxon historian the Venerable Bede died in 735, he bequeathed to his brethren a tiny collection of spices and scented woods that included, amongst them, a scrap of sugar.[4] After that, there isn't another mention of sugar in the records until the Crusades three-and-a-half centuries later. It has been theorised that Eleanor of Aquitaine, spouse of Henry II, came back from campaign after the Second Crusade with knowledge of – and some personal samples of – sugar and spices. When returning knights brought sugar back after the close of the First Crusade, it was mere curiosity, but when Eleanor brought it back with her seal of approval, her great celebrity encouraged its 'swift adoption' by the gentlemen and – more importantly – the ladies of her court, who were tasked to run their households. It was they who would compile food orders and hold the key to the closely guarded spice chest. When the mystic Lady Margery Kempe had a nervous breakdown, her keys to the spice chest were one of the first things to be taken away.[5]

The first record of a domestic sugar purchase in England can be seen in records of the household of Eleanor and Henry II, but only tiny amounts of it were purchased and it was strictly only to be consumed at court.[6] In the thirteenth century Henry III – Eleanor's grandson – bought sugar regularly. It was still very expensive and considered very special, but was now selling by the pound rather than the ounce.[7] In 1264 it cost him one shilling per kilogram, and, bearing in mind that a kitchen servant's annual wage amounted to around four shillings, it was special indeed.[8] Henry was not keeping the sugar for himself and his court because now it could be shared, but only with the most deserving; sugar was now a currency of diplomacy and receiving a gift of it was an esteemed honour.

In the thirteenth century sugar was coming into Western Europe in several forms and was often mixed with other – usually aromatic – ingredients such as violet, cinnamon, rose and saffron. Eleanor de Montford, a contemporary of Henry III, whose spouse was the highly regarded warrior-earl Simon de Montford, one of Henry's most trusted lieutenants, kept meticulous household accounts, and according to those accounts she purchased a significant amount of 'ordinary sugar', the cheapest available at the time.[9] It came in the form of sugarloaves and had to be laboriously broken down and ground by her staff. These loaves could vary in size considerably, weighing anywhere between 500g and 9kg, and were literally worth their weight in silver and well within the financial reaches of the upper classes. There is an account of the Countess of Burgundy buying fifteen loaves at the Fair of Lagny-sur-Marne in 1299, which must have been a pretty hefty haul, even if the loaves were on the small side.[10] Prices were highly variable, and doubled in the de Montford's accounts between the months of April and July of 1265. But families such as the de Montford's could easily bear such unpredictable costs and sugar was in constant use in one form or another.[11] By the 1330s prices fell to 15p per kilo and then again at very end of the fourteenth century, as more sugar and other derivatives of the sugar-making process, such as brown sugar and molasses, travelled along now well-worn and well-sailed trade routes.[12] However, it was still well out of the price range of the vast majority of people in Europe.

In the fourteenth century Richard used sugar as a seasoning in many foods, as *Forme of Cury* shows – it was common to find it in quiche-like egg tarts and dishes such as 'blanc mange', which at that time was not a wobbly dessert but a dish of capons stewed in almond milk.[13] Very popular was a dish known as 'sugar plate' which were essentially glasslike panes of sugar often dyed red and flavoured with rosewater. There were also sweetmeats like candied citrus peel, fruit preserved in syrup, and *blanchpoudre*, a mixture of sugar and ground dried ginger, all of which were imported by Venetian or Genoese merchants.[14] At table, Richard's frumenty (a type of wheat porridge) and wine were sweetened with sugar rather than honey, and there were spun sugar nests and impressive subtleties (*soteltes*) decorating the tables. Subtleties were theatrical foods, made to be looked at and admired rather than eaten, and included sugar knights and a tree laden with candied fruits.[15]

Impressive as these centrepieces must have been, they were just a 'modest … continuation of the magnificent festive food banquets' of the mediaeval Muslim Empire, especially those in Egypt.'[16] In 990 AD, for a feast celebrating the end of Ramadan, Egyptian confectioners made sugar trees, animals and castles, and Sultan Murad III ordered a parade of sugar animals including lions, elephants and giraffes and sugar fountains as well as a sugar castle to mark his son's circumcision.[17]

In his very extravagant later years Richard built a spicery that cost £35,000 per year to keep fully stocked.[18] Sugar even managed to make its way into ladies' fashion at court where 3-ft-high sugarloaf hats were

An example of an ornate sugar subtlety commissioned for a banquet hosted by Italian senator Francesco Ratta in 1693. (The J Paul Getty Trust)

worn (this was also the time of the infamous pointy shoes)[19], and it was Richard's – and his court's – high living and opulent lifestyle that would be one of the cues for his cousin Henry Bolingbroke to usurp the English throne to become Henry IV. Richard was imprisoned by Henry and starved to death in a dungeon; the dramatic irony not lost on the new king. The instigation of a more austere monarch's regime did nothing to lessen sugar's upward trajectory of popularity.

Indeed it was during Henry's reign that a ship docked in Bristol harbour weighed down with almost ten tons of the stuff.[20]

Sugar was much more common by the sixteenth century as it poured into European ports fresh from the Portuguese-Brazil colonies and was found in large amounts in all of the royal courts of Europe. Opulent banquets were frequently thrown, serving up a whole array of delicious sweetmeats and huge subtleties made from sugar and marchpane (the precursor to modern marzipan). In the ordinances of one banquet thrown in 1526 by Catherine of Aragon there is an entry for the 'wages of 7 cooks for making a subtlety, with a dungeon and a manor place, set upon 2 marchpanes, garnished with swans and cygnets swimming about the manor.'[21] Queen Elizabeth developed a particularly sweet tooth, and she regularly attended meals made entirely from sugar, the grandest of which was given by the Earl of Hertford in 1519. It included – amongst many other things – 'Her Majesties armes in sugar work', castles, drummers, lions, unicorns, tigers, elephants, apes, falcons, owls, vipers, dolphins and mermaids.[22]

Sugar prices were still prone to great fluctuation, but most of the upper-middle classes could enjoy sugar frequently, using it in similar ways to the mediaeval court. Tudor cookbooks contain recipes that are surprisingly similar to those found in fourteenth-century manuscripts, they were just cooked by a broader cross-section of society. *The Good Housewife's Jewel* (1596) by Thomas Dawson contains a short section on banquets, and in a list of thirty 'things necessary', sugar appears at the very top. Dawson gives instruction for making 'a paste of sugar, where of a man may make all manner of fruits, and other fine things with their form, as plates, dishes, cups, and suchlike things, wherewith you may furnish any table.'[23] This paste replaced the tricky-to-make sugar plate as the favoured sculpting medium, but aside from that the recipes are essentially the same as those in *Forme of Cury*, except they are not written for kings, but housewives, albeit very well-to-do ones. Sugar is used in various puddings and tarts more and more liberally, and there are chapters devoted to preserving foods in sugar in myriad forms: candies, jellies, jams, marmalades and syrups.

Sugar was not bought in such large amounts for mere opulence; there was a more serious use for it because it was believed to be an important medicine. Sugar's addictive qualities had been noted; the Flemish cartographer Abrham Ortelius said despairingly of its increasing ubiquity: 'what used to be kept by apothecaries for sick people [is] now only devoured by gluttony.'[24] It can't have all been pretence, however, as some medicines contained plenty of sugar but were not taken orally. For example, there was one preparation for treating conjunctivitis made up of powdered sugar, pearls and gold leaf that was blown directly into the eye.[25] The knowledge of Galen's theory of the Four Humours had spread with sugar along the Muslim Empire's trade routes, and several Muslim texts had been translated into Latin. Their teachings regularly recommend sugar to treat diseases of the loins, urinary tract, eyes and chest as well as headaches and inflammation.[26] It was also used in liberal quantities in remedies for complaints concerning the stomach and digestion: 'To make a syrup of quinces to comfort the stomach. To a great pint of the juice of quinces, a pound of sugar, and a good half pint of vinegar, of ginger the weight of five groats, of cinnamon the weight of six groats, of pepper the weight of three groats and two pence.'[27]

Sugar had become so revered in France that, in 1353, a Royal Decree was issued stating that honey should never be substituted for sugar if a physician prescribed it, and it wasn't long before adding 'a great deal of sugar' to medicines became a rule of thumb.[28] Precious honey – that manna from God Himself – was now playing second fiddle to sugar.

❡ Of penicles oz penettes.Ca.CCC.xxrb

D Enettes be hote ꝑ dꝛꝑe/and be maꝺe in this wꝑſe. Sugre is ſoden in water ſo longe that when a dꝛoppe thereof is dꝛoppeth on ſtone it wareth harde and bꝛꝑtꝙll and bꝛeketh. Than this ſugre ſo ſoden is layꝺ on a ſtone to coole/and than is hanged on naple and handleꝺ ꝑ chauf-feꝺ with handes tꝙll it ware whꝑte/ and

Of all its applications, it was considered most effective in treating ailments of the chest; for example, Edward I put his very ill son, Henry, under a regime of sugary foods in the hope it would cure, or at least ease, the infant's terribly weak chest. He was given sugar flavoured with rose, violets and liquorice, barley water and a sweet chicken potage. He also had thirteen widows who had been employed to pray for him. Unfortunately, neither strategy worked.[29] Sweet chicken soup was still getting prescribed for ailments of the lungs three centuries on. Richard Ligon spoke to a Doctor Butler who used sugar to treat the colonists in Barbados who was 'one of the most learned and famous Physitians that this Nation, or the world ever bred, was wont to say that, Sugar can preserve both Peares and Plumbs, Why can it not preserve as well our Lungs? And that it might work the same effect on himselfe, he alwayes dranke in his Claret wine, great store of the best refin'd Sugar, and also preferred it severall wayes to his Parents, for Colds, Coughs, and Catarrs; which are diseases, that reign much in cold Climats, especially in Ilands, where the Ayre is moyster then in Continents; and so much for our Health.'[30]

That said, the idea that sugar is a curative has endured, as this one piece of correspondence received by food historian Alice Thomas Ellis on the subject of the curative nature of sugar mice:

In 1920 when I was four years old an old woman who lived near my family in Radlett and whom I used to visit on every occasion I could find, would give me sugar mice to eat. These were made by skinning mice, which she had caught in an ordinary mousetrap, emptying them and then tying them by the tail to a wooden spoon where they were suspended into a strong sugar syrup in a cast iron saucepan over a slow heat. After some hours (or days) the mice became crystallised and, when they were cold, she would give me one to eat. They were *delicious* and even the bones were crisp and edible … I remember her saying that I would never have chest trouble if I ate the "sweetmeats".[31]

An extreme example perhaps, but many of us in the twenty-first century still have sugary drinks and syrups or glucose tablets when ill, all of which are widely available in pharmacies today. These, too, are the direct descendants of mediaeval medicine.

There are records of sugar being used for its medicinal value in Richard II's court. Because of its apparent cooling properties, his surgeon John Arnold made sure that there was sugar in his concoction of milk, violet oil, ptisan (a type of herbal tea) and almond oil which he injected into the urethra to treat gonorrhoea.[32] Richard, and Anne his queen, had difficulty producing children, so sugar was used to treat her and increase her fecundity – it was, after all, her primary function as queen. Her personal apothecary's list contained sugar in various forms including 'diverse syrups', 'sugar cooked in diverse waters', candy sugar and rose sugar. It seems that it never crossed anyone's mind to treat, or even question, Richard's fecundity.[33]

Sugar was also excellent for 'helping the medicine go down', or as one Hans Sloane would have it, 'a convenient vehicle' for medicines.[34] Yes, it was costly, but a little went a long way when taken with the oral administration of some of the rather more challenging curatives of the day. People were happy to pay through the nose if their prescribed boars' gall, or mouse dung in plantain juice went down and successfully stayed down.[35] The sugaring of unpalatable tablets is still widely practised today with common or garden drugs and medicines, such as paracetamol or ibuprofen covered in a sweet sugar shell.

It was at the apothecary that most people first tasted sugar, and apothecaries kept an array of different types: there was *caften* sugar, which came in loaves of plaited leaves; a very fragile white sugar called *cassonade*, which was the precursor to modern-day caster sugar; and there was *candy* from Crete. The most expensive was an Egyptian-made sugar called *muscarrat,* which had achieved almost mythological status. It was double refined and of extremely high purity for the time and was made exclusively for the Sultan of Babylon.

At the other end of the spectrum the very cheapest low-grade sugar available was known as *cypre* and was really a by-product of sugar-making rather than a type of sugar itself. It was intended only for sugar enemas, though unscrupulous apothecaries often cut their more expensive sugars with it.[36] The Church quickly noticed that sugar was being prescribed a little too lavishly, prompting its members to wonder whether all of these medicinal applications were really just an excuse to indulge. So the question was posed: was sugar medicine, nourishment or for pleasure? Thomas Aquinas stepped up to the plate and declared that sugar was not for nourishment or pleasure but for health, and was therefore permitted even during Lent.[37] There was little opposition.

If medicines were just a vehicle for sugar, then so were the new and exciting bitter drinks of tea, coffee and chocolate. These hot drinks had an invigorating effect on the body, but the bitterness put many off. Once they were mixed with a little sugar, however, they were delicious. As a result, sales in all three products skyrocketed, which increased sugar sales even more. Prices fell as demand increased and sugar trickled down from the upper to the upper-middle classes: as did the scourge of the sugar-eater – black teeth. Queen Elizabeth's rotten teeth are now infamous. She was described by visiting German tutor Paul Hentzer in 1598: 'next came the queen in the sixty-fifth year of her age, as we were told, very majestic; her face oblong, fair, but wrinkled; her eyes small, yet black and pleasant; her nose a little hooked; her lips narrow, and her teeth black; (a defect the English seem subject to, from their too great use of sugar).'[38]

It is the inevitable result of having a sweet, addictive substance that is also a status symbol; though it is a myth that the well-to-do wanted rotten, blackened teeth, showing off their hideous grins with pride as a splendid advertisement to all around of their great wealth. In fact, the opposite was true; the members of the Tudor court were just as self-conscious of their rotten gnashers as anyone would be today. Queen Elizabeth suffered with dental cavities from adolescence, and so, as an older woman in 1602, she had had most of her teeth extracted, and her face looked as though it had collapsed. To disguise this, she stuffed her mouth with cloth or covered the lower half of her face with a strategically-placed decorative fan, making it very difficult for anyone to understand anything she was saying.[39] The other infamous example of this is the Sun King Louis XIV, who had lost all of his teeth to sugar by the age of forty and had resorted to stuffing his sunken mouth with cotton to plump it out. So self-conscious was he that he banned smiling at court. Aside from suffering from poor oral health, it is highly likely that he also suffered from type-2 diabetes, another consequence of eating copious amounts of sugar.[40]

Man has always suffered from dental disease and pain, but it was only when eating large amounts of sugar became commonplace that poor dental hygiene became endemic. In pre-sugar days, the major dental issues were abscesses, jaw fractures and cancers, with tooth decay occurring infrequently. As mediaeval Europeans began to consume more and more sugar, tooth decay became so prevalent that by the end of the Middle Ages a new profession appeared, the Tooth Drawer, who specialised in dental surgery and tooth extractions.[41]

At first, the correlation between sugar and dental health was not picked up on because, presumably, sugar was considered so good for the health. The black pits and softened enamel and dentine were instead believed to be caused by the burrowing of parasitic tooth-worms, and it was their writhing within the teeth that caused the pain. This long-held belief can be traced back through the Islamic medical texts to Galen and right back to a Sumerian texts dated to 5000 BCE. Treatment for these worms was mainly with lotions and medicines or magicks. A favourite remedy was the use of henbane seeds, which purged the worms' eggs from infected teeth: 'If [the cavities] do come by worms, make a candell of waxe with Henbane sedes and lyght it and let the perfume of the candell entre into the tothe and gape over a dyshe of colde water and then you may take the worms out of the water and kyll them on your nayle.'[42]

To treat cavities, the rotten and soft parts of the tooth were cleaned away and packed with various materials, including ground dogs' teeth and salt wrapped in a 'fayre whyt cobweb'. Some were more sensible such as ground hartshorn, which expands slightly and forms a stiff gel when wet – an excellent temporary filling – and there are accounts of using gold leaf to fill teeth from the 1540s. The instruments used were rudimentary and clumsy, and so attempts at surgery would only occur in extreme cases. Instead, they preferred to apply materials they thought would break the teeth apart or make them fall out, such as ground partridge brains, cow dung and frog fat (it was widely believed that frogs made teeth fall out).[43] In the main, most treatments were just an attempt to manage discomfort or cover the stench of the bad breath associated with tooth decay: 'wash your teeth that be hollow and stink.'

Mediaeval medical texts highlight the importance of cleaning one's teeth, especially after every meal, and some even suggested avoiding sweet foods, especially sweet, spiced wines and mead.[44] All good advice of course, until they went on to suggest using a cloth covered in abrasives such as ground marble, or a mixture of honey and sugar, or worse a mouthwash of vitriolic (sulphuric) acid.[45] All of these dental problems were then made even worse by the upper-class diet of large amounts of meat and fish, stewed fruit and few vegetables (they were considered free of all nutriment). As a result, most suffered from mild vitamin C deficiency, a symptom of which is receding gums.

That tooth decay was an affliction of the wealthy was demonstrated in London in the 1940s when a German bomb exploded and exposed a communal grave of commoners dating from the 1640s, all of whom were plague victims. Luckily for the archaeology team, the bodies had been buried in heavy clay soil, effectively sealing them in anaerobically and preserving their remains very well. Upon inspecting the teeth of the children and adolescents, they discovered very little evidence of tooth decay. However, when the skulls of deceased children of the rich were inspected – children who would have eaten a lot of sweetened puddings and confections – they were found to be riddled with tooth decay.[46]

If one looks even further back to prehistoric Britain there are very few cases of significant poor dental health in children or adults. Then the Romans, who were very partial to syrupy drinks and fruits preserved in honey, turned up and cases of cavities increase markedly. Only when they left, and the Anglo-Saxon period began with its more modest way of life, did dental health improve again. It generally remained good after the Norman conquest, only to fall again in the late Middle Ages.[47] As time went on and sugar became available to more and more people, the dental health of the Western nations plummeted and '[d]ental disease [became] the almost universal disease of modern man.'[48]

Chapter 11

Sugar for All

[S]ugar was an ideal substance. It served to make a busy life seem less so; in the pause that refreshes, it eased … the changes back and forth from work to rest; it provided swifter sensations of fullness or satisfaction than complex carbohydrates did; it combined easily with many other foods … No wonder the rich and powerful liked it so much, and no wonder the poor learned to love it.

Sidney Mintz[1]

Sugar was part of the everyday middle-class diet from the 1750s, whether it was just a little chipped off a cheap sugarloaf at teatime, sprinkled on some bakery items, or lavishly doused upon more upmarket confections. The drive behind this increased consumption was the introduction of the popular bitter drinks tea and coffee. Coffee entered first, being the cheaper of the two, and fuelled by the caffeine and the accompanying sugar hit people became more talkative and enthused. It was quite the opposite to beer or brandy which dulled the mind rather than sharpened it. Soon, coffee houses sprang up everywhere, a great social melting pot of different classes, backgrounds and ideas. And to help the bitter drink to go down, there was, of course, plenty of sugar.

Tea was more expensive – it was traded and transported by the mysterious Chinese who set high prices and did not use slave labour. King Charles II was one of its earliest consumers after his new queen, Catherine of Braganza, brought a dowry consisting of several barrels of the stuff. Later Queen Anne, last of the Stuart monarchs, cemented its presence in the royal court by drinking it regularly with her ladies. Just a year after her death in 1717, tea had become popular enough for the first tea room to open, owned by a certain Thomas Twining.[2] Few could afford it, but in tea's favour it was easy to make in a domestic setting and required little paraphernalia. Then the United East India Company made a deal with China to trade with them directly, meaning that tea was suddenly available to new parts of society.[3] Now the upper and upper-middle classes could enjoy the drink, and soon the notion of 'teatime' emerged; essentially a snack that kept one going in the afternoon. In

An illustration of Mr Chivery's sparce tea table of bread and jam from Dickens' *Little Dorrit* (1857). (Archive.org)

grander houses dinner was served in the evening, so there was quite a wait between a noon-time lunch and dinner. This 'low tea' – low because it was served from side tables rather than dining tables – was served between three and four o'clock in withdrawing rooms alongside bread and butter and a few sweet baked goods, as well as the new must-have piece of tableware, the sugar bowl.[4]

This novel institution was mainly viewed as a good thing; tea and cakes were considered both refined and restrained – no alcohol was consumed – and it brought the household together in a relaxed and informal way. What began as a way to stave off the hunger pangs in the afternoon rapidly became a ritualised part of daily life, and everyone who could afford it had their low tea. The lower classes aspired to be as 'refined' as their 'betters', but this required tea to fall substantially in price for them to purchase it for themselves. Tea was passed around by domestic servants; after all, they were the ones buying, brewing and serving it alongside the delicious and dainty sweet treats that accompanied it. In more generous households servants were allowed a taste of tea made from previously brewed tea leaves, and they probably surreptitiously sequestered some to take back to their rooms.[5] It was nigh-on impossible to get hold of unused leaves, however, because in most houses the key to the tea caddy was kept with the lady of the household, just as the key to the spice chest had been in mediaeval and Tudor homes. Only she, and perhaps her highest ranking staff, were privy to the tea chest's fragrant contents.

In the eighteenth century prices dropped again. Trade in commodities such as tea and coffee were, by now, well-practised and imported on an ever-increasing scale. Duties on these imports were reduced too, and tea (albeit often of dubious quality) was suddenly affordable to everyone. Purchasing these items would, however, render them next to useless if there wasn't also sugar to make it palatable. The working classes used molasses at first, but as prices dropped with increased free trade it was swapped for unrefined sugars and then eventually pure, white granulated sugar.

Urban diets were very different to that of the rural: ale, once the working man's primary source of calories, had been ditched in favour of sugary tea, and workers' relatively varied diet of vegetables, wholegrains and porridge were swapped for white bread with butter or dripping. Desperately poor workers found themselves toiling shifts of twelve hours or more, living in squalor and foregoing their rural diet: 'studies of consumption, nutrition, heights, mortality, working hours and child labour have all concluded that life was getting worse for workers during the industrial revolution.'[6] The working class now paid extortionate rents for cramped hovels with no gardens in which to grow their own vegetables or keep their own livestock. For households in which just the 'man of the house' worked, sixty per cent of the family income was spent on food (compare this with twenty per cent today), though they often could not afford the fresh ingredients or the fuel which with to cook them.[7] However, factory workers in the mid-nineteenth century spent twice the amount on sugar and tea compared their agricultural counterparts.[8] Foods that were once aspirational were now bog-standard commodities, and the industrialisation of the bread-making process made it, for the first time, cheaper to buy bread than to make it.[9]

The tea that was served in these working-class homes was called 'high tea' because it was eaten on the high table – i.e., the kitchen or dining table. Sweet tea, bread and butter became the main evening meal rather than an afternoon snack, a distinction held in England to this day with northerners calling their early evening meal 'tea' and southerners typically calling their main evening meal 'dinner'. In homes where only the husband worked, his wife and children had bread and tea, while he was served the meat. This was a standard social norm at the time; the one who went out to work received the most nutritious food, resulting in the curious situation of households being made up of relatively fit and healthy men, and underfed, malnourished women and children.[10]

Britain's insatiable appetite for sugar transformed the landscapes of its city ports as well as its diet. The first sugar refineries were built in London from 1544 where they quickly began to pepper the shores of the Thames, their numbers increasing in tandem with sugar production in the Americas. Refineries began to populate the other large ports in England – Bristol and Liverpool – and then spread further north to other port cities such as Hull and Glasgow.

Refining sugar on an industrial scale was a filthy business. The process required dissolving the raw sugar under great heat into a super-saturated sugar syrup which was sent through several stages of clarification, passed through charcoal or burnt animal bones, then mixed with eggs and then filtered through cotton before being dried under intense heat. The ensuing stench from this process was so offensive that no one wanted to live in the vicinity of a refinery, and the smell was even worse when ox blood was used in place of eggs in the purification process. Working conditions were filthy too, the refining rooms coated 'with a thick preserve of sugar and grime. The floor was black … the roof was black, and pendant from the great supporting posts and bulks of timber were sooty, glistening icicles and exuding like those of a gum tree.'[11] Similar patterns occurred across the rest of Europe and North America: 'Amsterdam boasted forty sugar refineries, despite local attempts to curb the coal-based pollution belching from the refineries' chimneys.'[12]

In the same way that the infrastructure of the sugar plantations had evolved and production and scale increased to cope with demand and falling prices, so too were refineries forced to merge and become huge, creating an economy of scale. As a result, the landscape of many cities across the West changed:

> The great refineries which line the water-front of Brooklyn and Jersey City are enormous piles of brick, often more than a hundred feet high, with a dozen or more rows of windows one above the other, with no pretentions to architectural show, but by their very size and massiveness making an impressive feature of the river landscape. They are contrived so as to take the sugar as it is landed, and carry it through one process after another with the least possible waste of power, time, and space, until the "shining sand" emerges purified and ready for consumption. Accordingly the refineries are alongside deep water, and at their wharves vessels of all sorts, from West Indian coasters to the great steam "tramps" that roam the world over in search of a job, may be seen, three and four together, unloading their cargoes into the voracious maw of the great cook-shop.[13]

Working life in the refineries was filthy and dangerous, because as the sugar purified, it became hotter and more viscous and would regularly catch fire and explode. Accidents and deaths were relatively common as were scaldings and injuries sustained from falling or moving hogsheads. Even cleaning the machinery caused deaths, as the case of German worker Johann Cordes sadly illustrates. In 1853 the *Daily News* reported that he had been working at the Hall & Boyd refinery on Breezers Hill, London:

> on Sat 30 March proceeded with a lighted candle to clean out a tank filled with charcoal. The morning was dark, and on removing the lid he placed his legs inside the tank, when the foul air ignited, and blew him backwards about ten feet against a wall. The deceased was found by Hermann Henckin and John Buck in a dreadfully disfigured state, being burnt over the arms, face and body to a considerable extent. He was taken home, and subsequently was conveyed in a cab to the London Hospital, where he lingered and died on Sunday evening last.[14]

Sugar refineries became huge, the companies consolidating and amalgamating until a single British refiner remained – as it does to this day – the colossus that is Tate and Lyle.

In the nineteenth century sugar was well-established as a preservative, with many a country kitchen garden's summertime glut of seasonal fruit boiled up with sugar and carefully potted to be eaten at breakfast or low tea throughout the remainder of the year. The working city dweller ate a great deal of jam too, but like the bread it was spread upon, it was an industrialised product. Their jams were made from fruit of inferior quality or even the left-over pulp from some other food manufacturing process, and only made up around a third of the jam by weight.[15] It was advertised as nourishing and good value, and soon '[m]illions of people found their basic sustenance in sweet jams spread on bread made from flour with added sugar, and all washed down with tea. Not surprisingly, perhaps, the emergent dental profession found abundant evidence to dental decay among working-class children in the late nineteenth century.'[16]

The working-class family's food no longer had to be cooked at all, that process had been outsourced by the food industry and 'these skimpy, badly balanced and sugar-saturated meals fuelled not only the working classes but also the Industrial Revolution that their labour made possible.'[17] And if there was a sugar crash come the afternoon, factory or mill workers could be topped up with more in their afternoon break of more sugary tea and factory-made biscuits. The middle classes

A selection of sweetened puddings and desserts popular with the middle and upper classes. From *The Everyday Cook and Recipe Book* (1891) by Miss E. Neil.

were not missing out on their sugar either; their diet too was becoming progressively sweeter. They had become inclined to having a sweet course for their 'afters', usually a pudding with a sweet sauce. Indeed, it is this time in history that the great British pudding became an institution in itself, with hundreds devised; quite the feat seeing as they are all essentially a combination of refined flour, fat, and sugar or other sweet ingredients like syrup, jam or dried fruits.

As working families became more dependent upon factory foods, sugar consumption greatly increased, inspiring food manufacturers to increase the diversity of their products. Cakes and biscuits were now bought in such numbers that they too could be sold at a lower cost than either the home cook or baker could produce them. By 1900 there were 400 varieties of biscuit alone. The most popular in the United Kingdom is the iconic McVitie's Digestive biscuit, the recipe, devised by Alexander Grant de Forres, has remained unchanged since 1892.[18] It was marketed as a food that could promote healthy digestion because it contained some wholewheat flour and oats, as well as plenty of stomach acid-neutralising bicarbonate of soda, all made delicious with added sugar. Accompanying them on the shelves were products still available today, such as sweetened condensed milk and the requisite array of sugars: powdered, cubed, granulated, plus Demerara and moist (soft dark brown) sugar. One addition is still very much enjoyed today, the breakfast cereal. Eccentric American entrepreneur John Harvey Kellogg invented the concept in 1899. He promoted it as a health food and the people in Britain were quick to latch onto this new, transatlantic convenience 'health' food. By 1921 there were sixty brands of breakfast cereal available, most liberally laced with sugar.[19]

The grocer also sold a small array of sweets and chocolates, but to fully appreciate what was available one had to visit the local confectioner's shop where sweets were available to suit every pocket. Working with sugar is a complex process, but sugar chemistry had progressed by the late nineteenth century, resulting in 'a fuller scientific comprehension of sugar's remarkable variety.'[20] And what a variety: barley sugars, rock, liquorice allsorts, fruit pastilles, Pontefract cakes, pear drops and humbugs were all available at the end of the nineteenth century, and at the turn of the twentieth they were joined by more favourites – gobstoppers, aniseed balls, jelly babies and wine gums. All were almost one hundred per cent sugar and are thought of today with great nostalgia. In his 1984 memoir, *Boy*, author Roald Dahl, reminisces about the sweet shop he visited as a child:

> Sherbet Suckers were … two a penny. Each Sucker consisted of a yellow cardboard tube filled with sherbet powder, and there was a hollow liquorice straw sticking out of it … You sucked the sherbet through the straw and when it was finished you ate the liquorice. They were delicious, those Sherbet Suckers. The sherbet fizzed in your mouth, and if you knew how to do it, you could make white froth come out of your nostrils and pretend you were throwing a fit … Pear Drops were exciting because they had a dangerous taste. They smelled of nail-varnish and they froze the back of your throat. All of us were warned against eating them, and the result was that we ate them more than ever.[21]

Then of course, there was chocolate. It had been available as a drink, as cocoa powder, and in bar form since the late eighteenth century. As a bar was it always very bitter, stodgy and cloying in texture, sold more for its medicinal benefits than for its taste. But when chocolate company Fry's produced their *Five Boys* bar in 1902, containing a large proportion of milk and sugar, chocolate became a desired product for the masses. Fry's had turned a niche product into a delicious confection by watering it down and sugaring it. Then Fry's main rival, Cadbury's, became a major player in the chocolate world when they began to produce dainty boxed chocolates – chocolate as a highbrow gift – before cornering the Easter egg market after their chocolatiers came up with a formula for a chocolate that could be poured when warm, yet set hard and brittle when cool.[22] Then in 1905, they eclipsed Fry's and all the other chocolate manufacturers with the invention of their iconic *Dairy Milk* chocolate which promptly became the country's favourite chocolate brand.[23]

However, there was another critical element beside palatability to these chocolate manufacturers' business strategies that ensured success: advertising. Advertisements were everywhere: on posters; billboards; slapped on the side, front and back of trams and buses; huge painted signs on the sides of grocers' shops; and printed in newspapers, journals and magazines. They were advertised as both everyday treats and must-haves for special occasions like Easter and Christmas. Sweets and chocolates were also sold as the perfect romantic gift from a 'perfect husband', fiancé or date.[24] The demographic that was quickly targeted – because they were both consumer and buyer – was the housewife. It was sold as something she should buy for herself, but also to please her children. And if she was worried sweets were bad for her child, the ads were sure to point out that their chocolate was in some way nourishing – we were told then as now that *Dairy Milk* contains a glass and a half of milk for example. They were also billed as the only sweet or candy her discerning little angel would eat when it came to sweet treats. Fry's *Five Boys* bar used this strategy too, very successfully: 'each piece [of chocolate] had a boy's face moulded onto it, running through the canonical expressions of "Desperation … Pacification … Expectation … Acclamation … Realization … it's Fry's."'[25] In advertisements and on wrappers the five boys were dressed in cute Edwardian sailor outfits, used to convey that the boys' parents were the upwardly mobile sort. Fry's were specifically targeting the aspirational parents of an ever-growing population of grammar school children. Author Mick Jackson sums up the tuck shop favourite: 'The faces on the *Five Boys* chocolate bar wrapper just about managed to encompass a child's entire emotional range, from the pitiful

child at the beginning to his gleeful counterpart at the other end. All one had to do, the wrapper seemed to suggest, in order to bring about such a happy transition was to give in to your boy's demands.'[26]

Mass advertising had begun, helping annual sugar consumption to increase from 31kg per person in 1880 to 41kg in 1914.[27]

An advertisement for the upmarket children's chocolate treat Fry's *Five Boys* c.1910.

British chocolate manufacturers were also making handsome profits exporting their goods to the US, enjoying no real competition from the Americans at all. That all changed in 1900 when Milton S. Hershey began producing chocolate bars and the ever-popular *Hershey's Kisses*. By 1915 they were churning out 4.5 tons of chocolate per day. Hershey's chocolate empire grew happily, almost unrivalled, until a failing chocolatier named Frank Mars devised a most delicious confection made of whipped malt surrounded by a thin layer of chocolate: the *Milky Way*. Its whipped centre was mainly sugar and air[28] and the chocolate coating was very thin, making it cheap to produce whilst being much larger than Hershey's bars. It sold in its hundreds and thousands.[29] Hershey and Mars's bitter rivalry kept prices very competitive and in by the 1910s both Britain and the US were enjoying plenty of sweet and milky low-quality chocolate.[30]

But then everything changed. The onset of the Great War meant that Britain's once dependable European beet sugar supply suddenly evaporated. European sugar beet had taken off after Napoleon's defunct programme collapsed and had been enthusiastically picked up by neighbouring Germany who, having no sugar-producing colonies itself, made a great success of it, producing a million tons per year by 1886 and exporting sugar to the world's two largest consumers, the United States and Great Britain.[31] Germany was the primary producer of European sugar, and at the onset of the First World War in 1914 it was such an important source that when she stopped exporting it to the US and Britain, both countries had to ration it. Seeing Germany's success, many other European countries began a domestic sugar industry of their own, including France, who managed to produce enough domestically to make up a third of its consumption.[32] Britain had attempted to manufacture its own sugar after Dutch investors convinced some Norfolk farmers to grow it, but gave up after a couple of wet and unproductive years.[33]

To keep the sugar coming in, the government set up the Royal Commission for Sugar Supplies, its function to ensure a steady supply of cane and beet sugar by purchasing them wholesale, either from the empire or other allied countries.[34] Sugar was a luxury food no longer, but a necessity like bread and bacon. It was a must for soldiers' rations too, both as a source of ready calories and as a taste of home. A soldier's standard ration was crammed with jam, sugar and tea. Sugary food and drink undoubtedly gave the men a physical and psychological boost. Sugar was comfort, and jams and confections were reminiscent of home.

It was absolutely essential that Britain's bravest, standing in their alien, grim trenches maintained this link; a constant reminder of what they were fighting for. Sugar – it was hoped – would win the war. Many commanders thought that the inclusion of so many sweet things was namby-pamby and effeminate and suggested that rum would be much more appreciated, especially when some Dutch courage was required to settle nerves before going 'over the top'.

Soldiers had been receiving something sweet in their rations since the Boer War campaigns in 1900 after Queen Victoria requested from George Cadbury a tin of Christmas chocolate for her men posted in Africa. A staunch Quaker and pacifist, he considered the Boer War the 'most diabolical' of all. In fact, just a few years prior to Victoria's request, Mr Cadbury had paid for the printing and distribution of three million anti-war pamphlets. He refused, but not taking his 'no' for an answer, the queen put her foot down and insisted he produced the chocolate. Cadbury approached Fry and Rowntree – also Quakers – and they agreed to share the 'burden' amongst themselves, producing 200,000 tins between them. But being men of principle, they left the tins unbranded and took no profit.[35] However, George Cadbury's reputation was damaged soon afterwards when it was reported that the cocoa in his chocolate bars was made in São Thomé by slave labour. Not only that, it was alleged that he knew all about it. Quakers were staunchly anti-slavery and Cadbury took those responsible for making the malicious allegations to court. He won the case, but mud sticks and his reputation was forever tarnished. As a final injustice, he was awarded just a farthing in compensation.[36]

To keep sugar, sugar products and rum pouring into the British Isles, the Royal Commission strengthened its ties with the British West Indies and Cuba. It also gave financial support to farmers, as well as subsidies to kick-start a British sugar beet industry. The Commission's great efforts, however, did not come up to scratch. For the first time, the unrelentingly upward trajectory of sugar consumption was interrupted and took a downturn. Without their daily doses of sugar, the British people 'regarded [sugar rationing] as among the most painful and immediate of the petty hardships caused by the war.'[37]

Chapter 12

The Rise of Junk Food

Sugar is the new tobacco.[1]

The First World War came to a close and Britain was damned if it was going to go through any more 'petty hardships'; it was a case of once bitten, twice shy. The government had realised just how dependent Britain had become on its imports, and they knew exactly what the British people's priorities were and went about creating an incentive for farmers to cultivate sugar. The Sugar Industry (Subsidy) Act 1925, promoted sugar beet cultivation by offering attractive subsidies that would be protected for ten years for anyone who cared to farm it, and farmers were paid a very reasonable minimum 44s per ton of sugar beet.[2] It was a huge success, the amount of land cultivating sugar increased almost eight-fold in three years, with 20,000 farms providing fifteen factories with sugar beet for processing.[3] Success 'was immediate' and soon enough the British taxpayer was happily paying for its own sugar to be cultivated, and then buying it all over again in the local grocer's shop.[4] To be on the safe side, the Commission for Sugar Supplies also increased its sugar imports from its sugar-producing colonies such as Australia, South Africa and Fiji. However, the result of this huge push for cheap and plentiful sugar led to an overproduction of the stuff, making the seemingly limitless supply cheaper than ever before – so cheap in fact that its consumption was now evenly distributed through all classes. By the 1930s the British were eating five times that of the 1900s, and sugar joined bread and potatoes as a major source of carbohydrate in the British diet. How it was consumed changed too, because forty per cent of that sugar was not being purchased in paper bags as an ingredient for cooking and baking, but in the form of mass-produced industrial food: chocolate and confectionary, preserves and relishes, cakes and biscuits.[5]

At the same time, the burgeoning modern science of nutrition and food science was identifying what our food was made up of, discovering that proteins were made up of amino acids, and that there were trace substances – vitamins and minerals – found in a range of foods that were essential for good health. Scientists realised that when it came to feeding the poor it was not the amount of food they ate but the types of food that were important. It was possible to eat a lot of food and still be malnourished, and if one were to receive the full suite of vitamins and minerals, one needed a varied diet of fresh fruit and vegetables, dairy, fish and wholegrains. Refined bread, dripping, jam and sweet tea were just not going to cut it. Inevitably, science turned its beady eye towards sugar itself and found it contained no vitamins or minerals of any kind. An absence of nutrition does not necessarily make a foodstuff detrimental to health, but it was evident to anyone who dared look to see that sugar was rotting the teeth of the nation's children.[6]

With the onset of the Second World War, sugar – alongside butter and bacon – was almost immediately rationed. The burgeoning British sugar beet industry had not quite got on its feet; there had been a series of poor growing years and it continued to rely on government subsides, meaning that Britain was still importing the vast majority of its sugar.[7] German submarines in Britain's and its allies' waters interfered with importation and very quickly other foods containing or associated with sugar were rationed too: jam, biscuits, breakfast cereals and tea. The weekly ration varied throughout the war, but averaged at 340g per person, though it sank as low as 225g. This 'lack' of sugar made civilians thoroughly depressed. It may appear rather a lot by today's standards,[8] but compare that to the ration of a British soldier who received a whopping 850g per week, and that's not including his extra jam and syrup rations. Sugar was expected, once more, to help win a war.

Nutritionists look back at the war years rather misty-eyed, lauding wartime rationing for improving the nation's health. While it is true that fat consumption fell by sixteen per cent, meat by twenty-one per cent and sugar by thirty-one per cent, as well as a seventeen per cent increase in the consumption of grain products, there is little data to support this claim. Diseases associated with high sugar and fat intake, such as coronary heart failure, did not change significantly before, during or after the war. One thing we can say is, however, that the British were not a changed people. As soon as rationing was lifted in 1949, the need and greed for sugar was so 'voracious and entrenched' that it had to be rationed again for a further four years.[9]

The Ministry of Food created the system of rationing, and it worked with British sugar growers and refiners to control sugar production. It bought sugar in bulk from the Commonwealth countries that produced it and sold it on to British sugar refiners. The vast majority of it went to Tate and Lyle who were now the dominant sugar manufacturers in the UK and had been since 1921 when Mr Tate's and Mr Lyle's companies merged. However, this relationship between government and manufacturer would carry on well into peacetime much to Tate and Lyle's benefit. They had a source of cheap unrefined sugar from the British government, and a population who continued to eat more and more sugar, reaching a per capita consumption of 3.25kg in 1958.[10] That this level of consumption was possible was thanks to the newly created Sugar Board whose function was to support the British sugar industry by controlling and supporting sugar exports and domestic production, and it did so extremely effectively, negotiating excellent prices from the Commonwealth. At the same time, the Board established the areas in the UK that would be set aside for the cultivation of sugar beet which would be processed by the British Sugar Corporation, later to become Silver Spoon in 1972.[11] It remains Britain's favourite sugar brand, but despite its popularity most Britons are unaware that it is produced entirely from UK-grown sugar beet.

The huge Tate & Lyle Canning Town plant, *River Thames*, 1955. (Ben Brooksbank)

The post-war Labour government led by Clement Attlee could see that sugar was part of the fabric of British life; indeed it was so essential that it had caught up with starch as the nation's primary source of carbohydrate. Riding high on the National Health Service's success, Attlee's government decided that the sugar industry needed nationalising too and he made it a pledge to do so as part of Labour's campaign in the run-up to the 1951 General Election. Tate and Lyle were not best pleased and responded with a hard-hitting propaganda campaign led by Mr Cube, a cartoon sugar cube armed proudly with sword and Tate and Lyle shield, his function to personify the relationship between the British government and hard-working families' personal sugar supply. Mr Cube found his way onto every packet of Tate and Lyle sugar as well as the sides of buses, and inside newspapers and journals, 'informing' the people what the effects of nationalisation would have on their precious, bargain-price sugar with simple messages written to garner empathy from the public such as: 'Tate not State' and 'Leave it to private enterprise.'[12]

It was audacious behaviour: the British sugar industry had been dependent upon the British government and Crown throughout its entire history. Indeed, it is because of its protective and financial support that the industry was as dominant as it was, and it was *their* government that was buying sugar at such low prices on Tate and Lyle's behalf in the first place. Bearing all this in mind, it could be argued that it was time to give something back. Well, Mr Cube was having none of it, and his gripes were plastered everywhere. When recalling the campaign,

Tate and Lyle's campaign strategist said, 'we were strongly advised to have a cartoon character who, if he caught the public's imagination, could say the

Tate & Lyle's propaganda weapon, Mr Cube – equipped with sword and shield – is dispatched. The campaign was a great success and sugar avoided being nationalised. (Rennart)

most outrageous things and get away with it.'[13] He said things like: 'State control will make a hole in your pocket and my packet,' conveying, very effectively, that if the government got their hands on the country's sugar, prices would increase and quality would drop.[14] The knives were well-and-truly out, and as a result, the nationalisation of sugar became one of the major issues of the 1951 election campaign. The Conservatives, led by Sir Winston Churchill, made it clear to the public that nothing would change, and its sugar would be safe. Upon Churchill's re-election, Tate and Lyle breathed a sigh of relief as the notion of nationalising the industry was officially dropped, and they put Mr Cube out to pasture.

Under the new Conservative government, the Sugar Board continued to buy up Commonwealth sugar and to subsidise beet sugar. Britain then entered the European Economic Community, the 'United States of Europe' that Churchill had so wanted to protect Britain and Europe from future conflicts and to harness frictionless trade. The EEC helped make war, and the rationing that accompanied it, a distant memory, but it also made the Sugar Board less relevant now that beet sugar could be imported from Continental Europe unhampered.

***

The 1950s was a time of technological revolution in the home, and a whole host of labour-saving devices were purchased, such as vacuum cleaners, washing machines and electric food mixers. As time went on, more and more were added to the list of must-haves, whether for entertainment – video players and video games – or for easier cooking or housework – microwave ovens, dishwashers and the Fly-Mo. The 1950s was also the decade that driveways and garages began to fill up as a significant proportion of families invested in a car. And with all of the free time these things provided, television became the king of mod-cons; and with television came advertisements, beamed straight into the home, including those for sugar-laden foods, enticing us to consume all of those calories we no longer needed.

Before homes had an electricity supply and a little run-around car, folk walked to and from work, scrubbed floors, beat carpets, whisked eggs by hand and walked home with the shopping. Our free time, if there even was such a thing, was not spent sat in front of the television being drip-fed advertisements. Now people drove to their sedentary jobs, and were too busy or tired to exercise. As a result, people burnt away far fewer calories than ever, just as they were consuming record-breaking volumes of sugar and fat. These factors crystallised in the latter decades of the twentieth century into a range of health issues, including obesity, coronary heart disease, type-2 diabetes and a host of cancers. Our primaeval brains were still telling us to consume, safeguarding us from imminent famine, forcing our willpower to crumble, but in the West there were tough times no longer; instead, there was an overproduction of food stoking our never-sated hunger for foods that didn't even require effort to prepare.

The aggressive nature of advertising accelerated in the television age because with it came children's television programmes, which required commercial breaks to be filled just like any other show. A brand-new demographic was born, and for the first time adverts for junk food, chocolate and sweets could be beamed straight to the primary consumer, bypassing the parent altogether. The child didn't even need to know how to read; it was told everything it needed to know by a jolly animated character, puppet or clown. These empowered little consumers could now pull at sleeves, whinge and pressurise their parents until they gave in. And why not? It keeps them quiet and only costs a bit of spare change. This is 'pester power', and it is big money. By the 2000s the advertising budget in Britain was £450 million, and three-quarters of that budget went to advertising directly to children; and of that, ninety-nine per cent promoted some kind of junk food.[15] Pester power appeared in a different guise; rather than giving away free toys and stickers[16], some food businesses gave away vouchers for schools or free meal vouchers, easing the guilt associated with giving in to the child and providing them with junk food by the thought that 'at least it is doing some good.'[17]

Now the children of both the US and Britain were getting fat. Something had to be to blame, and all eyes turned to sugary cakes, biscuits, drinks and confections. It was hardly a secret that rich and sweet foods made one fat, but if one ate them in moderation, there should be no reason to avoid them. The trouble was that Big Sugar did not want anyone to cut down, and so, in the 1960s they – and those companies that used a lot of sugar in their products – began to panic as it looked like they were being singled out as the ones to blame. Big Sugar took a leaf out of Big Tobacco's book and went on a campaign to show that sugar was not damaging to health, and just like Big Tobacco, they worked with well-respected professors at highly esteemed institutions such as Harvard to produce data showing that sugar did not cause any ill effects. But *something* was causing it, and Big Sugar's scientists pointed the finger firmly at fat.[18] It was the obvious target: the link between the fat we consume ending up on the hips is rather more tangible than the more tenuous metabolic processes that transform sugar into fat. Sugar had got away scot-free and was ladled into all of our processed foods – even the health foods – with abandon.

The next strategy taken by the food and drink companies was to use a bit of sleight of hand and surreptitiously sneak in a whole load of sugar into our pantries, refrigerators and freezers, simply by making them 'good for us'. We are all familiar with them; those so-called healthy alternatives that are also delicious. The pioneers of this strategy were manufacturers of yoghurts and breakfast cereals, and they are still going strong.

The health benefits of fermented foods like yoghurt were well known. Historically, it was only eaten in the Middle East, Turkey and Southwestern Europe.[19] But yoghurt is also the perfect product to sell to a nation that has accrued a vast milk lake. The trouble is that yoghurt tastes sour, and therefore isn't to many people's taste, but if sweetened and flavoured with a small amount of cooked fruit it is perfectly palatable, though any health benefits are more than offset with the inclusion of lashings of sugar. Later, when fat had been singled out as the enemy, the yoghurt industry was happy to make a low-fat or fat-free alternative laced with even more sugar, as well as a large dose of beef or pork gelatine to make up for the fact that fat-free yoghurts lose all their structure once the fat is taken out. Now people could avoid the junk food and have these treats instead, safe in the knowledge that what they were eating was 'healthy'.

Ever since their inception, breakfast cereals have been marketed as a health food. They have also contained a large amount of sugar and highly processed, starchy grains. Selling them as the healthy choice allowed manufacturers to add vast amounts of sugar, and make their bland food appetising. Children were attracted further by the colourful characters on the packets. They also appeared on the television advertisements, usually announcing what free toy, sticker or transfer there was inside the box that month. So sure were they that sugar content was not an issue for consumers, manufacturers such as Quakers gave them names like *Sugar*

Puffs[20], but there were other infamous varieties: Kellogg's *Ricicles* was a cereal made up of puffed rice covered with a frosting of sugar and came in at a whopping thirty-seven per cent added sugar. There were many others too, of course, with Kellogg's *Frosties* and *Coco Pops*, and the US favourite, *Lucky Charms*, all containing similar amounts.

To demonstrate to parents that they were making good choices during their weekly shop, Kellogg's 'fortified' their products with vitamins and minerals such as iron and niacin, and made sure everyone knew it, printing it on the front of every box. Worst offenders, such as *Ricicles*, upped the ante, proudly stating that there were '7 essential vitamins and iron in every bowl'. *Frosties* packets told parents that the contents were 'supercharged' with extra B1, Niacin and B6, and laboured the point further with diagrams on the box showing both parent and child how

Tony and "friend" on the Garry Moore Show

Garry Moore says: "Won't they tell even you, Tony?"

US TV personality Garry Moore appears in a Kellogg's *Frosties* advertisement alongside mascot Tony the Tiger in 1955. (Life magazine)

these added nutrients help keep bodies healthy. What they were really doing was adding back just some of the nutrients stripped away during the refining process. They did not mention the 38g of sugar per 100g of cereal. Then, with the invention of the toaster pastry – *Pop Tarts* – they went to town on the sugar: sweet fruit or chocolate filling with sweetened pastry and covered in icing. Kellogg's no longer felt the need to dress up their foods as healthy now that the population was fully hooked, and gave us dessert for breakfast. Grown-ups fall for it too: Kellogg's *Crunchy Nut Cornflakes* and *Special K*, and the huge array of different nut clusters and mueslis are all aimed at adults, are laced with sugar and have their 'virtues' well presented on the packet – they are low fat, contain wholegrains, are a source of protein, etc.

Why are we surprised? By the turn of the twenty-first century several generations of the nation had grown up on sugary cereals. Many adults today eat the cereals they ate as children, and it is proving difficult to wean ourselves from these foods. Sugar was indeed the new tobacco. As for the foods' fortifications, no studies on the supplementation of nutrients 'has been able to show a decrease in the incidence of chronic diseases'. These foods are no more than 'junk with added nutrients'.[21]

A textbook example of the fortification trick came in the late 1990s with the launch in the UK of the extremely popular, though oddly brightly coloured orange 'juice' *Sunny Delight*. It was marketed to parents as the healthy choice because it contained vitamins A, C and E. The trouble was it wasn't orange juice but an orange-flavoured drink, its vitamins had to be added, and its main ingredient – after water – was sugar. The advertising campaign was so successful that it became the UK's third best-selling soft drink after Coke and Pepsi. Children across the country drank gallons of the stuff, and parents were happy that their kids were drinking fruit juice instead of Coke. *Sunny Delight*'s day-glo colour was achieved with an orange dye, and in one notorious case one child drank so much of the stuff that their skin turned a distinct shade of orange. *Sunny Delight* was exposed as a fraud, and parents were angry. According to the BBC, brand manager Jan Walsh said, 'we stayed in our little castle thinking if we don't say anything the debate would go away.' It didn't go away, and was forced to relaunch as *Sunny D*, with more vitamins and a higher proportion of orange juice.[22] By then it was too late, and it disappeared from the shelves as quickly as it arrived.

In the 2000s a new phenomenon appeared when a significant cohort of workers and students stopped bothering with breakfast time altogether. Cereal companies were quick to respond and produced a whole range of cereal-based foods for 'on the go': breakfast bars, biscuits and drinks. They all boasted something healthy; 'wholegrain', 'high protein' and 'low fat', but left the amount of sugar in the small print, where a busy worker would be unlikely to look. We still fall for it: granola anyone? 'This period of joyless fat-free eating,' says Carolyn Steel in *Sitopia*, her great thesis of the world's food issues, 'saw the steepest rise in obesity and diet-related disease in history.'[23]

America has influenced Britain more acutely than the rest of Europe because of the 'special relationship' they share. Consequently, Britain was quickest to ape its culture, pushing towards motorised vehicles, chest freezers, televisions, shopping malls, multiplex cinemas and its junk food. Britain 'was a rollover' and was the first country in Europe to consume *7-Up*, McDonald's and Kentucky Fried Chicken.[24] It was brash, and it was exciting, and the king of these was – and still is – Coca Cola, and it requires our special attention.

***

Sweet drinks flavoured with fruit, herbs, spices and other aromatics have a long history, their origin being medical or therapeutic. In the US at the end of the nineteenth century, they were concoctions made by pharmacists such as sarsaparilla and root beer. They were doubly good for you too, because not only were they medicinal, they were also alcohol-free and were therefore enthusiastically endorsed by the temperance movement. They became a real hit when combined with carbonated water which was also sold as a drink with health-giving properties.[25] Aside from pharmacies, sodas were drunk in the many soda fountains that sprang up across America's southern states, where sugary sodas were combined with sugary ice cream to make delicious floats. Carbonated soda drinks became very popular very quickly and launched some iconic American brands, all with health-enhancing properties; for example, the *pep* in Pepsi refers to the 'fact' that it was good for settling an acid stomach. Another early brand was Dr Pepper, but there was another waiting in the wings that would eclipse everything and become arguably the greatest player in the obesity and diabetes pandemic. It has reached almost every country on the planet and has cost health services hundreds of billions of dollars: Coca Cola. This is not hyperbole; other foods, drinks and factors have contributed to the epidemic, but Coca Cola set a precedent, and a ruthlessly cynical one at that.

Coca Cola got ahead of its other competitors for a variety of reasons. First, it contained extracts of the coca leaf, giving it the kick of 8mg of

An example of an early medicinal soda fountain, St Louis, Missouri, USA, 1887. St Louis is home to the USA's oldest soda fountain. From such fountains sarsaparilla and root beer were dispensed. Considered a health tonic, these drinks were laced with lots of sugar, and sometimes cocaine, in the case of Coca Cola. (Gerstein, University of Toronto)

cocaine per glass, as well as a good hit of caffeine from the kola nut. Add to this the ample amounts of sugar and the drinker received quite the buzz. The cocaine was removed from the drink by 1903, though coca leaves are still used in its production; the cocaine is extracted from the drink and sold on to drugs companies to produce a range of anaesthetics.[26] Second, the Coca Cola Company advertised right across the country, blazing a trail by installing brash vending machines wherever there were people, including schools: *especially* schools. Third, riding on the back of their advertising success, their economies of scale meant they could sell a bottle of Coke for just five cents, a price that would not change for decades. Other companies played catch up with great success, and the annual consumption of sweetened fizzy drinks over the next hundred years rose sharply from an average of 2.27 *l* in 1889 to 88.6 *l* in 1969, and then to 168.5 *l* in 1985; a seventy-five fold increase. Its winning

An 1890s Coca Cola advertisement. With government support, Coca Cola managed to keep its price set at five cents a bottle until the close of the Second World War.

business tactics made Coca Cola the largest consumer of sugar globally by 1910, aided by the government sugar subsidy and sugar quota system that kept sugar prices dependently stable and low, something it would benefit from until the 1970s.[27]

By the Second World War Coca Cola was part of the cultural fabric of the United States, but it was at this point the Coca Cola Company really exploded. First it increased its national distribution by selling it in every possible corner of the US so that no matter how rural or cut off you were there would always be a supply. Then they took it to the rest of the world, using war itself as the mechanism for propagation. Company owner Robert Woodruff worked closely with the US Army, promoting the drink – alongside cigarettes – as essential for the war effort. His lobbying gained political support, and Coca Cola was sent to every US base around the world. It was so crucial that it even found itself exempt from sugar rationing; as Woodruff famously said: 'We will see that every man in uniform gets a bottle of Coca Cola for five cents, wherever he is and whatever it costs the company.' Their monopoly allowed them to build up bottle works wherever men were stationed, and rather than *costing* the company money, it *made* it a huge amount. Between 1941 and 1945 the US military purchased ten billion bottles from the Coca Cola Company. The patriotic love for the brand made it as proudly American as Mom's apple pie, yet it was now manufactured wherever the United States stationed their men. It was now a world product.[28]

Coca Cola's next wave of domination came in the 1960s with its association with US fast food. The culture – headed by the beef burger – arose in the 1950s and 1960s with the arrival of such big names as McDonald's, Burger King and Pizza Hut. And it was in the 1950s that Coca Cola became the sole supplier to McDonald's burger restaurants, first in the USA and then around the globe. This second monopoly allowed them to increase their production vastly with very little change to their infrastructure; there was no need for more bottling works, because they sold the syrups direct. It was 'a unique symbiotic relationship', with Coca Cola even allowing McDonald's to use its offices as it began its own worldwide expansion.[29]

However, in the 1970s the soft drink industry hit a hurdle when Congress ended the sugar quota system that acted as a buffer against fluctuating prices after sugar prices had risen to 'unusual heights' in 1974. The origins of the sugar quota can be traced back to the country's colonial days. It benefitted domestic sugar producers by keeping prices stable and predictably cheap.[30] With the quota lifted, prices increased and fluctuated wildly. This stochasticity affected profits and Coca Cola were forced to search for an alternative source of sweetness. It did not take long to find the perfect replacement: high fructose corn syrup (HFCS), which is produced by extracting the syrup from the pithy stalk of maize plants. Like sugarcane, maize is a tall grass species with a sweet pithy centre, the juice of which was extracted by the indigenous people of South America. It has even been theorized that maize was first cultivated not for its cobs, but its pith.[31] It was an expensive process at first, but when farmers were encouraged to grow corn on a vast scale, prices fell, and with generous government subsidies substituting sucrose for HFCS it became a viable business strategy. What is more, on taste tests no one could tell the difference, and it was sweeter than sucrose, so less of it was required. By the 1980s all Coca Cola Company drinks made in the US were sweetened with HFCS. This paved the way for almost all companies who manufactured sweetened commercially produced foods to swap sugar for HFCS too.

HFCS it is not a crystalline substance, which limits its uses, so it could never displace sucrose completely, nevertheless it has become almost ubiquitous in cheap processed foods and is the States' most subsidised foodstuff. It was made on such a massive scale that it cost very little to sweeten and flavour drinks. So little, in fact, that in the final years of the twentieth century the Coca Cola Company suggested combining burger, fries and soda into a 'value meal'.[32] It was a great success, and off the back of it, McDonald's introduced the concept of 'going large' where French fries and sodas were upgraded to large portion sizes. It cost the customer less than a dollar, but cost McDonald's and Coca Cola next to nothing. As Carolyn Steel asserts: 'all they were really doing was sneaking high profit (and high calorie) items such as Coke and fries under the radar,' and as if by magic the calories in a McDonald's meal rose from 590 in the 1980s to 1550 by the mid-nineties.[33] Riding on that wave, they invited their loyal customers to 'supersize' their meal. In the US, a 'supersized' soda was 64fl oz (1.9 l) in volume and contained the equivalent of an eye-popping forty-four teaspoons of sugar.[34]

McDonald's and Coca Cola had hit on a magic formula: they had taken our evolved adaptation to find salt, fat and sugar pleasurable, refined it and exploited it on a massive scale. This left us in a world where highly calorific food, full of sugar, white wheat flour, meat and animal fat could be eaten in vast amounts – something once only available to the richest in society – and were cheaper than unprocessed, natural, healthy food; and it made us sick. HFCS is the main culprit, and it is so bad that even sugar – that is, sucrose – tried to distance itself from it. HFCS is a major cause of type-2 diabetes. When it is consumed, it does not need to be digested and is absorbed directly into the bloodstream, giving the drinker an immediate sugar rush. Our bodies' homeostatic feedback mechanisms quickly restore these levels, but if these aggressively oscillating physiological changes occur frequently, the mechanisms uncouple, causing diabetes. If we combine this physiological onslaught with the obesity associated with the consumption of that same sugar, the short circuit occurs all the more readily. Sucrose does this too, but being a disaccharide it has to be digested by enzymes first, and therefore is assimilated into the bloodstream at a slower rate. According to the World Health Organisation, there were 171 million people with the condition in the year 2000, and it estimates that this number will inflate to 366 million by 2030.[35]

Obesity and diabetes cause a range of associated complications like heart disease and stroke, and the less well-known such as vision loss, loss of feeling, kidney disease, sores and skin infections, and poor circulation. For the latter, the only viable life-saving treatment is to amputate limbs. Obesity *per se* is, in fact, not the issue, and some see it as almost a distraction; around twenty per cent of obese people are perfectly healthy, but forty per cent of them have metabolic syndrome, and it is this syndrome that is linked to insulin resistance and diabetes. This occurs when fructose enters the bloodstream and binds to insulin, preventing it from fulfilling its function to lower blood sugar levels, leading to type-2 diabetes.[36]

Theoretically, any one could be susceptible to the diseases related to this diet, but in reality it is not evenly spread throughout society. The poor, as usual, are hit the hardest with children from the poorest families twice as likely to be obese than children belonging to moderately wealthy ones. It is also associated with race, with Afro-Americans being fifty per cent more likely to be obese than Caucasians and therefore more prone to high cholesterol, hypertension, insulin resistance, type-2 diabetes, metabolic syndrome and colorectal cancer, as well as depression.[37] It was – and still is – the poorest in society who are most vulnerable to sugar's ill

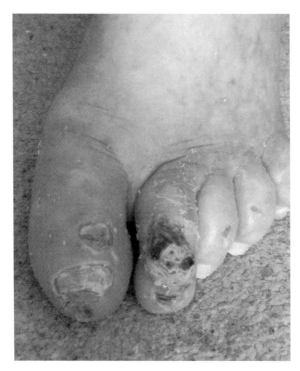

An ulcerated foot of a patient with poor circulation brought on by type-2 diabetes and obesity. It is likely that toes, and perhaps foot, may be amputated. This may be an extreme effect of sugar on the body, but it is becoming increasingly common in the West, especially in the United States. (Bondegezou)

effects because it is they who buy the cheapest foods; foods that are full of sugar and other refined ingredients, foods that do not spoil easily, and foods that require the least amount of time and fuel to prepare. Healthy foods, however, do take time and energy to prepare and have short shelf lives; they are not subsidised by governments and are therefore more expensive.[38] What is more, decades of consuming convenience foods stripped us of our cooking skills, traditionally a families' way to be thrifty. The claim that eating these foods is a choice is an illusion: a choice between cheap junk foods and expensive fresh food, which needs skill to prepare and refrigeration to prevent spoilage,[39]is not an option; it is a Hobson's choice. This is what 'being on the bread line' meant – and still means – at the turn of the twenty-first century. But it is not a new phenomenon. George Orwell pointed that out very clearly in his 1937 book *The Road to Wigan Pier*:

> The miner's family spend only tenpence a week on green vegetables and tenpence half-penny on milk (remember that one of them is a child less than three years old), and nothing

on fruit; but they spend one and nine on sugar (about eight pounds of sugar, that is) and a shilling on tea. The half-crown spent on meat might represent a small joint and the materials for a stew; probably as often as not it would represent four or five tins of bully beef. The basis of their diet, therefore, is white bread and margarine, corned beef, sugared tea, and potatoes – an appalling diet. Would it not be better if they spent more money on wholesome things like oranges and wholemeal bread or if they even, like the writer of the letter to the New Statesman, saved on fuel and ate their carrots raw? Yes, it would, but the point is that no ordinary human being is ever going to do such a thing. The ordinary human being would sooner starve than live on brown bread and raw carrots. And the peculiar evil is this, that the less money you have, the less inclined you feel to spend it on wholesome food. A millionaire may enjoy breakfasting off orange juice and Ryvita biscuits; an unemployed man doesn't … When you are unemployed, which is to say when you are underfed, harassed, bored, and miserable, you don't want to eat dull wholesome food. You want something a little bit 'tasty'. There is always some cheaply pleasant thing to tempt you … Run out and buy us a twopenny ice-cream! Put the kettle on and we'll all have a nice cup of tea! That is how your mind works when you are at the P.A.C. level. White bread-and-marg and sugared tea don't nourish you to any extent, but they are nicer (at least most people think so) than brown bread … Unemployment is an endless misery that has got to be constantly palliated, and especially with tea, the Englishman's opium. A cup of tea or even an aspirin is much better as a temporary stimulant than a crust of brown bread.[40]

We need to start to undo the damage that sugar and its refined comrades, fat, white wheat flour and salt, are doing to the world's population. Can we realistically be free from sugar's ill effects when it is so plentiful, cheap and normalised to consume it? Will it forever be the new tobacco?

Chapter 13

Fifty Words for Sugar

> Industrial cooking has taken a substantial toll on our health and well-being. Corporations cook very differently from how people do (which is why we usually call what they do "food processing" instead of cooking). They tend to use much more sugar ... than people cooking for people do; they also deploy chemical ingredients seldom found in pantries.[1]
>
> *Michael Pollan*

We can be in no doubt today that eating too much sugar is bad for our health, but sugar has always been mistrusted by some, even if their ideas were unpopular. Notions that sugar caused disease rather than cured it began to gain traction from the late seventeenth century – the first time a large cohort of society was habitually consuming large amounts of it. Physician Thomas Willis described diabetes in the 1640s, naming it *diabetes mellitus* – mellitus meaning 'honey' – because he noted that the urine of a sufferer of the condition tasted honey-like,[2] though it was not until the eighteenth century that sugar was shown to be responsible for the sweet taste.[3] It wouldn't be until the 1930s that H.P. Himsworth would differentiate between the two forms of the disease: type-1 caused by a 'deficiency' in the hormone insulin; and type-2, caused by being 'insensitive' to it, and related to diet.[4]

In the early eighteenth century Danish physician Steven Blankaart condemned the excessive sweetening of food and drinks with sugar and questioned its ubiquity in medicinal preparations. Others began to argue that sugar was harmful rather than healthy, with Blankaart's contemporary, Christoph Schroer, agreeing: 'for all sweet things produce sharp, acidic humours, from which evolve countless diseases.' He also noted that it was particularly dangerous if combined with fat in the diet.[5]

Sugar was deemed responsible for a whole smorgasbord of other illnesses and conditions too: diabetes, hyperactivity, hypoglycaemia and cravings. Dr Thomas Willis blamed nutrition-devoid sugar as 'one cause of our universal scurvy.' However, rather spurious connections were made too, including bubonic plague, criminal behaviour, hair loss, freckles and worms.[6] Sugar even got the blame for causing spots and acne.[7]

The idea that sugar was deleterious to health endured through the centuries, but it ended up getting eclipsed by the more pressing ethical debate around the use of slave labour to produce the sugar in the first place.[8] It was only when we reach the twentieth and twenty-first centuries do we see a serious push, not only to understand better the connection between sugar and health, but also to determine just what it is about sugar that led us down this path in the first place. The knowledge of sugar's link to obesity and diabetes gave it a bad name, and now there was competition between those who considered themselves on the moral high ground who wanted us all watch our sugar intake, and the food manufacturers who wanted us to keep on eating their sugar-laden products. Big Sugar was not prepared to let a lot of do-gooders put a dent in their industry.

Once it was established that sugar was a critical factor in causing obesity, artificial sweeteners became very popular, the most famous – or perhaps infamous – examples being aspartame and saccharine. These chemicals are many times sweeter than sugar and therefore only needed in tiny amounts; so tiny that they add no significant nutritional value to the foodstuff to which they have been added. At first they were not used to attract the calorie-counting cohort of society, but as a cheap alternative to the sugar in soda pop after Congress ended the United States' long-running sugar quota system in the 1970s. Though used with abandon in fizzy drinks, coffee and tea, many were sceptical about these laboratory-made too-good-to-be-true artificial sweeteners, and in due course links to cancer began to be questioned.[9] However, these correlations only seem to be biologically or statistically significant when consumed in vast amounts, and manufacturers insist that their products have been tested rigorously and are perfectly safe for human consumption.[10] All that said, many consider the consumption of any synthetic foodstuff intrinsically bad, a fact that soda and cereal manufacturers have been able to use to their advantage, announcing with pride that sugar is an all-natural product. Many felt they had a point, and food scientists looked at identifying 'natural' sweeteners, the best known of these being the extract of the Stevia plant.[11]

More intriguing is the data that shows a positive correlation between obesity, heart disease and diabetes, and consumption of diet soft drinks.[12] This curious link is not because artificial sweeteners are calorific or cause these diseases – they do not – but the real link tells us a lot about human behaviour. Most people who like a lot of sweetened drinks also tend to eat food high in calories, so to reduce energy intake some people make the change to diet soft drinks but fail to address the rest of their diet. This dietary tactic only slows the weight gain and does not reduce it. When data is collected from studies in fully controlled conditions some weight loss is observed, but it is only in conjunction with a calorie-controlled diet supplemented with exercise that weight loss is significant. The changes we make need to be more drastic than swapping our Coca Cola for Coke Zero.[13]

Two major problems soda companies had with convincing consumers to switch *en masse* to the diet alternative were 'mouthfeel' and the feminisation of their products. Pleased as they must have been with the discovery that tiny amounts of artificial sweeteners could be used in lieu of lashings of sugar or corn syrup, a consequence of this swap was that the drinks were less syrupy and dense than the full-sugar version. Indeed, the lack of syrupy viscosity is so important in the experience of drinking these beverages that it put people off much more than the hyper-sweet taste of the artificial sweetener itself.[14] The issue of feminisation arose because diet drinks, particularly Diet Coke when it was released in 1983, were advertised directly to women who were watching their weight. The Coca Cola Company realised that if they were to get a wholesale shift toward low-calorie drinks they needed a gender-neutral drink, or even one that's a little bit macho, so that men would not feel their masculinity was being compromised in any way. The company released Coke Zero in 2006 with an updated formula more like the original Coke.[15]

The consumer's problem with a calorie-controlled diet is that most do not, will not or cannot count the calories or grams of sugar they are consuming. In a bid to make this easier, several governmental and NGO-led initiatives have been implemented over the last few decades to help consumers make better decisions as they rush around the supermarket filling their trolleys. The first of these began to be introduced in Europe in the 1960s where the packaging included a list of every ingredient in the product from smallest to largest by weight.[16] Now consumers could compare directly between products and they saw that for many products sugar was one of the largest constituents. But food manufacturers were quick to find ways of making their products appear to have less sugar than they really did, sparking off a sort of packaging information arms race between food manufacturers and government. In this case, food manufacturers responded to this by giving different types of sugar different names: maltodextrin, corn syrup, partially inverted glucose syrup and so on, allowing sugar to be dispersed in the ingredients list so that it would no longer stand out at the top of it. By 2018 there were at least fifty-six names in use for sugar in ingredients lists.[17]

Then in the 1970s came the familiar nutritional information box that divides up the nutrients – rather than ingredients – per 100g of product into sugars, fats, salt and calories, giving a more objective overview of the product's nutritional make-up.[18] This was confusing for many because no one eats their food in 100g portions: Britain, like the US, was still a mainly pounds and ounces country. Was 100g a lot, or not much? One hundred of anything *sounds* a lot. To help make the information more relatable, manufacturers added an extra column with the amounts shown in a typical portion, and later how much of one's recommended daily intake was contained within that portion. This is all well and good, but the problem was the shopper in a hurry wasn't looking at all this data on the back of each and every food packet, so although the information was there, it wasn't easy to quickly digest, especially if relegated to the back or side of the box or hidden behind a flap on some plastic packaging.

To make choosing healthy foods easier, this nutritional information was moved to the front of the packet showing how much of your recommended daily allowance of food calories that sugar, salt, etc. contained within. In the United Kingdom, the Food Standards Agency recommended extending this to a traffic light system in 2006. The dangerously high levels of sugar should have been easy to spot, but manufacturers would often provide nutritional data for ridiculously small portions that bore no resemblance to the amount of food people were really consuming. For example, Kellogg's *Special K*, a breakfast cereal that has always been promoted as a healthy food; it's 'healthy'

Is our No.1 ingredient

Each 3 pieces contain

Energy	Fat	Saturates	Sugars	Salt
408kJ 98kcal	5.7g	3.4g	9.5g	0.06g
5%	8%	17%	11%	1%

of an adult's Reference Intake (RI)*
Energy Per 100g: 2265kJ/542kcal

Nutritional information has been represented by a traffic light system since 2006. The sugar in one serving of this chocolate bar is high – 11% recommended daily allowance (RDA) of an adult. Note that the serving size is just three pieces. Eating the whole bar would contain the equivalent of 104% of one's RDA of sugar. (Neil Buttery)

because it is low in fat, but it also contains a large proportion of added sugar. Kellogg's calculated the nutritional information from an unrealistically small portion size, so when the size of portions people actually gave themselves were compared, it was found that they had consumed more sugar than if they had eaten a *Krispy Kreme* doughnut. The upshot of using the 'serving size' loophole by food manufacturers meant the legislation had little success: in the UK sales of ready meals shot up, not down, and its effectiveness to aid those with 'low self control … remains to be seen.'[19]

Another way manufacturers managed to maintain high sugar levels in their sweet foods was to introduce the 'no added sugar' label. This sounds most appealing, a sweet food sweetened naturally without refined white sugars. However, ingredients containing a large amount of sugar were used, such as concentrated apple or grape juice. The result were foods high in sugar, but with no sugar present on the ingredients list. Even fresh 'not from concentrate' fruit juices contain a lot of sugar, so switching from sodas to juice is doing no one any favours with respect to sugar consumption (they do, of course, contain a whole suite of vitamins and minerals). But how can this be? The problem is that when we drink fruit juice we are not consuming the roughage that usually comes with eating the fruit; to make 500ml of orange juice you need six good-sized oranges. This amount of fruit contains over 100g of sugar – that is, a solution of twenty per cent sugar weight-by-volume. However, sit down and try and eat six good-sized oranges and you will soon see it is impossible to consume that amount of sugar; 'in nature [there is no food] rich in fructose and devoid of fibre.'[20] We may not think of it as such, but fruit juices are a processed food, and although the processing is so simple you can do it at home, it just shows how it can completely change the nutritional profile of a foodstuff.

In 2016 the United Kingdom's Sugar Reduction Programme was launched, its purpose to significantly reduce children's sugar intake by 2020. Companies were expected to reduce sugar in their products either by proportion or by portion but were given time to adjust their recipes and were expected to have significantly lowered the sugar in their offerings by 2018.[21] Wanting to be seen as proactive and on board with this important programme, food giant Nestlé almost immediately produced a low-sugar alternative to the perennial children's favourite Milkybar, containing thirty per cent less sugar. Companies such as Cadbury's and Heinz quickly followed suit.

There was good progress after a year: big offenders such as yoghurts and breakfast cereals reduced their sugar content by 10.3 per cent and 8.5 per cent respectively. However, manufacturers quickly realised that they could simply use the old trick of 'reducing' the amount of sugar in a serving by decreasing the size of the bar or container, or reducing the amount considered to be one serving, so a chocolate bar once assumed to be one serving was now smaller, and if one cared to look at the small print, considered now to be two, or even three, servings. If the consumer ate their bar in one go, that was on them. One of the major intrusions into the food manufacturers' activities came in 2007 with the banning of highly sugared and calorific junk food on children's television. Soda companies responded by producing smaller sized cans, and Quakers even dropped the word 'sugar' from their Sugar Puffs, renaming it Honey Monster in an attempt to appear more wholesome.

Some tried to meet the consumer halfway. In 2014 the Coca Cola Company proved themselves ahead of the curve when they announced a lower sugar alternative, Coke Life, in 2014. This new drink contained thirty-five per cent less sugar than regular Coca Cola and was sweetened with 'natural' Stevia, but even with a strong advertising push and resplendent green can, by 2016 'its days were numbered'.[22] The low-sugar Milkybar also suffered the same fate. It seemed that given a choice, the average consumer did not want half measures. In their 2018/19 audit, Public Health England saw that sugar consumption had fallen, but by a dismal 0.1 per cent.

At the same time as the Sugar Reduction Programme, the UK government announced a 'key milestone in tackling childhood obesity':

the infamous Sugar Tax. Sugary soft drinks were to be taxed, just like alcohol and tobacco; there would be an additional cost of 24p per litre for drinks containing 8g or more of sugar per 100ml, and 18p for those containing between 5 and 8g of sugar per 100ml.[23] The levy turned out to be 'unexpectedly successful', leading to a fall in sugar consumption via soft drinks by thirty per cent.[24]

***

Now that sugar was fully exposed as bad – bad for health, bad of you for eating it, and bad of the food companies for making it so cheap and inviting – one might imagine high-sugar products to be difficult to find, yet all of these products are available today and still cheap. Cans of full sugar and salt baked beans, 500ml bottles of Coca Cola, sugary Dairy Milk, all of which contain more than one serving (according to their packaging), have not disappeared from the supermarket shelves. Why? Because we still want to eat them, even though we can input our food items into smartphone apps and count every gram of sugar that passes our lips. It is clear: we cannot help ourselves.

The only real way we are going to reduce sugar intake to a healthier level is to change how we make and consume the food we buy in our supermarkets or on our high streets. If we really want to ditch the sugar, we need to ditch industrially produced refined foods, foods that are devoid of fibre, bran and – most importantly – the flavour that once gave them their character[25], leaving us with empty calories and, perhaps, a few vitamins and minerals added back in. Cooking from scratch with natural foods that fill you up with fewer calories provides a full suite of nutrients, and requires your body to work at digesting it. We need to start doing this now because the fate of the world's population is wobbling on a knife's edge. Now, as our dark history of sugar has reached the present day, we need to decide just how dark sugar's legacy will be.

Chapter 14

Legacy

'Over the past 50 years, a typical British meal has morphed from meat and two veg to sticky chilli chicken, via burgers, Coke and fries.'

Carolyn Steel[1]

Who could have possibly imagined that when the first trickle of sugar found its way to Europe from the mediaeval Muslim Empire in Persia almost a thousand years ago, it would leave two-thirds of the world's population obese[2] and teetering on diabetes with mouths riddled with gum disease and cavities? Those genes of ours, honed and selected in a past environment where sweetness was scarce, highly valued and required work to obtain it when present, now find themselves in a world of unlimited choice and a never-depleting supply, all at a bargain price. Our genes, unfortunately, do not know this. We cannot stop eating it and it shows, and it continues to worsen: in 2017 there were 43,000 dental operations in the UK to extract rotten teeth from the mouths of children and adolescents, an increase of twenty per cent in just five years.[3] Even those kids who do not have their teeth removed have mouths dotted with decay; children with cavities have an average of three or four affected teeth. Over the centuries dentistry has improved, even if reining in our sugar consumption has not, but even today with the lifetime of care we receive from our healthcare systems worldwide, poor oral hygiene is extremely common. Between 2011 and 2014 nearly 26,000 children between five and nine years of age were admitted to hospital in England for 'extensive tooth extraction under general anaesthetic'.[4] In more recent years things have improved slightly, but with sugar ever-present in our preparatory foods it makes things very difficult. It's not just the obvious ones like chocolate, fizzy drinks and biscuits either, but also in places where people may not expect it to lurk, such as pasta sauces, chili con carne and barbeque ribs. Only when we leave added sugar behind will we say goodbye to this public health nightmare. But bearing in mind this sugar binge has been going on for 500 years, it is unlikely to stop anytime soon.

What's more, there is a stark difference between the mouths of children from different socio-economic backgrounds, with 'children from the most deprived areas having more than twice the level of decay than those from the least deprived.'[5] The same disparity is found in adults too of course, and this inequality can be extended to obesity and diabetes.

Recently, focus has returned to the issue of advertising and promotion of junk food. McDonald's long-running Monopoly promotion, which is aimed at adults and adolescents, came under fire in 2019 for its shameless promotion of high-calorie foods, with advertisements found on television, buses, billboards and social media. The idea behind it is simple: diners are encouraged to collect matching tokens to win prizes, and they receive tokens when they buy McDonald's food. Tom Watson, ex-deputy leader of the Labour Party, said of it: 'McDonald's "Monopoly" promotion is a grotesque marketing ploy that encourages people to eat more and more junk food by offering sugar-filled desserts as rewards. It is a danger to public health.'[6] He went even further in an open letter addressed to McDonald's in March 2019 saying:

> It is unacceptable that this campaign aims to manipulate families into ordering junk food more frequently and in bigger portions, in the faint hope of winning a holiday, a car, or a cash prize many would otherwise struggle to afford ... Businesses have a moral responsibility to their customers, and as a society we have a responsibility to safeguard the health of our children ... I am requesting that you urgently rethink this strategy: McDonald's must stop playing on people's hopes and prioritising profit over public health. I urge you to cancel this marketing campaign.[7]

The UK government intends to ban the advertising of sugary or calorific food before the 'watershed' (9pm) after it was found that two-thirds of the television watched was aimed not at them but at their parents. Sugar's 'tobaccofication' continues on its trajectory as big food and drinks companies are exposed as ruthless agents cynically preying on a population addicted to their products. Any new legislation needs to be effective too if we are to be anywhere close to the World Health Organisation's recommendation of consuming a proportion of no more than ten per cent sugar in our diets. But will ditching the junk food work? Perhaps not, for sugar has one thing that tobacco does not, and that is a place in our hearts: rose-tinted memories of the penny sweet shop, ice cream floats at the diner, birthday cakes with candles and Grandma's jam roly-poly pudding with lashings of sweet custard. No one says that sort of thing about Richmond's Superkings or Marlborough Lights. Indeed, the success of television programmes such as the *Great British Bake Off* depends on us having this misty-eyed nostalgia. During the lockdown months of the Covid-19 pandemic, we baked more than ever, but at least some of us got to see the amount of sugar that actually goes into a simple sponge cake, and perhaps cut thinner slices, or reduced the frequency of such treats.

Let's not be fooled by this though: we are living in a world populated with sugar junkies. Some are very quick to point out that sugar is not technically a drug, citing two reasons: first, it is an essential foodstuff, we would die without it; and second, it does not infiltrate and affect the nervous system directly as drugs do. Things are never that straightforward of course, because when sugar is consumed, our bodies detect it and there is an 'intense release of opioids in the brain': sugar is a drug by proxy. There can little doubt that sugar, like drugs, affects behaviour, and it certainly makes us behave like addicts with phenomena such as 'bingeing, craving, tolerance [and] withdrawal' all common. There is also a strong correlation between attention deficit hyperactive disorder (ADHD) and sugar consumption, and it has been hypothesised that the disorder is the manifestation of sugar withdrawal.[8]

Treating the diseases associated with sugar consumption is buckling our healthcare systems, costing the world a staggering amount of money. In the UK alone, obesity and diabetes cost the National Health Service £6.1 billion and £8.8 billion respectively in 2014/15.[9] In the United States, over twenty per cent of all medical spending goes into treating obesity and the complications associated with it. In 2012 it cost the country $190.2 billion, and of that, $14 billion was spent on treating childhood obesity.[10]

There has been some success, such as the sugar levy. Unfortunately, some food and drink manufacturers feel it has been rather too successful and are worried that their stars may be fading in the West; in particular, our friend, the Coca Cola Company. To address this, they have turned their focus toward the Developing World. Speaking in 2016, the then CEO of Coca Cola, Muhtar Kent, said, 'last decade we invested about $5.5 billion in total in Africa. This decade we've earmarked to invest about $17 billion.' Other companies too, such as Pepsi, are attempting to sink their claws into the lucrative African market. Coca Cola's approach is exactly the same as the one they took to spread through the US and the rest of the Western World: by opening up bottling plants and encouraging local sellers to do the legwork. By 2016 they had opened 145 bottling plants across Africa and employed over 70,000 people.[11]

The world's diabetes epicentre is shifting from the West too. The highest rates of increase of the condition are found in India and China, especially in urban areas, where the population of adults suffering from type-2 diabetes is verging on twenty per cent.[12] And what's to blame? Increased consumption of sweetened soft drinks, especially fizzy drinks, and processed, refined foods, though there also appears to be a genetic component at work compounding the problem, making people of Asian descent more prone to developing the disease than Caucasians. Asian women are also more prone to gestational diabetes, which, in turn, considerably increases their children's chances of developing type-2 diabetes.[13] It would appear that soft drinks are well into their second phase of world domination.

Sugar has also left its mark on the health of the planet, and its injuries are deep and long-lasting. The 2020 Sugar Report made the current situation very clear: 'Sugarcane cultivation [has] harmful environmental impacts, such as air pollution and greenhouse gas … emissions that result from sugarcane field burning before manual harvesting. It can also contribute to water stress due to overconsumption and agricultural runoff. Approximately 30 per cent of sugarcane production takes place in high or extremely high water stress areas, and agricultural runoff coupled with the overapplication of fertilizers and pesticides have polluted water bodies.'[14]

The World Wildlife Fund reckons that sugar is 'responsible for more biodiversity loss than any other crop.'[15] Ever since the sugar trade expanded to the Canary Islands and Madeira and on to the Americas, it devasted forests, first for timber to fuel the fires of the boiling rooms and then to make room for the sugarcane itself. As the English took the industry to new 'heights', they cleared land at an even faster rate. The pristine Barbados forest was almost completely destroyed by 1650, and the spread of sugar to the other islands meant that Jamaica, Guadeloupe, St Domingue and Antigua all lost the majority (if not all) of their forests within a century. Neat, organised and ordered cane fields replaced the apparent disorder and viciousness of nature, reducing biodiversity and leaving the land prone to soil erosion, the trees and understorey no longer providing the soil with its structure, strength or resilience. With forests receding, indigenous people became more and more exposed, eventually exploited and worked to death. Two million natives had already died between the 1490s and 1540s, well before the wholesale trade in slaves from Africa.[16]

The widespread use of chemical pesticides is having a devastating effect upon what is left of plantations' natural fauna, especially on the surrounding aquatic habitat, with chemical leachate from the fields causing widespread eutrophication of rivers and lakes, with species such as blue-green algae growing in vast numbers, depleting the oxygen

The Indian mongoose was introduced to several islands of the West Indies to predate the rats that were destroying sugarcane roots. The scheme was only successful on one island, and they are responsible for the extinction of several island species. (Aniketan Math)

179

dissolved in the water and blocking out sunlight to other plants.[17] The leachate from the cane fields of Queensland, Australia, contains no fewer than four 'photosynthesis-inhibiting herbicides', a cocktail of chemicals that quickly kills the corals' symbiotic algae. Once these tiny plants are gone, so is the rest of the food chain, leaving the community to die from the bottom up, leaving a ghostly underwater desert in its wake.[18]

The biological control of pests has had a devastating effect on the habitats surrounding cane fields. The Indian mongoose was released into the cane fields of the West Indies and Hawaii to control the rat population which, aside from spreading disease, was destroying sugarcane. The mongoose was introduced in the 1870s and was particularly populous on the Caribbean Islands where they greedily tucked into the rats they were there to control. Unfortunately, various reptile and ground-nesting bird species are equally delicious to a mongoose (as were the contents of residents' poultry pens), and even after a decade-long trapping and poisoning regime, they are still found in substantial numbers, happily polishing off vulnerable indigenous species. On Jamaica, at least, they did manage to wipe out the rat population, but now the mongoose eat so many of the local seabirds' eggs at nesting times that the birds have chosen to give the island a wide berth and breed elsewhere.[19] Despite the unexpected devastating effects of introducing this animal, it was still – somehow – thought a good idea to introduce the cane toad as pest management in Australia and Hawaii in the 1930s. It was introduced to control an insect pest called the sugarcane beetle which, if allowed to go unchecked, can decimate entire crops by eating the stems and roots of the canes. The disaster that unfurled was three-fold: first, the large toads were too bulky to climb or jump up to the beetles and larvae that sat high up on the canes; second, the toads are highly toxic, and have poisoned a diverse range of animals, from dingoes to kangaroos, cats to honeybees;[20] lastly, they have no natural predators in their novel environments, and so they bred at such an alarming rate that by 2017 there were approximately 1.5 billion cane toads at large in Australia.[21]

Sugar is even getting in the way of improving habitats. In the United States, from the late nineteenth century, the Florida Everglades have had their water diverted so that swampland could be converted into agricultural land. The extent of the drainage means that freshwater no longer meets saltwater downstream, and as a consequence the water

Introduced to Australia and Hawaii in the 1930s as pest management, the cane toad largely avoided its intended victim, the cane beetle. By 2017 there were 1.5 billion toads at large in Australia alone. (Patrick Gijsbers)

is too salty. These saline waters have killed the keystone plant species seagrass, which was important for both food and shelter for a whole range of animals. Without this resource, baitfish could not find food, and in turn neither could the population of brackish and freshwater waders and other waterfowl. The same goes for the larger species of fish.

With populations crashing, something had to be done. The solution was to build reservoirs to the north of these areas, which could flood the Everglades' southern tracts, restoring the habitat, at least to some degree. The perfect land for the proposed reservoirs was government owned, something that should have been a major benefit to the project, but the land was already leased to America's Big Sugar company Florida Crystals. In 2015, amid widespread protest, their lobbyists managed to influence the Florida Water Committee and made sure that Florida Crystals' lease was extended.[22] But then in 2019 cracks started to appear in the company's hold over government when Republican governor Ron DeSantis began to undo the damage, determined that the reservoir project would go ahead in 2024. He is meeting resistance of course, but his message is clear: sugar is stopping the Everglades from being saved.

DeSantis has flatly refused to take any funding from sugar companies, and his influence was far-reaching: President Trump signed the Water Infrastructure Act in October 2019 which, among other things, will fund those reservoirs. However, the very next month there was 'outrage' when the committee rushed through a motion extending Florida Crystals' lease for a further eight years. Its legality is being contested because there was no public notice declaring that the hearing was taking place. No doubt fines will be issued, fines that Florida Crystals can easily absorb.[23] Big Sugar's exploitation of the planet is not over yet.

The modern sugar industry also continues to exploit its workers, and is still considered to have a poor labour rights record. In 2019 the International Institute for Sustainable Development's report cited several 'documented occurrences of forced and child labour', and observed that occupational health and safety issues at plantations and mills are not uncommon, even in some of the largest producing countries, such as Brazil.'[24] Brazil is particularly notorious for its poor workers' rights record in general, but even so, when charities liberated workers from gruelling and illegal work regimes fifty per cent came from sugar plantations. The workers may not be slaves, but they are considered so because conditions are 'degrading' and there is a 'significant element of unfreedom.'[25] Mexico's sugar workers are dying in their forties from kidney failure associated with chronic dehydration. Under those criteria, then, we must also include the workers in Florida in the 1980s and 1990s. There is also the Dominican Republic.

The Dominican Republic is a client state of the United States and shares an island with Haiti. The Republic was occupied by the Americans in 1916 where they immediately began cultivating sugarcane with labour sourced not domestically but from the British West Indies. In the 1930s, when the Republic was run by dictator Rafael Trujillo, his regime purchased workers from neighbouring Haiti in what was essentially a new form of slave trade, and it continues to this day. The Haitians are only allowed to work the fields by hand, which is gruelling enough, but added to this is the use of large amounts of chemical fertilizers and pesticides. 'I've been working for this company for forty-five years,' says one worker, 'I've cut the sugarcane, cultivated it, carried it. Then I sprayed the sugarcane. This has been very bad for me. It has destroyed my leg and hand. My knee gets swollen. I can't work properly. I'm old. I'm seventy years old, and I'm fucked.'[26] With no real prospects and no window or communication to the outside world, living in squalid villages that sit like tiny islands in vast seas of sugarcane, life here is also 'unfree', but the planters made sure they did not work them quite as hard as slaves. That way they would not die quickly. Instead, plantation owners have learned to temper the workload so that the drudgery can be extended, dragged out to a full lifetime. What's more, because the Haitians are foreigners with no official legal paperwork, they receive no pension. They have nowhere to go, nothing to do, and nothing to show for their labour; no property and no nest egg, just broken bodies.[27] And so it continues: it is the most vulnerable who are coaxed into working in modern-day cane fields, usually migrant workers trapped by their alien status or residents who are trapped by their own poverty.

This legacy of exploitation originates from the use of slave labour. In the US, with the emancipation of the slaves came the Thirteenth Amendment to the United States Constitution. From 1865, a black person could be a chattel no more:

> Section 1. Neither slavery nor involuntary servitude, except as a punishment for crime whereof the party shall have been duly convicted, shall exist within the United States, or any place subject to their jurisdiction.

> Section 2. Congress shall have power to enforce this article by appropriate legislation.

But great inequality remained and became entrenched, and with it a lack of opportunity and widespread violence and abuse. With the civil rights movement in the 1960s came a modicum of hope that there would be progress, acceptance, and a fairer and more equal society.[28] It did not, and the violence towards black people in the US continued, which was catalysed by Richard Nixon's presidential campaign of 1968 which addressed the persecution of black people in the US not as a racist war, but a 'War on Drugs'. Nixon's aide John Ehrlichman, admitted this to a journalist in 2016:

> The Nixon campaign in 1968, and the Nixon White House after that, had two enemies: the antiwar left and black people. You understand what I'm saying? We knew we couldn't

make it illegal to be either against the war or blacks, but by getting the public to associate the hippies with marijuana and blacks with heroin, and then criminalizing both heavily, we could disrupt those communities. We could arrest their leaders, raid their homes, break up their meetings, and vilify them night after night on the evening news. Did we know we were lying about the drugs? Of course we did.

The 'War on Drugs' morphed into the 'War on Crime' as it was developed by future prospective Republican candidates Ronald Reagan and George Bush Senior. The policy sufficiently disrupted the black movement and maintained a fear of black people in the white American public; a fear that can be traced right back to the plantations when the white slavers were outnumbered by, and terrified of, their own slaves. This fear, they felt, justified their terrible treatment of them. The violence that the black population received at the hands of both the police and public was turned back at them: black people were the ones instigating violent crime, and whites were the innocent victims. When a journalist asked black rights activist Angela Davis if she took part in this violence, she baulked, physically deflated that his line of enquiry was put in terms of acts of violence by black people:

> I remember the sounds of bombs, our house shaking. I remember my father having to have guns at his disposal at all times because of the fact that at any moment we expected to be attacked. That's why when someone asks me about violence, sir, I just find it incredible because what it means is the person who is asking that question has absolutely no idea what black people have gone through, what black people have experienced in this country since the time the first black person was kidnapped from the shores of Africa.'

And let's not forget why the vast majority of black people were kidnapped from Africa: sugar. This governmental approach and the associated police brutality continued and has led to an overrepresentation of black people in America's prisons.[29]

The reality of this situation captured the imagination of the West in the 2020s in numbers never before seen, thanks to social media and smartphones. Today, recorded evidence can shoot around the world in seconds without editing, or being hidden or dismissed by police chiefs, presidents, national media groups or government officials. Today we are being shown what is happening on the ground every day to the descendants of sugar slaves, untainted by the political agenda of the television channel or newspaper. It is the secret of the success of the Black Lives Matter movement, and it has made it very clear just how stark the difference is between almost every aspect of life between black and white people in society. Public historian Michael Wood has said: 'this year's [2020's] events in the US (and in Britain too) suggest progress has been slower than we hoped. And that, ultimately, is because of the legacy of slavery.'[30] A reminder – just in case we need one – that the current situation we find ourselves in is a direct result of the cascade of events that took us from the comparatively modest sugar *ingenios* of the Mediterranean coast and Atlantic islands to slavery in the Americas.

In the United Kingdom, the disparity between the government's perceived worth of black people compared to white was made all too apparent in 2016, when the Home Office's actions resulted in the deportation of black people, and other ethnic minorities, from the UK on the grounds that they resided in the country illegally. This was the Windrush Scandal. In the years following the Second World War, the UK had reached out to the people of the Commonwealth to help rebuild the country. The British government expected the vast majority of the people signing up to be white people from Australia and New Zealand – countries that were, in their minds, culturally more similar to Britain. Instead, they received people from Asia, Africa and the West Indies. Those from the West Indies were descendants of sugar slaves, whose back-breaking, unpaid and unrecognised toil had helped make Britain great.

Though not what they were expecting, the government rushed in these subjects of the empire, the process of immigration being made simple with many not requiring papers: the Commonwealth was considered an extension of Great Britain after all. In 1948 the HMT *Empire Windrush* docked in England, with 492 passengers fresh from the West Indies eager to help Britain back on its feet. Then in 2016 this uncharacteristically unbureaucratic system was abused when the Home Office issued letters to those of the 'Windrush Generation', announcing their expulsion from the country if they could not provide papers showing the legality of their residence – the very papers that were supposedly not required. Some believe that this was no oversight, but a continuation of the exploitation of black people. Many were deported, including individuals who were just children in 1948, forced to move back to the land 'where they came from', a land completely alien to them, often without extended family to support them. Though a major news story, the scale of the deportations was underreported. According to Houn Wardle and Laura Obermuller this is because, '[t]he thousands of expulsions happening under the UK's "hostile environment" policies go unremarked because the human beings targeted are already marginal and unprotected.'[31] So let us be in no doubt that the 'legacy of slavery … still at work in American society'[32] is very much present in the UK.

Perhaps the most iconic moment of the Black Lives Matter protests of 2020 in the UK, was the tossing of the statue of slaver Edward Colston into the dock at Bristol. Protestors took it upon themselves to make an example of those who played a part in the trade and expose them. As it turned out for Colston's case, they were only just slightly ahead of the curve because the statue had already been earmarked for removal by the local council;[33] the protestors simply hurried the process. In other places, things are not so clear cut. Take Penny Lane in Liverpool, named after slave trader James Penny, but made famous in the Beatles song. There are several other streets named after slave and sugar traders in Liverpool, and in 2007 local councillors decided it was about time these street names were changed, but because the Beatles song *Penny Lane* is so iconic and important to Liverpool's culture and tourism, the changes were not made.[34] This may seem like a cynical decision, but we must consider the Beatles were strongly influenced by early rock and roll, which is an extension of African American slave culture. Just how do we square those circles? Monuments can be removed, and buildings can have their names changed, but what do we do with the Penny Lanes of this world that are much trickier, piled in layers of history and heavy with nuance? The strategy seems to be educating Britain about the British Empire, and how it is built on slavery, and therefore sugar. Continuing this logic then, much of black history is British history and *vice versa*, and the white British people who were key in the trade of black slaves, like Colston and Penny, need to be taken to task. Black Lives Matter has helped British and Americans alike to see history from different viewpoints. Some of these things are difficult to swallow; pride is now mixed with some shame, and once stalwart patriotism is now being questioned. With time to let all of this sink in, nations like the UK and the US can appreciate that not everything that was done in their countries' name was done for good. This cannot be achieved, however, if we continue to sweep inconvenient truths under the carpet.

Slave trader Edward Colston's empty pedestal, the day after his statue was thrown into the dock at Bristol during the Black Lives Matter protests of 2020. (Caitlin Hobbs)

Afterword

A Brighter Future?

With environmental destruction, widespread inequality, exploitation of workers and a sick population, sugar's legacy appears grim indeed, yet I felt I couldn't leave this dark history without wondering if a bright future could ever be gleaned from sugar's dark past?

The most pressing issue is our sugar consumption. The current scourge of type-2 diabetes is so worrying because it seems almost too big a problem. However, sugar's effects can be reversed, and in as little time as twenty-four hours it has been shown that one day of complete fasting can reverse the disease.[1] Low carbohydrate diets work too but take longer. Unfortunately, once someone has developed type-2 diabetes, their body is prone to developing it more readily, so careful work and support needs to go out to sufferers to help them keep on the straight-and-narrow; and the best way to do that is to avoid processed foods.

How do we cut down on our sugar then? My answer is always to learn to cook because that's what I did. We desperately need our cooking skills back so that we don't depend on ready-made foods – both sweet and savoury – with their large amounts of added sugar. I have a rule in my house: if I want a cake, I have to bake one. Home cooking always requires less sugar and contains fewer additives than the stuff bought in supermarkets. By cooking, we see the sugar that goes into our foods, and then we might be more inclined to find a recipe that uses less of it. However, I realise that everyone cooking their own food from scratch might be a little unrealistic. Still, it is possible to give up sugar without giving up sweetness now that we have naturally occurring low-calorie sweeteners that don't have the stigma of being laboratory-made.

If we don't want to cut down our sugar for own health, maybe we should for the sake of the planet's (and by extension the health of all who reside there). The sugar industry's impact upon the environment is massive; sugar has ravaged our planet of its resources and significantly contributed to pollution and biodiversity loss, but many of these effects can be muted, or even reversed. There is a growing number of activists, NGOs and smallholders who are adamant in their resolve that sugar can be grown sustainably by moving to organic farming. Organically produced crops use no chemical fertilizers, pesticides or herbicides,[2] which is a great benefit, not only to the environment but also to the worker, who is no longer being slowly poisoned working the cane fields. Growing sugarcane organically means that the fields are fertilized naturally and sustainably by traditional crop rotation and companion planting methods. The productivity may be lower, but the losses are offset by the money saved from buying and safely storing dangerous, aggressive agrochemicals.[3] Runoff from organic fields is significantly less hazardous to wildlife. One encouraging thing about the shocking effects the runoff from cane fields of Queensland have had on the Great Barrier Reef is that the effects of the chemical leachate is completely reversible.[4]

Sugar is making its name in the world of environmental sustainability as an important biofuel. Sugar is fermented into ethanol and used to fuel road vehicles, or is converted into electricity. In Brazil in the 2010s, fifty per cent of 'fuel used for transportation by light vehicles' was sugar-derived ethanol. Not only is it sustainable, but it makes us less reliant on fossil fuels that spew out poisonous gasses and particulates. Combusting ethanol produces only water vapour and carbon dioxide, and the latter can be converted back into biomass via the growth of more cane (or indeed any other plant species). Sugar-derived ethanol is proving popular in ex-colonies and developing countries, allowing them to be more self-sufficient and less reliant on the big Western petroleum companies.[5] Even leftover bagasse has found a new use: as an alternative to wood in papermaking.

Organic sugar also makes for a lower carbon footprint: the burning of the fields prior to harvest does not take place, and it is less processed than regular cane sugar. From field to fork regular white sugar has a carbon footprint twice that of the organic product, and high fructose corn syrup has a footprint up to three times that of organic sugar.[6] Using this approach in countries such as Argentina has meant that small plantations that were no longer sustainable in Big Sugar's world have reopened, creating local jobs in safer environments.[7] Organic sugar is not always available of course, so as an alternative you could reduce your carbon footprint instead by using beet sugar or by swapping your white sugar for unrefined and raw sugars.

Some parts of the sugar industry have made a stance about the exploitation of workers too, and the island of Mauritius is a proud outlier in this respect. When under control by the British Empire, half a million Indians were sent to work the fields, and any gaps in the workforce were filled with West Indian workers. The same story of exploitation and violence played out, but when Mauritius became independent in 1968, all races united in cultivating sugar as cooperatives.[8] A similar pattern occurred in India too (sugarcane cultivation has now gone full circle), the old system of plantations were rejected, and a fairer system was devised. This was made easier by the fact that Indians, though huge consumers of sugar, preferred unrefined *gur* to make their sweets and so the industrialisation associated with producing pure, snow-white sugar is not needed.

Big Sugar exploits people. It is 'a powerful industry … with vast wealth and poverty woven into the fabric of its culinary history.'[9] Kicking this trend is the Fairtrade movement which has made some great leaps forward in reducing poverty associated with sugar production. In 2020 they worked with over 55,000 smallholders to make sure that they received a reasonable price for their product and fair wages for their workforce.[10] There are products easily available to us in supermarkets that are Fairtrade, and a quick internet search will surprise you with the variety and choice. Companies are proud to make Fairtrade products, and display this fact on their packaging. If the company that makes your favourite sweet food or drink is not making claims to be Fairtrade, you can safely assume it is not traded fairly.

A future of sustainably grown sugar that's produced without exploiting workers is possible if the pressure to stock them is there. Manufacturers should be using refined sugars in smaller amounts, topped up with natural sweeteners if need be, but this won't happen if we don't ditch Big Sugar. The best way to make our message clear would be to use the abolitionists' approach: be vocal and tell people, and then vote with your wallet and take your custom elsewhere.

There is so much we need to consider that it seems like an impossible task. We don't necessarily have the time to research and then seek out an unrefined organic sugar alternative to the chocolate biscuit that goes into the family's packed lunches. It feels like Big Sugar and the supermarkets have got us over a barrel in this respect because it's hard to shop ethically. In order for us to make better decisions, the supermarkets and grocery stores need to do their part in seeking out more ethically produced foods. This may sound too good to be true, but there are businesses around the globe that are doing this. An example of this is a grocery store in south Manchester in the United Kingdom. Unicorn seek 'a more transparent and consistent position regarding foods that contain sugar', and avoid savoury foods containing added sugar. If sugar must be present, it is used sparingly, is ethically sourced and 'minimally processed'. What's more, there is such choice in the store that no one even notices their 'restrictions'.[11]

Cutting out refined sugar does not mean we have to eat boring food; we just need to see that it can be done so that using less sugar becomes normalised. So how do we do it? We need to be proactive, but being proactive doesn't necessarily mean making drastic and unsustainable changes to our lifestyles. Just once a month, make one change: find just one product that is fairly traded, or has less sugar in it, learn one new recipe and ditch the Dolmio sauce, or ask for the sugar-free alternative when asking for a flavoured syrup in your latte, or bake with unrefined sugars (cakes and meringues still rise perfectly). Small acts made by many add up. No one can change sugar's dark history, but we can try to play our part to give it a brighter future.

Notes

The full citation of a source is given the first time it is used in a chapter, thereafter only the author's name and publishing date are provided.

Introduction

1. Beeton, I. (1861) *The Book of Household Management* p.696 (from facsimile of the original book published by Lightning Source).
2. *A Concise Anglo-Saxon Dictionary*. Available at: https://www.gutenberg.org/files/31543/31543-h/files/dict_hn.html.
3. Aykroyd, W. D. (1967) *Sweet Malefactor: Sugar, Slavery and Human Society* p.7.
4. Toussaint-Samat, M. (1992) *History of Food* p.17.
5. Chaucer, ever the professional diplomat, was also in attendance at Richard's usurper's – Henry Bolingbroke – coronation feast in 1399 where Bolingbroke was crowned Henry IV.
6. This is Nevill Coghill's classic Penguin translation: Chaucer, G., & Coghill, N. (1952). *The Canterbury Tales* p.181.
7. Toussaint-Samat, M. (1992) p.19.
8. This was in Rome in the fifth century and they got the idea to do this because they knew that King Herod and his wife were buried in this way. It's perplexing why they tried to emulate him over anyone else. Arce, J. (2000) 'Imperial funerals in the later Roman empire: change and continuity', in Theuws, F. and Nelson, J. L. (eds) *Rituals of Power: From Late Antiquity to the Early Middle Ages* p.25.
9. He says so in the Georgics, translated quote taken from Toussaint-Samat, M. (1992) p.14.
10. Both of these quotes are taken from the King James Bible.
11. More precisely, the word sweet, in this case, is derived from the Greek *gleukos*, meaning 'sweet wine'.

12. In the United Kingdom, this is called your 'pudding stomach'.
13. The English may not have invented the plantation, but they did invent the word. When the first colonists arrived in the Americas, every settlement was a plantation, even those on the mainland where sugar was not grown. This is because the word didn't apply to the crop, but the people; the settlers themselves were the plantation.

Chapter 1. Innocent Times

1. Toussaint-Samat, M. (1992) *History of Food*, translated by Anthea Bell p.24.
2. They do not taste particularly sweet, but any starches present are digested into glucose as soon as they meet our mouths – chew a piece of white bread and very quickly it will begin to taste sweet as the amylase enzyme present in saliva immediately gets to work on digesting it into glucose.
3. Reviewed in Crittenden, A. N. (2011) 'The Importance of Honey Consumption in Human Evolution', *Food and Foodways* p.257.
4. Bowyer, P. (2018) *Minds Make Societies: How Cognition Explains the World Humans Create*. Introductory chapter.
5. Modern geneticists who attempt to untangle the knotted mass that is the genetic basis of behaviour have found genes that appear to be the major players in sugar craving and addiction. Wiss, D. A., Avena, N. and Rada, P. (2018) 'Sugar addiction: From evolution to revolution', *Frontiers in Psychiatry* pp. 6-7.
6. *Ibid.*
7. One might imagine that, because we too are great apes, that a common ancestor acquired the ability to collect honey and passed this adaptation down through the clade. However, methods differ between species (and even between societies of the same species) so honey-gathering as a trait probably developed many times independently. The important shared characteristic here is that all of the great apes have large brains capable of problem-solving.
8. Crittenden, A. N. (2011) pp. 265-6. They are also known as 'Lucy'.
9. *Ibid.* p259.
10. Reviewed in Crittenden p259; Toussaint-Samat, M. (1992) *History of Food* p.16.

11. Toussaint-Samat, M. (1992) p.24.
12. Crittenden pp.262-4.
13. See Friedman, H. (1955) *The Honey Guides*. This species of bird's binomial Latin name rather pleasingly is *Indicator indicator.*
14. Toussaint-Samat, M. (1992) p.26.
15. Deerr, N. (1949) *The History of Sugar Volume I* pp.5-6; Aykroyd, W. D. (1967) *Sweet Malefactor: Sugar, Slavery and Human Society* pp.12-3. Although they kept bees, they had not quite worked out how to collect the honey without killing the entire swarm, queen and all. It took the Hittites to work out a method of extracting the honey without killing the bees.
16. Macinnis, P. (2002) *Bittersweet: The Story of Sugar* p.1; Vaughan, J. G. and Geissler, C. A. (2009) *The New Oxford Book of Food Plants* p.18.
17. Galloway, J. H. (1977) 'The Mediterranean Sugar Industry', *Geographical Review* p.14.
18. At this the point applying the biological concept of species to them is almost futile. That said, plant phylogeneticists soldier on.
19. Ballard, C., Denham, T. and Haberle, S. (2013) 'Wetland Archaeology in the Highlands of New Guinea', in Menotti, F. and O'Sullivan, A. (eds) *The Oxford Handbook of Wetland Archaeology.* p.233.
20. The New Guineans grew other plants for carbohydrates, such as yams.
21. Reviewed in Warner, J. N. (1962) 'Sugar Cane: An Indigenous Papuan Cultigen', *Ethnology.* p.405.
22. Vaughan and Geissler (2009) p.18.
23. It could be that there were several hybridisation events. *S robustum* hybridised with *S spontaneum* again in India to produce another species called *S barbari*. Later, the two species hybridised once more, but this time in China to produce yet another species. You can see why botanists scratch their heads so. Reviewed in Denham, T. (2017) 'Domesticatory Relationships in the New Guinea Highlands', in Golson, J. et al. (eds) *Ten Thousand Years of Cultivation at Kuk Swamp in the Highland of Papua New Guinea.* pp.33-5.
24. Macinnis, P. (2002) p.2.
25. Sugarcane cultivation had spread to China around the same time, but there it was consumed as the New Guineans had intended – chewed as a delicious treat. Sugar refining as a small industry was introduced around 200 BCE. Sugar was used mainly as medicine

and sometimes to sweeten drinks, but because it wasn't in great demand, it did not evolve much further than a kind of dark-coloured rock candy. Smith, A. F. (2015) *Sugar: A Global History*. Reviewed in chapter 1, e-book.

26. Vaughan and Geissler (2009) p.18.
27. Macinnis, P. (2002) p.2.
28. McGee, H. (1984) *On Food and Cooking: The Science and Lore of the Kitchen* pp.648-9.
29. Other foodstuffs such as ghee and milk fall into this category and these ingredients are used to make delicious sweets (*barfi*) that are distributed and shared on special occasions.
30. Reviewed on the website Hinduism Today: *Significance Of Sugarcane During Hindu Festivals* (2013) Available at: https://www.hinduismtoday.com/blogs-news/hindu-press-international/significance-of-sugarcane-during-hindu-festivals/12637.html.
31. Macinnis, P. (2002) p.2.
32. Why sugarcane took so long to spread west is unknown, but one has to assume that the vast swathes of dry scrub and desert between the two areas were an ecological barrier as well as an anthropological one. Long days travelling by camel caravan in the searing heat must have desiccated many samples; assuming there was interest in the plant in the first place. Though there are some suggestions that it did manage to travel a certain distance along the coast of the Persian Gulf. Aykroyd, W. D. (1967) p.13.
33. Aykroyd, W. D. (1967) p.13; Deerr (1949) pp.69-70.
34. Deerr (1949) pp.68-9.
35. Aykroyd, W. D. (1967) p.13.
36. Deerr (1949) p.69.
37. Phillips, W. D. (2004) 'Sugar in Iberia', in Schwartz, S. B. (ed.) *Tropical Babylons: Sugar and the Making of the Atlantic World, 1450-1680* p.32.
38. Deerr (1949) p.73.
39. Galloway, J. H. (1977) 'The Mediterranean Sugar Industry', *Geographical Review* p.183.
40. Sato, T. (2014) *Sugar in the Social Life of Medieval Islam* pp.35-41.
41. Caramel, aside from being a delicious foodstuff, was also used by women as a hair wax. Toussaint-Samat, M. (1992) pp.497-8; Tannahill, R. (1973) *Food in History*. 3rd edn. p.142.

42. Toussaint-Samat, M. (1992) pp.497.
43. Galloway, J. H. (1977) p.177.
44. *Ibid.* p.117.
45. It also became a very important industry in Tunisia in the eleventh century; Galloway, J. H. (1977) p.180.
46. Galloway, J. H. (1977) p.180; Schwartz, S. B. (1985) *Sugar Plantations in the Formation of Brazilian Society: Bahia, 1550-1835* p.4.
47. Phillips, W. D. (2004) pp.29-30.
48. Galloway, J. H. (1977) p.183.
49. *Ibid.* p.184.
50. *Ibid.* pp.184-6.
51. Phillips, W. D. (2004) p.28.

Chapter 2. Enter the White Man

1. Schwartz, S. B. (1985) *Sugar Plantations in the Formation of Brazilian Society: Bahia, 1550-1835* p.6.
2. Phillips, W. D. (2004) 'Sugar in Iberia', in Schwartz, S. B. (ed.) *Tropical Babylons: Sugar and the Making of the Atlantic World, 1450-1680* pp.31-2.
3. Aykroyd, W. D. (1967) *Sweet Malefactor: Sugar, Slavery and Human Society* p.13.
4. Riley-Smith, J. (2014) *The Crusades: A History* p.104; Curtin, P. D. (1998) *The rise and fall of the plantation complex.* 2nd edn. p.4; Cordeiro, G. *et al.* (2007) 'Sugarcane', in Kole, C. (ed.) *Pulses, Sugar and Tuber Crops* p.175.
5. Toussaint-Samat, M. (1992) *History of Food* p.498.
6. Curtin, P. D. (1998) p.5.
7. Prinsen Geerligs, H. C. (2010) *The World's Cane Sugar Industry* p.74.
8. Jacoby, D. (2005) 'Aspects of Everyday Life in Frankish Acre', in Kedar, B. Z., Phillips, J. P., and Riley-Smith, J. (eds) *Crusades: Volume 4* p.83.
9. Prinsen Geerligs, H. C. (2010) p.6.
10. Jacoby, D. (2017) 'The Venetians in Byzantine and Lusignan Cyprus: Trade, Settlement, and Politics', in Jacoby, D. (ed.) *Medieval Trade in the Eastern Mediterranean and Beyond*, chapter 2, e-book.

11. Macinnis, P. (2002) *Bittersweet: The Story of Sugar* p.22; Prinsen Geerligs, H. C. (2010) p.7.
12. Deerr, N. (1949) *The History of Sugar Volume I* p.72.
13. Macinnis, P. (2002) pp.20-1.
14. Until, that is, the refining element was translocated to mainland Europe; Schwartz, S. B. (1985) p.575.
15. Aykroyd, W. D. (1967) p.15.
16. Moore, J. W. (2000) 'Sugar and the expansion of the early modern world-economy. Commodity frontiers, ecological transformation, and industrialisation'.
17. Aykroyd, W. D. (1967) pp.4-5.
18. O'Connell, S. (2012) *Sugar: The Grass that Changed the World* Chapter 2, e-book; Schwartz, S. B. (1985) p.8.
19. Moore, J. W. (2010) 'Madeira, sugar, and the conquest of nature in the "first" sixteenth century, Part II: From regional crisis to commodity frontier, 1506-1530' p.1.
20. Aykroyd, W. D. (1967) p.14.
21. Phillips, W. D. (2004) p.35.
22. Macinnis, P. (2002) pp.20-1.
23. Phillips, W. D. (2004) p.35, 38.
24. Abbot, E. (2008) *Sugar: A Bittersweet History* p.19.
25. *Ibid.* p.8; Aykroyd, W. D. (1967) pp.14-15.
26. Abbot, E. (2008) p.18.
27. O'Connell, S. (2012) Chapter 2.
28. Schwartz, S. B. (1985) p.6-7.
29. Moore, J. W. (2000) p.413.
30. O'Connell, S. (2012), Chapter 2.

Chapter 3. Pioneers of the New World

1. Macinnis, P. (2002) *Bittersweet: The Story of Sugar* p.35.
2. Quote from Walvin, J. (2017) *How Sugar Corrupted the World* p.34. Scholars had long since known that the Earth was spherical in shape, and they had estimated the curvature of the Earth and extrapolated from it the size of the globe. The trouble was their estimate was way off and the Earth was rather a lot bigger than anybody had expected and there was rather a lot more to be discovered than at first suspected.

3. Walvin, J. (2017) p.34.
4. Macinnis, P. (2002) *Bittersweet: The Story of Sugar* pp.31-2.
5. Abbot, E. (2008) *Sugar: A Bittersweet History* pp.22-3.
6. *Ibid.* (2008) p.25.
7. Quoted in Abbot, E. (2008) p.25.
8. Quotes from Sale, K. (1991) *The Conquest of Paradise: Christopher Columbus and the Columbian Legacy* pp. 196-7; Abbot, E. (2008) p.27.
9. Abbot, E. (2008) pp.31-2.
10. Flannigan, M. (1844) *Antigua and Antiguans: A Full Account of the Colony and Its Inhabitants from the Time of the Caribs to the Present Day, Interspered with Anecdotes and Legends.*
11. Abbot, E. (2008) pp.31-2.
12. *Ibid.* (2008) p.24.
13. Sloane, H. (1707) *A voyage to the islands Madera, Barbados, Nieves, S. Christophers and Jamaica Volume I* p.xxvii.
14. Macinnis, P. (2002) pp.34-5; Abbot, E. (2008) pp.29-30.
15. Abbot, E. (2008) p.28.
16. Quoted in Abbot, E. (2008) p.24.
17. *Ibid.* (2008) pp.23-4.
18. Though it does seem that Columbus's own sugarcane plants failed. Rodriguez Morel, G. (2004) 'The Sugar Economy of Espanola in the Sixteenth Century', in Schwartz, S. B. (ed.) *Tropical Babylons: Sugar and the Making of the Atlantic World, 1450-1680* p.86.
19. Quoted in Dennis, Y. W., Hirschfelder, A. and Flynn, S. R. (2016) *Native American Almanac: More Than 50,000 Years of the Cultures and Histories of Indigenous Peoples.* Available as an e-book.
20. Mintz, S. W. (1985) *Sweetness and Power: The Place of Sugar in Modern History* pp.34-5.
21. Abbot, E. (2008) p.25.
22. Rodriguez Morel, G. pp.100-1.
23. *Ibid.* pp.88-9,105-6.
24. Abbot, E. (2008) pp.26-7.
25. Rodriguez Morel, G. pp.107-8.
26. Mintz, S. W. (1985) p.33.
27. Quoted in Abbot, E. (2008) p.33.
28. Abbot, E. (2008) p.33.
29. *Ibid.* (2008) pp.28-30.
30. Abbot, E. (2008) p.29; Macinnis, P. (2002) p.35.

31. Quote from Abbot, E. (2008) p.34; this was in his *Very Brief Account of the Destruction of the Indians* in 1542.
32. Macinnis, P. (2002) p.34.
33. Abbot, E. (2008) pp.35-6.
34. Macinnis, P. (2002) p.35.
35. Extended quote from Williams, E. (1970) *From Columbus to Castro: The History of the Caribbean.* Available as an e-book.
36. Macinnis, P. (2002) p.33.
37. *Ibid.* (2002) pp.43-4.
38. Schwartz, S. B. (2004) 'A Commonwealth within Itself: The Early Brazilian Sugar Industry, 1550-1670', in Schwartz, S. B. (ed.) *Tropical Babylons: Sugar and the Making of the Atlantic World, 1450-1680* p.159.
39. Walvin, J. (2017) pp.35-6.
40. Silva, L. *et al.* (2000) *Dutch Brazil* p.23, 25.
41. Walvin, J. (2017) p.36.
42. Silva, L. *et al.* (2000) p.17.
43. Schwartz, S. B. (2004) p.188.
44. *Ibid.* (2004) pp.188-9.
45. Silva, L. *et al.* (2000) pp.23,25.
46. Quoted in Schwartz, S. B. (2004) p.161.
47. Schwartz, S. B. (2004) pp.161-2,189-90.
48. Walvin, J. (2017) p.36.
49. Silva, L. *et al.* (2000) p.29.
50. Schwartz, S. B. (2004) pp.163-4.
51. Silva, L. *et al.* (2000) p.27.
52. Schwartz, S. B. (2004) p.166; Silva, L. *et al.* (2000) pp.49-51.
53. Schwartz, S. B. (2004) pp.170-1.
54. *Ibid.* (2004) p.171.

Chapter 4. Life on the Sugar Colonies

1. Harlow, V. (1925) *Colonising Expeditions to the West Indies and Guiana, 1623-1667.* Edited by V. Harlow p.xiv.
2. Dunn, R. S. (1972) *Sugar & Slaves: The Rise of the Planter Class in the English West Indies, 1624-1713* p.10; Macinnis, P. (2002) *Bittersweet: The Story of Sugar* pp.45-8.

3. The Right Honourable Privy Council (1789) *No abolition; or, An attempt to prove to the conviction of every rational British subject, that the abolition of the British trade with Africa for negroes, would be a measure as unjust as impolitic, fatal to the interests of the nation, ruinous to its sugar colonies etc* p.1.

4. Dunn, R. S. (1972) p.10.

5. Macinnis, P. (2002) p.47.

6. That is, if one could find the archipelago in the first place: according to an account of the Voyage of Sir Henry Colt in 1631 the 'land is low, hard to find & stands alone … Barbados may well admitt of this simile, to be like sixpence throwne downe uppon newmarkett heath, & you should command such a one to goe & finde itt out.' Harlow, V. (1925) p.63.

7. Dunn, R. S. (1972) p.8.

8. Harlow, V. (1925) p.xix.

9. Dunn, R. S. (1972) pp.12-13,17,21.

10. *Ibid.* pp.xxi-xxiii, 10.

11. Macinnis, P. (2002) p.45.

12. *Ibid.* p.49.

13. Dunn, R. S. (1972) pp.14, 17.

14. Harlow, V. (1925) pp.xxxvii-xxxviii.

15. Ligon, R. (1657) *A True & Exact History Of the Island of Barbados* p.24-5.

16. Harlow, V. (1925) pp.xxxix-xl.

17. *Ibid.* p. xxxviii.

18. 'The Dutch sell their Commodityes, after the rate at a penny for a pound of sugar. Browd & brimd, white or black hatts yield here 120 lb of sugar, & 140 lb & some 160 lb; Broune thred is at 36 pence will yeeld 40 lb of Sugar a paire; mens shoes 16 lb; new fashioned shoes 25 or 30 lb the paire.' Letter in Harlow, V. (1925) dated 1651 p.51.

19. Harlow, V. (1925) p.I.

20. Ligon, R. (1657) p.40.

21. The list goes on 'New England brought cheap, low-quality goods for the slaves…staves for the sugar hogsheads, and horses to work the mills.' The people of the English sugar islands gained a reputation for hard drinking, especially on Jamaica, and because that too was imported and we have accounts of amounts of alcohol that were consumed, for example in a single year 719 tons of wine and spirits

were imported onto the island, compare that to 756 tons of meat and fish and 315 tons of wheat, bread and other provisions. Dunn, R. S. (1972) p.210.

22. And as a result, stank, the heavy clothes making them overheat and they had to heavily-perfume their clothes to mask the terrible body odour that would emanate from them.
23. Dunn, R. S. (1972) pp.263, 270.
24. Data is available in table 25 p.170 of Dunn, R. S. (1972) as well as p.267.
25. *Ibid.* p.267.
26. The untitled enactment can be found in what is now known as the Egerton manuscript, which can be found at the British Museum or online.
27. There was a word for it: they had been 'Barbadoed'.
28. Macinnis, P. (2002) p.50, 53.
29. Ligon, R. (1657) p.44.
30. *Ibid.* p.58.
31. Harlow, V. (1925) pp.44-5.
32. *Ibid.* p.43-4.
33. *Ibid.* p.xxviii-xxix.
34. Sloane, H. (1707) p.xiv.
35. Ligon, R. (1657) p.68.
36. Harlow, V. (1925) p.65.
37. Ligon, R. (1657) p.62.
38. Harlow, V. (1925) p.65.
39. Ligon, R. (1657) p.62; a curry comb is used to brush horses of dead hair and is covered with raised dimples or blunt hooks.
40. Sloane, H. (1707) p.lxviii.
41. Ligon, R. (1657) p.62.
42. *Ibid.* p.65.
43. Dunn, R. S. (1972) p.284.
44. Ligon, R. (1657) p.27.
45. Dunn, R. S. (1972) p.289.
46. Harlow, V. (1925) p.liv.
47. Dunn, R. S. (1972) pp.42-3.
48. Quotes from Equiano, O. (1793) *The Interesting Narrative of the Life of Olaudah Equiano, or Gustavus Vassa, the African* p.151; and Sloane, H. (1707) p.xliv.

49. Dunn, R. S. (1972) p.43.
50. Harlow, V. (1925) p.lv.
51. Sloane, H. (1707) p.xxviii.
52. Harlow, V. (1925) p.93; A Quaker trader on the North American mainland received an order in 1699 from just ten customers on Jamaica for: '83 casks, 174 half-barrels, 66 quarter barrels and 9 [full] barrels', enough to bake bread for the entire island; Dunn, R. S. (1972) p.273.
53. Dunn, R. S. (1972) p.278.
54. Ligon, R. (1657) p.31.
55. *Ibid.* pp.33, 113.
56. *Ibid.* p.37.
57. Sloane, H. (1707) p.x.
58. Ligon, R. (1657) p.37.
59. *Ibid.* p.50.
60. Ligon lists them in amongst other livestock several times in his accounts, e.g., 'we breed both Negres, Horses and Cattle' Ligon, R. (1657) p.113.
61. They almost listed amongst livestock in accounts. For example, in *A Comparison Between the British Sugar Colonies and New England, as They Relate to the Interest of Great Britain. with Some Observations on the State of the Case of New England. to Which Is Added a Letter to a Member of Parliament* (1732) planters are praised for their hard work considering the loss in potential profits because of the 'Expence in Negroes, Cattle and Mules' p.23.
62. It was only until the very of the seventeenth century that the English would allow black slaves to convert to Christianity.
63. Sloane, H. (1707) p.lvi.
64. Quote from Sloane, H. (1707) p.xlviii; Dunn, R. S. (1972) p.250.
65. 'An Act for the Governing of Negroes' (1688) in *The Laws of Barbados*, pp. 137-144.
66. Epstein, D. J. (1963) 'Slave Music in the United States before 1860: A Survey of Sources (Part 1)' p.196.
67. Levine, L. W. (1978) *Black Culture and Black Consciousness: Afro-American Folk Thought from Slavery to Freedom* p.7.
68. Camp, S. M. H. (2002) 'The pleasures of resistance: Enslaved women and body politics in the plantation South, 1830-1861', *Journal of Southern History* p.568.

69. Dunn, R. S. (1972) p.226.
70. Quoted in Dunn, R. S. (1972) p.224.
71. *Ibid.* p.313.
72. Ligon, R. (1657) p.54.
73. Equiano, O. (1793) p.143.
74. Ligon, R. (1657) p.37; there is another example where he describes a female mistress of a planter: she was a 'Negro of the greatest beautie and majestie together that ever I saw in one woman. Her stature large, and excellently shap't, well favour'd, full eye'd & admirably grac't.' p.12.
75. Ramsay, J. (1784) *An essay on the treatment and conversion of African slaves in the British sugar colonies By the Reverend James Ramsay* p.75.
76. Ligon, R. (1657) p.48.
77. Sloane, H. (1707) p.lii; Richard Ligon also chipped in that once they 'have had five or six Children, their breasts hang down below their navells, so that when they stoop at their common work of weeding, they hang almost down to the ground, that at a distance, you would think they had six legs.' Ligon, R. (1657) p.48. There are many examples of these comments, but I felt it gratuitous to include any more.
78. Dunn, R. S. (1972) p.252.
79. *Ibid.* p.240.
80. *Ibid.* p.254.
81. Mullatoes were considered a rank above black slaves, receiving less harsh jobs such as domestic service or working a trade. On the islands a person was considered white after three generations. Dunn, R. S. (1972) p.255.
82. *Ibid.* p.256.

Chapter 5. Making Sugar

1. Ramsay, J. (1784) An essay on the treatment and conversion of African slaves in the British sugar colonies By the Reverend James Ramsay pp.59-60.
2. Dunn, R. S. (1972) *Sugar & Slaves: The Rise of the Planter Class in the English West Indies, 1624-1713* pp.188-9.
3. *Ibid.* p.189.

4. *Ibid*. p.229.

5. Walvin, J. (2017) *How Sugar Corrupted the World* p.40-1.

6. *No abolition; or, An attempt to prove to the conviction of every rational British subject, that the abolition of the British trade with Africa for negroes, would be a measure as unjust as impolitic, fatal to the interests of the nation, ruinous to its sugar colonies* published by The Right Honourable Privy Council (1789).

7. Dunn, R. S. (1972) p.204.

8. *Ibid*. p.189.

9. Ligon, R. (1657) *A True & Exact History Of the Island of Barbados* p.95.

10. Dunn, R. S. (1972) p.198.

11. Ligon, R. (1657) p.110.

12. *Ibid*. p.114.

13. Rodriguez Morel, G. (2004) 'The Sugar Economy of Espaniola in the Sixteenth Century', in Schwartz, S. B. (ed.) *Tropical Babylons: Sugar and the Making of the Atlantic World, 1450-1680* p.101.

14. Dunn, R. S. (1972) pp.198-200.

15. *Ibid*. (1972) pp.248-9.

16. Ligon R. (1657) p.55-6.

17. Dunn, R. S. (1972) pp.190-1.

18. Sloane, H. (1707) *A voyage to the islands Madera, Barbados, Nieves, S. Christophers and Jamaica Volume I* p.xlvi.

19. Ligon, R. (1657) p.48.

20. Sloane, H. (1707) pp.87-8 .

21. Littleton, E. (1689) *The groans of the plantations, or, A true account of their grievous and extreme sufferings by the heavy impositions upon sugar and other hardships relating more particularly to the island of Barbados* p.16.

22. Ligon, R. (1657) p.50.

23. *Ibid*. (1657) pp.88-9. Rats were a major pest away from the cane fields too, Ligon tells us 'when the great down-falls of rain come, which is in November and December, and in the time of the Turnado, they leave the field, and shelter themselves in the dwelling houses where they do much mischiefe.'

24. Ligon, R. (1657) p.89; Dunn, R. S. (1972) p.192.

25. Dunn, R. S. (1972) p.240; Ramsay, J. (1784) pp.61-2; Schwartz, S. B. (2004) 'A Commonwealth within Itself: The Early Brazilian Sugar

Industry, 1550-1670', in Schwartz, S. B. (ed.) *Tropical Babylons: Sugar and the Making of the Atlantic World, 1450-1680* p.176.

26. Walvin, J. (2017) p.44.
27. Ligon, R. (1657) p.89.
28. Walvin, J. (2017) p.46; the whips were used throughout the day for punishment and communication. On many plantations, slaves were woken first thing in the morning by the sound of the whip, the origin of the idiom 'the crack of dawn'.
29. Schwartz, S. B. (2004) pp.176-8.
30. Ramsay, J. (1784) p.61.
31. Schwartz, S. B. (2004) p.177.
32. Ligon, R. (1657) pp.88-9.
33. Schwartz, S. B. (2004) pp.176-8.
34. Littleton, E. (1689) p.17.
35. Ligon, R. (1657) p.90.
36. *Ibid*. p.85 'The five black Rounds are the Coppers, in which the Sugar is boyled, of which, the largest is called the Clarifying Copper, and the least, the Tatch'; see also Dunn, R. S. (1972) p.194.
37. Schwartz, S. B. (2004) p.176; the colonies had no access to copper ore, and had not the skills needed to work expensive copper metal.
38. Ligon, R. (1657) pp.90-1.
39. Schwartz, S. B. (2004) p.179. And they used vast amount of timber too: approximately 740kg of fuel per *ingenio* per day was used: Morel points out the depressingly obvious: 'This situation caused considerable deforestation as well as speculation in the sale of firewood and in the price of lands close to forested areas.' Rodriguez Morel, G. (2004) 'The Sugar Economy of Espanola in the Sixteenth Century', in Schwartz, S. B. (ed.) *Tropical Babylons: Sugar and the Making of the Atlantic World, 1450-1680* p.101; The vast forest providing them with 'an Infyntt of Brasyll Wood' as well as more room for more cane fields; Ligon, R. (1657) p.23.
40. Littleton, E. (1689) p.17. Birdlime was the very sticky syrup of boiled down mistletoe berries that was used to catch wild birds by smearing it on the branches of trees. Depending upon the species caught, these birds would have been kept in cages as pets or eaten.
41. Ligon, R. (1657) p.90; Pudsey, E. in Silva, L. *et al.* (2000) *Dutch Brazil* p.18.
42. Ligon, R. (1657) pp.91-2.

43. Dunn, R. S. (1972) p.240.
44. Ligon, R. (1657) p.92; Schwartz, S. B. (2004) p.180.
45. Sloane, H. (1707) p.lxii.
46. Ligon, R. (1657) p.85.
47. Sloane, H. (1707) p.xxx.
48. Because rum was cheap to make, it became the most widely drunk form of alcohol on the West Indies. The English planters were well known as heavy drinkers, but rum drinking caused more than gin blossoms and a dodgy liver; it induced 'the most mysterious malady of the seventeenth century: excruciating cramps in [the] stomach and bowels,' and loss of the use of the patients' limbs. The reason rum caused this malady is unknown, but it is most likely the symptoms of lead poisoning; the lead leaching from the pipes into the distillate as the rum was processed on the plantation. Dunn, R. S. (1972) p.306.
49. Macinnis, P. (2002) *Bittersweet: The Story of Sugar* p.58.
50. Ligon, R. (1657) pp.92-3.
51. Quote in Schwartz, S. B. (2004) p.176.
52. Thomas, K. (2018) *In Pursuit of Civility: Manners and Civilization in Early Modern England* p.244.
53. Quote in Thomas, K. (2018) p.237.
54. Quote in Dunn, R. S. (1972) p.200.

Chapter 6. Fear of Freedom

1. Dunn, R. S. (1972) *Sugar & Slaves: The Rise of the Planter Class in the English West Indies, 1624-1713* p.246.
2. 'An Act for the Governing of Negroes' (1688) in *The Laws of Barbados* p.137.
3. Dunn, R. S. (1972) pp.224-5.
4. *Ibid.* p.239.
5. 'An Act for the Governing of Negroes' (1688) p.137.
6. *Ibid.* p.144.
7. Dunn, R. S. (1972) p.239.
8. Dunn, R. S. (1972) p.284; Ligon, R. (1657) *A True & Exact History Of the Island of Barbados* p.109.
9. Though murder or unfounded maiming could result in a fine of around twenty-five pounds Dunn, R. S. (1972) p.140.

10. Dunn, R. S. (1972) pp.140-1.
11. Equiano, O. (1793) *The Interesting Narrative of the Life of Olaudah Equiano, or Gustavus Vassa, the African* pp.138-9.
12. Abolitionist James Ramsay noted it: 'there have been instances of slitting of ears, breaking of limbs, so as to make amputation necessary, beating out of eyes, and castration.' Ramsay, J. (1784) *An essay on the treatment and conversion of African slaves in the British sugar colonies By the Reverend James Ramsay* p.73.
13. Dunn, R. S. (1972) p.246.
14. 'An Act for the Governing of Negroes' (1688) pp.142-3.
15. *Ibid.* p.141.
16. *Ibid.* p.142.
17. *Ibid.* p.147.
18. Dunn, R. S. (1972) p.240.
19. Sloane, H. (1707) *A voyage to the islands Madera, Barbados, Nieves, S. Christophers and Jamaica Volume I* p.lvii. There are countless examples of this I could have used, and Olaudah Equiano also wrote on this subject: 'One Mr. D----- told me that he had sold 41,000 negroes, and that he once cut off a negro-man's leg for running away' p.125.
20. Thomas, K. (2018) *In Pursuit of Civility: Manners and Civilization in Early Modern England* pp.155-6.
21. Equiano, O. (1793) p.125.
22. Ligon, R. (1657) *A True & Exact History Of the Island of Barbados* p.50.
23. *Ibid.* p.50-1.
24. *Ibid.*
25. Dunn, R. S. (1972) pp.244-9.
26. de la Fuente, A. (2004) 'Sugar and Slavery in Early Colonial Cuba', in Schwartz, S. B. (ed.) *Tropical Babylons: Sugar and the Making of the Atlantic World, 1450-1680* p146.
27. Davis, D. B. (1966) *The Problem of Slavery in Western Culture* p.249.
28. Dunn, R. S. (1972) p.241.
29. Ligon, R. (1657) p.105.
30. 'An Act for the Governing of Negroes' (1688) pp.142-3.
31. Sloane, H. (1707) p.lvii .
32. 'An Act for the Governing of Negroes' (1688) p.142.

33. Sloane, H. (1707) p.lvii. There were slave revolts on all of the colonies at one time or another, but they usually occurred not in an attempt to ignite revolution, but to escape their poor treatment.
34. Dunn, R. S. (1972) p.256.
35. See Ligon, R. (1657) pp.45-6 for his account of the uprising.
36. Harlow, V. (1925) *Colonising Expeditions to the West Indies and Guiana, 1623-1667* p.lv
37. Dunn, R. S. (1972) p.258-9.
38. Quote in Dunn, R. S. (1972) p.260.
39. Macinnis, P. (2002) *Bittersweet: The Story of Sugar* p.171.
40. The industry was extremely important on a social level; it was estimated that at its peak, the French sugar industry paid the wages for 700,000 working families, Abbot, E. (2008) *Sugar: a Bittersweet History* pp.178-80; Walvin, J. (2017) *How Sugar Corrupted the World* p.140-2.
41. Abbot, E. (2008) p.214; Macinnis, P. (2002) pp.71-2.
42. The French, unlike the English, used bagasse as fuel.
43. Abbot, E. (2008) p.214; Macinnis, P. (2002) p.72.
44. Abbot, E. (2008) p.216; Macinnis, P. (2002) p.73.
45. Macinnis, P. (2002) p.74
46. Abbot, E. (2008) pp.216-7.
47. In 1802 William Wordsworth wrote a sonnet to the great hero of the Haitian Revolution *To Toussaint L'Ouverture,* William Wordsworth.
48. Abbot, E. (2008) pp.217-8.
49. Macinnis, P. (2002) *Bittersweet: The Story of Sugar* p.76.
50. Abbot, E. (2008) pp.181-3; Walvin, J. (2017) p.181-3.
51. Abbot, E. (2008) p.218.

Chapter 7. The Slave Trade

1. Rankin, F. H. (1836) *The White Man's Grave; a visit to Sierra Leone in 1834 Volume II* p.72.
2. Hogerzeil, S. J. and Richardson, D. (2007) 'Slave purchasing strategies and shipboard mortality: Day-to-day evidence from the Dutch African Trade, 1751-1797', *Journal of Economic History* p.184.
3. Steckel, R. H. and Jensen, R. A. (1986) 'New Evidence on the Causes of Slave and Crew Mortality in the Atlantic Slave Trade', *The Journal of Economic History* pp.58-63, 78.

4. Eltis, D. (1989) 'Fluctuations in Mortality in the Last Half Century of the Transatlantic Slave Trade', *Social Science History* p.327.
5. Steckel, R. H. and Jensen, R. A. (1986) p.75.
6. Parker, M. (2011) *The Sugar Barons* p.56.
7. *Ibid.* p.56.
8. Quote in Parker, M. (2011) p.70.
9. Harlow, V. (1925) *Colonising Expeditions to the West Indies and Guiana, 1623-1667* p.liv.
10. Parker, M. (2011) pp.70-4.
11. Co. Royal Adventurers (1667) pp.5, 10-12.
12. Parker, M. (2011) p.126.
13. Which, after the abolition of the slave trade was utilised by the Africans and warehouses for timber. Rankin, F. H. (1836) p.70-1.
14. Parker, M. (2011) p.126.
15. Dunn, R. S. (1972) *Sugar & Slaves: The Rise of the Planter Class in the English West Indies, 1624-1713* p.232.
16. Quote in Parker, M. (2011) p.172.
17. Planter Henry Drax said of the indentured servants 'the fewer the better'; Parker, M. (2011) p.126.
18. Quote in Dunn, R. S. (1972) p.232.
19. The Right Honourable Privy Council (1789) *No abolition; or, An attempt to prove to the conviction of every rational British subject, that the abolition of the British trade with Africa for negroes, would be a measure as unjust as impolitic, fatal to the interests of the nation, ruinous to its sugar colonies* p.11.
20. Abbot, E. (2008) *Sugar: a Bittersweet History* p.148.
21. *Ibid.* pp.149-50.
22. Mintz, S. W. (1985) *Sweetness and Power: The Place of Sugar in Modern History* p.31.
23. Parker, M. (2011) p.148.
24. Shaw, C. (2020) *Liverpool's Slave Trade Legacy, History Today.*
25. Abbot, E. (2008) p.153.
26. *Ibid.* pp.154-5.
27. Equiano, O. (1793) *The Interesting Narrative of the Life of Olaudah Equiano, or Gustavus Vassa, the African* p.3.
28. Rankin, F. H. (1836) p.70.
29. Dunn, R. S. (1972) p.122; Geggus, D. (2001) 'The French slave trade: an overview.', *The William and Mary Quarterly.*

30. Over one hundred languages were spoken, Dunn, R. S. (1972) p.235; Ligon also notes that '[t]hey are fetch'd from severall parts of Africa [and] speake severall languages, and by that means, one of them understands not another.' Ligon, R. (1657) *A True & Exact History Of the Island of Barbados* p.46.
31. Dunn, R. S. (1972) pp.236-7.
32. *Ibid*. p.237.
33. Rankin, F. H. (1836) p.89.
34. Equiano, O. (1793) p.19.
35. *Ibid*. p.4.
36. *Ibid*. p.14.
37. *Ibid*. p.15.
38. *Ibid*. pp.17-18, 31-40.
39. *Ibid*. pp.31-40.
40. *Ibid*. (1793) p.15.
41. *A Short Account of the African Slave Trade, collected from local knowledge, from the evidence given at the Bar of both Houses of Parliament and from tracts written upon that subject.* (1788) Anonymous p.7.
42. Sloane, H. (1707) *A voyage to the islands Madera, Barbados, Nieves, S. Christophers and Jamaica Volume I* p.lvii.
43. Eltis, D. and Richardson, D. (1997) p.13.
44. Reviewed in Hogerzeil, S. J. and Richardson, D. (2007); see also Eltis, D. (1989) p.315.
45. Equiano, O. (1793) p.46.
46. This occurred after the British had ended their slave trade, but before other nations followed suit.
47. Eltis, D. (1989) p.333.
48. Cohn, R. L. (1985) 'Deaths of Slaves in the Middle Passage', *The Journal of Economic History* p.687.
49. Glickman, J. A. (2015) p.81.
50. Eltis, D. (1989) p.334.
51. Sloane, H. (1707) p.xlvii.
52. Geggus, D. (2001) p.124.
53. Hogerzeil, S. J. and Richardson, D. (2007) p.186.
54. Steckel, R. H. and Jensen, R. A. (1986) pp.65-6.
55. Geggus, D. (2001) pp.128-9.
56. 'The Du Bois Institute dataset lists 4,033 slaving voyages by French-registered ships destined for the Americas that said between 1669 and 1864.' Reviewed in Geggus, D. (2001).

57. Equiano, O. (1793) p.51.
58. Eltis, D. and Richardson, D. (1997) 'The Numbers Game and Route to Slavery', in Eltis, D. and Richardson, D. (eds) *Routes to Slavery: Direction, Ethnicity and Mortality in the Transatlantic Slave Trade* p.9.
59. Steckel, R. H. and Jensen, R. A. (1986) pp.64-71.
60. Rankin, F. H. (1836) pp.119-123.
61. Glickman, J. A. (2015) *A War at the Heart of Man: The Structure and Construction of Ships Bound for Africa.* University of Rhode Island thesis p.25-6.
62. Eltis, D. (1989) pp.333-4; Hogerzeil, S. J. and Richardson, D. (2007) p.186.
63. Ligon, R. (1657) pp.56-7.
64. Hogerzeil, S. J. and Richardson, D. (2007) p.186.
65. Glickman, J. A. (2015) p.25. Olaudah Equiano witnessed such an event: 'two of my wearied countrymen, who were chained together ... preferring death to such a life of misery, somehow made through the nettings, and jumped into the sea.' Equiano, O. (1793) p.53.
66. Equiano, O. (1793) p.48.
67. *Ibid.* pp.52-3.
68. These are the words of Sir George Yonge in a collection of speeches made in Parliament on the subject of abolition. Houses of Parliament (1789) *The Speeches of Mr. Wilberforce, Lord Penrhyn, Mr. Burke, Sir W. Young, Alderman Newnham ... &c. &c. on a Motion for the Abolition of the Slave Trade, in the House of Commons, May the 12th, 1789.*
69. Equiano, O. (1793) p.49.
70. This meant that there were densities of just 1.5 and 1.4 slaves per ton respectively, which seems very low, but because the space taken up for the crew, supplies, etc. was not excluded in the calculation, it skewed the data and made the packing appear much lighter than it was; what really mattered was the space the slaves were kept in. If one calculates packing with this figure, the deleterious effect of packing would have been very clear. See Garland, C. and Klein, H. S. (1985) 'The Allotment of Space for Slaves aboard Eighteenth-Century British Slave Ships', *The William and Mary Quarterly.*
71. Equiano, O. (1793) p.124.
72. Rankin, F. H. (1836) p.125.

73. Ligon, R. (1657) p.46-7.
74. Equiano, O. (1793) pp.56-7.
75. Curtin, P. D. (1969) *The Atlantic Slave Trade: A Census*; reviewed in Eltis, D. and Richardson, D. (1997) 'The Numbers Game and Route to Slavery', in Eltis, D. and Richardson, D. (eds) *Routes to Slavery: Direction, Ethnicity and Mortality in the Transatlantic Slave Trade.*
76. Dunn, R. S. (1972) p.237.

Chapter 8. Abolition & Aftermath

1. Pitt, W. (1792) *The speech of the right honourable William Pitt, on a motion for the abolition of the slave trade, in the House of Commons, on Monday the second of April, 1792.*
2. Although he did make an exception for prisoners of war who were forced into labour in the more traditional sense.
3. Parker, M. (2011) *The Sugar Barons* pp.153-4.
4. Abbot, E. (2008) *Sugar: a Bittersweet History* pp.221-3; Parker, M. (2011) p.317.
5. Parker, M. (2011) pp.314-5.
6. There were exceptions of course – many were frustrated that attention was being diverted away from their plight, but they were the minority.
7. Abbot, E. (2008) pp.226-7, 239.
8. Macinnis, P. (2002) *Bittersweet: The Story of Sugar* p.116; Parker, M. (2011) p.348.
9. Ramsay, J. (1784) *An essay on the treatment and conversion of African slaves in the British sugar colonies By the Reverend James Ramsay* p.54.
10. *Ibid.* p.46.
11. Equiano, O. (1793) *The Interesting Narrative of the Life of Olaudah Equiano, or Gustavus Vassa, the African* pp.127-8, 357.
12. *Ibid.* pp.127-8.
13. *Ibid.* p.153.
14. *Ibid.* p.85.
15. *Ibid.* pp.147-8.
16. Abbot, E. (2008) p.232.
17. *A Comparison Between the British Sugar Colonies and New England, as They Relate to the Interest of Great Britain. with Some*

Observations on the State of the Case of New England. to Which Is Added a Letter to a Member of Parliament (1732) p.24.

18. *The Gentleman's Magazine*, 1789, vol 59.
19. Bisset, R. (1805) *Essays on the Negro Slave Trade. no. 1* pp.3, 7-9.
20. *A Comparison Between the British Sugar Colonies…* (1732) pp.15-16.
21. Neatly passing the buck squarely at the Portuguese, in a textbook example of 'We didn't start it, they did.' Bisset, R. (1805) p.5.
22. Norris, R. (1789) *A Short Account of the African Slave-trade* pp.12-13.
23. *Ibid*. p.32.
24. Quotes from Bisset, R. (1805) pp.45-6, 51.
25. Adair, J. M. (1790) *Unanswerable arguments against the abolition of the slave trade: with a defence of the proprietors of the British sugar colonies against certain malignant charges contained in letters published by a sailor and by Luffman, Newton, &c.* p.225.
26. *A Comparison Between the British Sugar Colonies…* (1732) p.8.
27. Norris, R. (1789) p.7.
28. *A Short Account of the African Slave Trade, collected from local knowledge, from the evidence given at the Bar of both Houses of Parliament and from tracts written upon that subject* (1788) p.7.
29. Bisset, R. (1805) p.29.
30. Abbot, E. (2008) pp.244-6; Parker, M. (2011) pp.351-2.
31. Abbot, E. (2008) pp.166-8, 177, 239-41.
32. *Ibid*. p.243.
33. *Ibid*. pp.247-8.
34. Macinnis, P. (2002) pp.111-2.
35. Abbot, E. (2008) pp.250, 253.
36. *Ibid*. pp.254-5.
37. *Ibid*. pp.258-60.
38. Equiano, O. (1793) p.165.
39. Mintz, S. W. (1985) *Sweetness and Power: The Place of Sugar in Modern History* p.70.
40. Abbot, E. (2008) pp.267-8.
41. Mintz, S. W. (1985) p.70.
42. Walvin, J. (2017) *How Sugar Corrupted the World* p.154.
43. *Ibid*. pp.123-4.
44. They were sent on their way by John Gladstone, father of future Prime Minister William Gladstone; Macinnis, P. (2002) p.150.
45. Abbot, E. (2008) p.315.

46. *Ibid.* p.320.
47. They were also sent to Cuba and Peru in huge numbers where the term of indenture was seven years.
48. Abbot, E. (2008) pp.321-2.
49. Mintz, S. W. (1985) p.72.
50. Walvin, J. (2017) p.124.
51. Abbot, E. (2008) pp.329-30.
52. Macinnis, P. (2002) pp.155-60; Walvin, J. (2017) pp.125-6.
53. Abbot, E. (2008) pp.326-8; Walvin, J. (2017) pp.124-5.
54. Walvin, J. (2017) pp.121-2.

Chapter 9. Sugar States

1. Walvin, J. (2017) *How Sugar Corrupted the World* p.148.
2. *Ibid*. pp.106-7.
3. Trethewey, R. J. (1969) 'The Economic Burden of the Sugar Act', *The American Economist* p.62. The seed had actually been sown in 1733 with the similar Molasses Act; an attempt to make the less lucrative by-product subject to duties. It was largely ignored and unenforced.
4. Parker, M. (2011) *The Sugar Barons* pp.325-6.
5. They had much more success with rum however, by trading cheap molasses with the West Indian colonies (or surreptitiously with the French) and made it themselves. However, a significant number eschewed rum altogether and tried their hands – rather successfully – distilling whiskey from their more than ample stores of cereal crops. Walvin, J. (2017) pp.109-10, 147.
6. Reviewed in Herzog, C. A. (2020) *Sailing Illicit Voyages: Colonial Smuggling Operations between North America and the West Indies, 1714-1776.*
7. Parker, M. (2011) pp.326-7.
8. Walvin, J. (2017) p.148.
9. Paquette, R. L. (2009) '"A horde of brigands?" The great Louisiana slave revolt of 1811 reconsidered', *Historical Reflections* p.81-2; Rankin, F. H. (1836) *The White Man's Grave; a visit to Sierra Leone, in 1834 Volume II* p.86.
10. Paquette, R. L. (2009) p.85.

11. Quoted in Paquette, R. L. (2009) pp.76-7. Anglo-Americans commented: 'Of all human barbarity and indelicacy, none can exceed that of the Creole-French of Louisiana.' They were obviously unaware of the practises on the English plantations.
12. Walvin, J. (2017) pp.148-9.
13. Heitman, J. A. (1987) 'The Modernization of the Louisiana Sugar Industry, 1830-1910', *History Faculty Publications* p.11.
14. Abbot, E. (2008) *Sugar: a Bittersweet History* p.282-3.
15. Rillieux was an 'quadroon', i.e. one-quarter African; planters called men and women who were one-eighth African 'octoroons'. Abbot, E. (2008) p.283; Heitman, J. A. (1987) pp.11-12.
16. Quote in Follett, R. J. (1997) p.27.
17. Abbot, E. (2008) pp.290-1.
18. *Ibid.* pp.283-8.
19. Follett, R. J. (1997) *The Sugar Masters: Slavery, Economic Development, and Modernization on Louisiana Sugar Plantations, 1820-1860* pp.306-7.
20. Statistics from Walvin, J. (2017) p.149.
21. Follett, R. J. (1997) pp.408-9.
22. Abbot, E. (2008) pp.285-7.
23. Statistics calculated from data in Abbot, E. (2008) pp.295-6.
24. Abbot, E. (2008) pp.296-300.
25. *Ibid.* pp.301-2.
26. Knight, F. W. (1977) 'Origins of Wealth and the Sugar Revolution in Cuba, 1750-1850', *The Hispanic American Historical Review* p.232.
27. Tomich, D. and Zeuske, M. (2008) 'The Second Slavery: Mass Slavery, World Economy and Comparative Microhistories', *researchgate.net* pp.2-5.
28. Walvin, J. (2017) pp.153-5.
29. Abbot, E. (2008) pp.274-5.
30. Walvin, J. (2017) p.156.
31. Morrill, J. S. (1875) 'Hawaiian Reciprocity Treaty: Speech of Hon. Justin S. Morrill, of Vermont'. Washington Government Printing Office pp.4-5.
32. Quote in Fleischman, R. K. and Tyson, T. N. (2000) 'The interface of race and accounting: The case of Hawaiian sugar plantations, 1835-1920', *Accounting History* p.11.
33. Walvin, J. (2017) pp.157-9.
34. *Ibid.* p.168.

Chapter 10. Sugar Takes Hold in Court

1. From *Brevarie of Health* (1552), quote found in Ring, M. E. (1968) 'Review of dental practices in Tudor England.', *Journal of the American Dental Association* p.1341.
2. Groom, S. (2013) *At the King's Table: Royal Dining Through the Ages* p.22.
3. It was expected that the cooks knew what they were doing in the kitchen, so they are not detailed step-by-step recipes with precise amounts, temperatures and timings as we have today, but lists of instructions or ingredients to help jog the memory of the cooks. Nevertheless they are extremely useful. The number of recipes changes depending upon which copy of *Forme of Cury* you are looking at. No two handwritten manuscripts are the same, and sometimes they have even been added to: after all, these were real working documents so if a new and tricky dish was added to the repertoire of the owner's master cook, he probably would have added to the end of the manuscript.
4. Information on this is scant, though I found mentions in MacFarlane (1873) *History of British India: From the Earliest English Intercourse* p.4; and Mintz, S. W. (1985) *Sweetness and Power: The Place of Sugar in Modern History* p.82.
5. Dickson Wright, C. (2011) *A History of English Food* p.45; Henisch, B. (2009) *The Medieval Cook* p.109.
6. Mintz, S. W. (1985) p.82.
7. Hammond, P. (1993) *Food & Feast in Medieval England* pp.10-11.
8. Dickson Wright, C. (2011) p.50.
9. Labarge, M. W. (1965) *A Baronial Household of the Thirteenth Century* pp.14-15, 96.
10. Toussaint-Samat, M. (1992) *History of Food* p.498.
11. Labarge, M. W. (1965) pp.95-6.
12. Hammond, P. (1993) pp.10-11; Labarge, M. W. (1965) p.96.
13. Don't balk at this idea; sugar in foods such as this was used in small amounts as a seasoning to heighten the taste of other foods. Thai food works on the same principle, as do things like British sauces, relishes and ketchups, so not strange at all. And I can personally vouch it as I have cooked it myself; see 'Mediaeval Blanc Mange'

blog post on *British Food: A History* (www.britishfoodhistory. com/2019/06/08/mediaeval-blanc-mange/) if you fancy recreating it yourself.

14. Other examples found in a later book by John Dussel called the *Boke of Nurture* included the following recipes: sugar and mustard with pheasant, curlews with sugar and salt, 'appuls & peres with sugre candy', and spice plates with sugar plums and other sweetmeats. Hammond, P. (1993) p.11; Hieatt, C. B. and Butler, S. (1985) *Curye on Inglysch: English culinary manuscripts of the fourteenth century* p.217.

15. Groom, S. (2013) p.28.

16. Lewicka, P. (2011) *Food and Foodways of Medieval Cairenes: Aspects of Life in an Islamic Metropolis of the Eastern Mediterranean.*

17. Abbot, E. (2008) *Sugar: A Bittersweet History* pp.21-2.

18. Groom, S. (2013) p.22.

19. Hooke, J. J. (1869) *Questions and Answers on English History* p.32.

20. Hammond, P. (1993) p.11.

21. Taken from the 'Eltham Ordinances', kindly provided by Elise Fleming, personal communication.

22. For the full list, see Stone, E. (1845) *Chronicles of Fashion From the Time of Elizabeth to the Early Part of the Nineteenth Century, in Manners, Amusements, Banquets, Costume, Etc. Volume 1* p.51.

23. Dawson, T. (1596) *The Good Housewife's Jewel.* 1996 Edition by Southover Press pp.117-8.

24. Quote in Macinnis, P. (2002) *Bittersweet: The Story of Sugar* p.18.

25. Mintz, S. W. (1985) p.107.

26. Sato, T. (2014) *Sugar in the Social Life of Medieval Islam* pp.101-2.

27. Dawson, T. (1596) p.137.

28. Henisch, B. (2009) pp.150-1; Macinnis, P. (2002) p.18.

29. Dickson Wright, C. (2011) pp.50-1; Labarge, M. W. (1965) p.97.

30. Ligon, R. (1657) *A True & Exact History Of the Island of Barbados* p.96.

31. Mice, and their faeces, have been thought to have magical or medicinal properties for centuries; Thomas Ellis, A. (2004) *Fish, Flesh and Good Red Herring* pp.30-1.

32. Thomson, T. (2011) *History of the Royal Society* p.166.

33. Reviewed in Geaman, K. L. (2016) 'Anne of Bohemia and Her Struggle to Conceive', *Social History of Medicine.*

34. Sloane, H. (1707) *A voyage to the islands Madera, Barbados, Nieves, S. Christophers and Jamaica Volume I* p.cviii.

35. There are many examples of sugar being used in this way; see Abbot, E. (2008) p.21, and Thomas Ellis, A. (2004) p.29.

36. Toussaint-Samat, M. (1992) p.499.

37. Macinnis, P. (2002) p.99.

38. Quote in Timbs, J. (1870) *Abbeys, Castles, and Ancient Halls of England and Wales Their Legendary Lore, and Popular History. By John Timbs: Volume 1* p.125.

39. La Trobe, B. (2012) *Of Diamonds and Dentistry* pp.180-1.

40. Mansel, P. (2019) *King of the World: The Life of King Louis XIV*, online e-book, chapter 14.

41. *Ibid.* chapter 14; Stoy, P. (1951) 'Dental Disease and Civilisation', *Ulster Medical Journal* p.145.

42. This is probably quackery at work. The 'eggs' were probably the seeds themselves. Quote by Boorde found in Ring, M. E. (1968) p.1341.

43. Boorde instructs us to collect 'as many lilte grene frogges, brething or sitting upon trees as thou canst get in the water,' and then skim the fat away after simmering. If an extraction was absolutely necessary, 'open the gums round about the tooth as much as possible with an instrument, then the roote. Anoint it with oyle where frogs have been decocted; when the tooth is very loose, then take it out.' Quotes and tinctures found in Ring, M. E. (1968) pp.1341-3.

44. The sweet wines – the favourite being hippocras and mead – were drunk hot or cold and laced with sugar or honey and were very popular in the higher echelons of mediaeval and early modern society.

45. Examples from Bifulco, M. *et al.* (2016) p.1; Guerini, V. (1909) *A history of dentistry from the most ancient times until the end of the eighteenth century* pp.153-4; and Ring, M. E. (1968) p.1343.

46. La Trobe, B. (2012) p.180.

47. There are some modern anthropological examples of this phenomena, though they are few and far between; some remote Inuit and Maori tribespeople have a natural very low frequency of tooth decay comparable to the European pre-sugar world because they eat large amount of fish or meat and very little carbohydrate. Stoy, P. (1951) pp.145-7.

48. *Ibid.* p.144.

Chapter 11. Sugar for All

1. Mintz, S. W. (1985) *Sweetness and Power: The Place of Sugar in Modern History* p.186.
2. Keane, B. and Portnay, O. (1992) 'The English Tearoom', in Walker, H. (ed.) *Oxford Symposium on Food and Cookery 1991: Public Eating: Proceedings* p.158.
3. Walvin, J. (2017) *How Sugar Corrupted the World* p.75.
4. Abbot, E. (2008) *Sugar: a Bittersweet History* pp.58-9.
5. *Ibid.* pp.66-9.
6. Griffin, E. (2018) 'Diets, hunger and living standards during the British industrial revolution', *Past and Present* p.76.
7. Abbot, E. (2008) pp.65-6; Griffin, E. (2018) p.84.
8. Griffin, E. (2018) p.87.
9. Mintz, S. W. (1985) pp.127-8.
10. Abbot, E. (2008) p.66.
11. Sugar Refining, *St George-in-the-East Church* website. Available at: http://www.stgitehistory.org.uk/sugarrefining.
12. Walvin, J. (2017) p.38.
13. *Harper's New Monthly Magazine* (1886) 'A Lump of Sugar', p. Vol 73, issue 433.
14. *The Daily News*, 18 August 1853. Source: http://www.mawer.clara.net/fatalities.html.
15. As opposed to home-made jams which are typically made from equal weights of fruit and sugar. Even jams and preserves today – no matter how posh – use more sugar than fruit.
16. Walvin, J. (2017) pp.178-9.
17. Abbot, E. (2008) p.67.
18. *McVitie's: Our Story*. Available at: mcvitiescanada.com/en/timeline.
19. Walvin, J. (2017) p.180.
20. Mintz, S. W. (1985) p.187.
21. Dahl, R. (1984) *Boy: Tales of Childhood* pp.31-2. If you have never read this book, stop what you are doing and go read it now.
22. Up until then, chocolate was rather soft, so eggs had to be solid, making them prohibitively expensive.
23. Abbot, E. (2008) pp.361-3.
24. French, M. (2017) 'Modernity in British advertising: selling cocoa and chocolate in the 1930s', *Journal of Historical Research in Marketing* p.11.

25. Bywater, M. (2005) *Lost Worlds What Have We Lost, & where Did it Go?* p.71.
26. Jackson, M. (2010) *Five Boys.*
27. Walvin, J. (2017) p.180.
28. There are two things, above all else, food manufacturers try to get into their products: air and water.
29. Abbot, E. (2008) pp.634-5.
30. British and US chocolate was considered far too sweet, milky and low-quality by continental Europeans who preferred their food with a bitter bite to it, but even they would succumb to brands such as *Milka* and *Kinder* in the coming decades.
31. Walvin, J. (2017) p.144.
32. Macinnis, P. (2002) *Bittersweet: The Story of Sugar* p.136.
33. Richardson, D. (2012) *The history of the sugar beet generation, Farmer's Weekly.*
34. *Monthly Labor Review: February* (1917) p.937; a report summing up the aims of the commission to the US government.
35. Abbot, E. (2008) p.368.
36. Richardson, T. (2004) *Sweets: The History of Temptation* p.275; Thompson, A. S. (2014) *The Empire Strikes Back?: The Impact of Imperialism on Britain from the Mid-Nineteenth Century* pp.35-6.
37. Mintz, S. W. (1985) p.187.

Chapter 12. The Rise of Junk Food

1. The phrase 'sugar is the new tobacco' has been attributed to various people, but it seems to originate from a talk given by Professor Robert Lustig in 2013 at a conference on the subject of sugar, obesity and metabolic syndrome. Ravichandran, B. (2013) *Sugar is the new tobacco, The BMJ Opinion.*
2. Bridges, A. and Dixey, R. A. (1934) *BRITISH SUGAR BEET TEN YEARS' PROGRESS UNDER THE SUBSIDY.* University of Oxford Agricultural Economics Research Institute p.9; Walvin, J. (2017) *How Sugar Corrupted the World* p.182; Ward, N. *et al.* (2008) 'Productivism, post-productivism and European agricultural reform: The case of sugar', *Sociologia Ruralis* p.122.

3. The area of farmland used for growing sugar beet rose from 6800ha in 1923 to 52,500ha by 1926.
4. Bridges, A. and Dixey, R. A. (1934) p.12; Ward, N. *et al.* (2008) p.122.
5. Walvin, J. (2017) pp.182-3.
6. Walvin, J. (2017) pp.183-4; there was a similar shock when working class lads' teeth were inspected when they were called to fight in the First World War.
7. Bridges, A. and Dixey, R. A. (1934) p.84.
8. It only seems a lot because we don't bake from scratch like we used to. Our preparatory foods and fizzy drinks contain more sugar.
9. Reviewed in Barker, D. J. P. and Osmond, C. (1986) 'Diet and coronary heart disease in England and Wales during and after the second world war'; Walvin, J. (2017) p.185.
10. Walvin, J. (2017) pp.185-6; Ward, N. *et al.* (2008) p.122.
11. Ballinger, R. A. (1971) *A History of Sugar Marketing*. US Department of Agriculture, Economic Research Service p.60.
12. Moran, J. (2010) 'Defining Moment: Tate & Lyle squares up to the Labour government, July 28 1949', *Financial Times*, 5 March; Walvin, J. (2017) pp.185-6.
13. Noon, R. (2001) 'Goodbye, Mr Cube', *History Today*, p. Vol. 51, No.10.
14. Moran, J. (2010).
15. In the UK Coca Cola spent £23 million annually, Walkers £16.5 million and Muller £13.15 million. Walvin, J. (2017) pp.209-10.
16. McDonald's give away free toys with their Happy Meals, and they sell so many that they are the UK's largest distributor, despite the toys being free of charge.
17. Brassington, F. and Pettitt, S. (2006) *Principles of Marketing* p.136.
18. Ravichandran, B. (2013); Walvin, J. (2017) p.236.
19. Benefits include: predigestion of nutrients, especially lactose, change in nutrient profile in the form of additional vitamins and the colonisation of symbiotic bacteria; see Katz, S. E. (2012) *The Art of Fermentation* p.22-4.
20. I must admit, a favourite of mine as a child, the name was changed recently to 'Honey Monster'.
21. Bonner, G. *et al.* (1999) *Fortification Examined: How added nutrients can undermine good nutrition* pp.46-50, 72-3.
22. Clayton, J. (2003) *The rise and fall of Sunny Delight*, *BBC News*. Available at: http://news.bbc.co.uk/1/hi/business/3257820.stm.

23. Steel, C. (2020) *Sitopia: How Food Can Save the World* p.72.
24. Steel, C. (2008) *Hungry City: How Food Shapes Our Lives* p.238. France was not a rollover, in fact the first McDonald's to sprout up in France 'was physically attacked', which goes to show how much of a culture shock this Americanised food was for mainland Europe. Depressingly by 2014 the residents of Saint-pol-sur-Ternoise felt so deprived living in a town without a McDonald's restaurant they went on a march demanding one was opened! Steel, C. (2020) p.59.
25. Walvin, J. (2017) pp.245-6.
26. You couldn't make it up. Reviewed in Janicka, M., Kot-Wasik, A. and Namieśnik, J. (2010) 'Analytical procedures for determination of cocaine and its metabolites in biological samples', *Trends in Analytical* Chemistry.
27. Walvin, J. (2017) pp.246-9.
28. *Ibid.* pp.252-4 Prior to entering the war, Coca Cola had no issue with selling its product to Nazi Germany, but once they entered the war, they had to stop. Germany had plenty of domestic sugar beet at their disposal, they plugged the gap by making their own soft drink from 'by-products of the production of cider and cheese, such as whey; like its colour, its taste conjured up oranges.' It was named *Fanta*, and 3 million cases of it were sold in 1943 alone; Pauwels, J. R. (2017) *Big Business and Hitler* p.207.
29. Gelles, D. (2014) 'Coke and McDonald's, Growing Together Since 1955', *New York Times.*
30. Ballinger, R. A. (1975) *A History of Sugar Marketing Through 1974* pp.i, 58.
31. See Smalley, J. and Blake, M. (2003) 'Sweet beginnings: Stalk sugar and the domestication of maize', *Current Anthropology.*
32. Gelles, D. (2014).
33. Steel, C. (2008) p.243.
34. Walvin, J. (2017) p.261.
35. Abbot, E. (2008) *Sugar: A Bittersweet History* p.399.
36. Ravichandran, B. (2013).
37. Reviewed in Lincoln, K. D., Abdou, C. M. and Lloyd, D. (2014) 'Race and socioeconomic differences in obesity and depression among black and non-Hispanic White Americans', *Journal of Health Care for the Poor and Underserved.*
38. This is much more apparent in US than UK supermarkets.

39. A point made by Professor Jason Harford, speaking at the same conference as Robert Lustig in 2013.
40. Orwell, G. (1937) *The Road to Wigan Pier* p.87-8.

Chapter 13. Fifty Words for Sugar

1. Pollan, M. (2013) *Cooked: A Natural History of Transformation* p.8; in the original quote, he also included sugar's mates, fat and salt.
2. The sweet taste had been independently observed previously and a reference to it appears in an Indian manuscript written by Avicenna (980-1037).
3. See Eknoyan, G. and Nagy, J. (2005) 'A history of diabetes mellitus or how a disease of the kidneys evolved into a kidney disease', *Advances in Chronic Kidney Disease.*
4. Himsworth, H. P. (1936) 'Diabetes mellitus. Its differentiation into insulin-sensitive and insulin-insensitive types', *The Lancet.*
5. Munt, A. H. (2004) *The Impact of Dutch Cartesian Medical Reformers in Early Enlightenment German Culture (1680-1720)* p.204; Smith, W. D. (1992) 'Complications of the Commonplace: Tea, Sugar, and Imperialism', *Journal of Interdisciplinary History* pp.269-70.
6. Fischler, C. (1987) 'Attitudes Towards Sugar and Sweetness in Historical and Social Perspective', in Dobbing, J. (ed.) *Sweetness* pp.14-15; Munt, A. H. (2004) p.204.
7. Sugar has been long associated with skin complains, though it is often dismissed as a bit of an old wives' tale: studies seem to suggest that the association is tenuous at best, with one meta-analysis from 2009 concluding that there is no association between sugar or chocolate with acne. There may be one link though, with one study finding an association with sugar consumption and seborrheic dermatitis, otherwise known as dandruff. However a recent study (2019) found a mysterious association between sugar intake and acne, but only if it was consumed in the form of a soda drink and if it exceeded one hundred grams of sugar per day. See Spencer, E. H., Ferdowsian, H. R. and Barnard, N. D. (2009) 'Diet and acne: A review of the evidence', *International Journal of Dermatology*; Bett, D. G. G., Morland, J. and Yudkin, J. (1967) 'Sugar Consumption in Acne

Vulgaris and Seborrhoeic Dermatitis', *British Medical Journal*; and Huang, X. *et al.* (2019) 'Daily Intake of Soft Drinks and Moderate-to-Severe Acne Vulgaris in Chinese Adolescents', *Journal of Pediatrics.*

8. Fischler, C. (1987) p.8.

9. Marinovich, M. *et al.* (2013) 'Aspartame, low-calorie sweeteners and disease: Regulatory safety and epidemiological issues', *Food and Chemical Toxicology* p.5.

10. Although recently there is some evidence that artificial sweeteners may have a detrimental effect on our gut microbiome. Reviewed in Ruiz-Ojeda, F. J. *et al.* (2019) 'Effects of Sweeteners on the Gut Microbiota: A Review of Experimental Studies and Clinical Trials', in *Advances in Nutrition.*

11. Belloir, C., Neiers, F. and Briand, L. (2017) 'Sweeteners and sweetness enhancers', *Current Opinion in Clinical Nutrition and Metabolic Care* p.3.

12. *Ibid.* (2017) p.5.

13. Reviewed in Pereira, M. A. (2013) 'Diet beverages and the risk of obesity, diabetes, and cardiovascular disease: A review of the evidence', *Nutrition Reviews.*

14. Stuckey, B. (2013) *Taste: Surprising Stories and Science about Why Food Tastes Good* p.219.

15. At least that what their website says: www.coca-cola.co.uk.

16. Lafuente, G. S. (2016) 'Labelling Standard Information and Food Consumption in Historical Perspective: An Overview of State Regulation in Spain 1931-1975', in Oddy, D. J., Atkins, P. J., and Amilien, V. (eds) *The Rise of Obesity in Europe: A Twentieth Century Food History* p.98.

17. The *Virta* blog lists 56 different names for sugar in the US, though others count over 60. Some of these names are: dextrose, fructose, galactose, glucose, lactose, maltose, sucrose, beet sugar, brown sugar, cane juice crystals, cane sugar, castor sugar, coconut sugar, superfine sugar, corn syrup solids, crystalline fructose, date sugar, Demerara sugar, dextrin, diastatic malt, ethyl maltol, Florida crystals, golden sugar, glucose syrup solids, grape sugar, icing sugar, maltodextrin, Muscovado sugar, panela sugar, raw sugar, sugar (granulated or table), sucanat, turbinado sugar, yellow sugar, agave syrup, barley malt, blackstrap molasses, brown rice syrup, caramel; Barnwell,

A. (2018) *Secret Sugars: The 56 Different Names for Sugar*, *Virta*. Available at: www.virtahealth.com/blog/names-for-sugar.

18. Reviewed in Hawley, K. L. *et al.* (2013) 'The science on front-of-package food labels', *Public Health Nutrition.*

19. See Koenigstorfer, J., Groeppel-Klein, A. and Kamm, F. (2014) 'Healthful food decision making in response to traffic light color-coded nutrition labeling', *Journal of Public Policy and Marketing*; and Sacks, G., Rayner, M. and Swinburn, B. (2009) 'Impact of front-of-pack "traffic-light" nutrition labelling on consumer food purchases in the UK', *Health Promotion International.*

20. Professor Lustig's words at the 2013 conference on the subject of sugar, obesity and metabolic syndrome. Ravichandran, B. (2013) *Sugar is the new tobacco*, *The BMJ Opinion.*

21. See Public Health England website (2000) *Sugar Reduction Programme.* Available at: www.actiononsugar.org/uk-sugar-reduction/sugar-reduction-programme/.

22. Brown, R. (no date) 'Is there life in Coke Life yet, or will it die a slow painful death?', *The Grocer.*

23. Data from gov.uk (2018) *Soft Drinks Industry Levy comes into effect.* Available at: https://www.gov.uk/government/news/soft-drinks-industry-levy-comes-into-effect.

24. Campbell, D. (2019) 'English consuming more sugar despite tax and anti-obesity drive', *The Guardian.*

25. Steel, C. (2008) *Hungry City: How Food Shapes Our Lives* p.237.

Chapter 14. Legacy

1. Steel, C. (2008) *Hungry City: How Food Shapes Our Lives* p.245.

2. Ravichandran, B. (2013) *Sugar is the new tobacco*, *The BMJ Opinion.*

3. *Tooth extraction 'epidemic' costs NHS millions* (2018) *Sky News.* Available at: https://news.sky.com/story/tooth-extraction-epidemic-costs-nhs-millions-11205389.

4. Walvin, J. (2017) *How Sugar Corrupted the World* pp.27-8.

5. *Child oral health: applying All Our Health*, *gov.uk*. Available at: https://www.gov.uk/government/publications/child-oral-health-applying-all-our-health/child-oral-health-applying-all-our-health.

6. Hornall, T. (2019) 'Junk food adverts could be banned before 9pm as part of government plans to fight "epidemic" of childhood obesity', *Independent*, 17 March.

7. Savage, M. (2019) 'Tom Watson urges McDonald's to cancel "danger to health" campaign', *The Guardian*, 17 March.

8. Reviewed in DiNicolantonio, J. J., O'Keefe, J. H. and Wilson, W. L. (2017) 'Sugar addiction: Is it real? A narrative review', *British Journal of Sports Medicine.*

9. gov.uk (2017) 'Health matters: obesity and the food environment'. Available at: www.gov.uk/government/publications/health-matters-obesity-and-the-food-environment/health-matters-obesity-and-the-food-environment--2.

10. Chan, T. H. *Obesity Prevention Source, Harvard School of Public Health.* Available at: https://www.hsph.harvard.edu/obesity-prevention-source/obesity-consequences/economic/.

11. Nurse, E. (2016) *The secret behind Coca-Cola's success in Africa, CNN.* Available at: https://edition.cnn.com/2016/01/21/africa/coca-cola-africa-mpa-feat/index.html.

12. This was found in Goa and was estimated at precisely 18.3%; Akhtar, S. and Dhillon, P. (2017) 'Prevalence of diagnosed diabetes and associated risk factors: Evidence from the large-scale surveys in India', *Journal of Social Health and Diabetes* p.31.

13. Zheng, Y., Ley, S. H. and Hu, F. B. (2018) 'Global aetiology and epidemiology of type 2 diabetes mellitus and its complications', *Nature Reviews Endocrinology* p.81.

14. Voora, V., Bermudez, S. and Larrea, C. (2019) *Global Market Report: Sugar.*

15. Hashem, K. *et al.* (2015) 'Does Sugar Pass the Environmental and Social Test?', *The Food Research Collaboration* p.2.

16. Walvin, J. (2017) pp.55-6.

17. Abbot, E. (2008) *Sugar: a Bittersweet History* p.381.

18. Coral Digest (2020) *The Impacts of the Sugar Cane Industry on the Great Barrier Reef, Coraldigest.org.* Available at: https://www.coraldigest.org/index.php/SugarCane.

19. Long, J. L. (2003) *Introduced Mammals of the World: Their History, Distribution and Influence* pp.306-7.

20. Abbot, E. (2008) pp.381-2.

21. Mercer, P. (2017) *The rapid spread of Australia's cane toad pests*, *BBC World News.*

22. Kennedy, L. (2019) 'Rotten: A Sweet Deal' available on Netflix.

23. Luscombe, R. (2020) 'Florida: Republican "green governor" seeks to reverse predecessor's legacy', *The Guardian.* 23 January 2019.

24. Voora, V., Bermudez, S. and Larrea, C. (2019).

25. McGrath, S. (2013) 'Fuelling global production networks with slave labour?: Migrant sugar cane workers in the Brazilian ethanol GPN', *Geoforum* p.1.

26. Kennedy, L. (2019).

27. See also pp.388-96 *Sugar: a Bittersweet History* (2008) by Elizabeth Abbot; she writes compellingly about the terrible treatment of the Haitians in the Dominican Republic in the 2010s.

28. Wood, M. (2020) 'Michael Wood on...the Civil Rights Movement', *BBC History Magazine*, August.

29. For more on this subject see the compelling documentary *13*[th]; director: A. DuVernay (2016). Available on Netflix.

30. Wood, M. (2020).

31. See Wardle, H. and Obermuller, L. (2018) 'The Windrush generation', *Anthropology Today.*

32. Wood, M. (2020).

33. The Bristol buildings named in his honour are also expected a name change.

34. Shaw, C. (2020) *Liverpool's Slave Trade Legacy*, *History Today.* Available at: https://www.historytoday.com/history-matters/ liverpool's-slave-trade-legacy.

Afterword

1. See Furmli, S. *et al.* (2018) 'Therapeutic use of intermittent fasting for people with type 2 diabetes as an alternative to insulin', *BMJ Case Reports.*

2. United States International Trade Commission (2001) *Sugar: Industry and Trade Summary* p.1.

3. Dankers, C. and Liu, P. (2003) *Environmental and Social Standards, Certification and Labelling for Cash Crops.* Food and Agriculture Organization of the United Nations p.52.

4. See *The Impacts of the Sugar Cane Industry on the Great Barrier Reef* on the coraldigest.org website. Available at: https://www.coraldigest.org/index.php/SugarCane.
5. See preface of *Fuel Ethanol Production from Sugarcane* (2019), edited by L. C. Basso and T. P. Basso.
6. See Klenk, I., Landquist, B. and De Imaña, O. R. (2012) 'The product carbon footprint of EU beet sugar (part I)', *Zuckerindustrie*.
7. Dankers, C. and Liu, P. (2003) p.52.
8. Abbot, E. (2008) *Sugar: A Bittersweet History* p.322-3.
9. Hashem, K. *et al.* (2015) 'Does Sugar Pass the Environmental and Social Test?', *The Food Research Collaboration* p.1.
10. Buying Sugar, Spreads and Oils (2020) *Fairtrade website*. Available at: https://www.fairtrade.org.uk/buying-fairtrade/sugar-spreads-and-oil/.
11. It's not just me who thinks this; it also won a much coveted *Radio 4 Food and Farming Award* in 2017 in the Best Retailer category. Unicorn's website: www.unicorn-grocery.coop.

Index

Page numbers written in bold denote illustrations, and those in italics refer the endnotes.

Ache people 4
Abbot, Elizabeth 126
Act for the Governing of Negros 66-70
advertising 144, 147-8, 155-8, **158**, 159, 162, **162**, 170, 173, 176
Africa 3, 10-11, 18-9, 22, 32, 34, 30, 38, 39, 80-1, 85, 87-8, 90, 107-8, 120, 178, 185
Aldeas people 31
Alexander the Great 7-8
Alexander VI 17, 22
Algarve 19
American War of Independence 75, 78, 119
American-Spanish War 127
Ancient Egypt viii-ix, **4**, 4-5
Anglo-Saxons 130, 138
Angola 18, 32, 87
Anne I 139
Anne of Bohemia 135
Antigua 35, 66, 70, 73, 179
Antilles, Greater 20, 22, 35
Antilles, Lesser 27, 35, 38
Antoinette 92

apothecaries 133, **134**, 135-6
apprenticeships 70, 111-2, 113
Aquinas, Thomas 136
Arana Cave 3
Argentina 189
Arnold, John 135
aspartame 169
Attlee, Clement 154
Australia 113, 115-6, 119, 151, 180, 185
Australopithecines 2-3

bagasse 62, 75, 98
Baghdad 10, 15
Bahamas 27
Barbados 35, 37, 38, 40, 41-2, **42**, 45, 49, 54, 65, 70, 72, 82, 83, 91, 97, 99-100, 179
Barbados Assembly 66-7
Baxter, Robin 99-100
Beatles, The 186
beehives 2-5
Beeton, Isabella vii
Benin 88-9
Biafra 91-2
Bible, The ix, 101, 107, 110, 123

Big Sugar x, 117, 125, 127, 128, 156-7, 169, 181, 189, 190-1
biodiversity loss 178, 179, 189
Birmingham 85
biscuits 144, 146, 151, 152, 156, 160, 175, 190
Black Lives Matter xi, 185, **187**
blackbirding 116
Blankaart, Steven 168
Boer War 150
boiling 10, **61**, 61-2
boiling house 15, 16, 28, 55, **61**, 61-2, 178, 105
Bonaparte, napoleon 77-9, 119, 149
Bonner, William 51-2
Boorde, Andrew 129
branding 51, 67, 68, 82, **97**, 98
Brazil 17, 20, 23, 27, 30-33, 49, 54, 55, 58, 63, 80, 125, 182, 189
Brazilian plantations 28, 30, 33, 57, 60, 64, 112
breakfast cereals 146, 152, 157-60, **158**, 171-2, 173
Bristol 17, 81, 84, 85, 86, 132, 142, 186
British Commonwealth 153, 155, 185
British Empire x-xi, 8, 84, 87, 113, 115-6, 149, 185, 186, 190
British Navy 54, 85, 101, 119
British Sugar Corporation see Silver Spoon
British-made sugar 153-4
Bronze Age 5
Brooks, The 95, 103
Bruges 11

buccaneers see pirates and piracy
Bush, George Snr 184

cachaça 55
Cadbury, George 150
Cadbury's 147, 150, 173
    Dairy Milk 147, 148, 174
caffeine 139, 162
Calendar of Cordoba 11
calories 1-2, 4, 63, 141, 149, 155-6, 164, 169-70, 171, 174, 176
Canada 116
Canary Islands 16, 17, 20, 21, 26, 126, 178
cancer 137, 156, 165, 169
candy xii, 15, 135, *195, 217*
cane toad 180, **181**
cannibalism 23
capitalism x, xii, 16, 23, 33, 112, 113
Caribbean 28, 36, 75, 78, 80, 116, 120, 128, 180
Caribs 23-4, 31, 35, **36**, 45
cartoons **95, 105**, 154, **154**
Castro, Fidel 127
Catherine of Aragon 132
cave art 3
Cayenne 36
Charles I 81
Charles II 82, 139
Chaucer, Geoffrey viii, *192*
Chesapeake pioneers 36
children's advertising 148, 156-159, **158**
China 7, 127, 140, 178, *194*
Chinese workers 114, 124, 126-7
chocolate 136, 146-151, 173, *219*
Chosroes I 9

Christianity 66, 99-100, 126

Church of Our Lady and St Nicholas 86

Churchill, Winston 155

Coca Cola 161-4, **162**, 173, 174

Coca Cola Company 161-4, 170, 173, 178, *222*

Coca Cola in Africa 178

Coca Cola, advertising 162

cocoa 38, 147, 150

coffee 85, 92, 136, 139, 141, 169

coffee houses 139

Coke Life 173

Coke Zero 170

colonialism xi, 18, 20, 27, 35, 41, 78-9, 80-1, 83, 91, 101, 105, 108, 118, 126, 163-4

Columbus, Christopher 21-26, **22**, 27, 29, *198*

Company of Royal Adventurers, The 39, 82

complex carbohydrates 1

Congress 163, 169, 183

cooking 166, 168, 174, 188

coolies 113

corn syrup 170

Colston, Edward 186, **187**

Countess of Burgundy 131

Covid-19 177

Crete 10, 15, 135

Cromwell, Oliver 38, 81

Crusades, The x, 11, 13-15, 129-30

Cuba 17, 28, 35, 112-3, 125-7, 150
   annexation of 126-7

Cunard Building 86, **86**

Curtin, Phillip D. 98

Cyprus 10, 15

Dahl, Roald 147

Davis, Angela 184

Dawson, Thomas 133

de Arana, Beatriz Enríquez 21

de Bobadilla, Francisco 25

de las Casas, Bartolomé 28-30

de Montford, Eleanor 130-1

de Vellosa, Gonzalo 26

deforestation 17, 26, 40, *205*

dehydration of workers 182

Democratic Republic of Congo 3, 91, 120

dental health 136-8, 144, 175-6

Desallines, Jean-Jacques 77-8, 79

DeSantis, Ron 181

Description of a Slave Ship 96, 96

diabetes 160, 165, 168-9, **166**, 170, 175, 176, 177, 178

diabetes mellitus 168

diabetes, gestational 178

Diet Coke 170

disaccharides ix-x, 1, 165

Dolben's Act 80, 91, 94, 96

domestic servants 19, 51, 55, 141, *203*

Dominica 23, 24, 36

Dominican Republic 182-3

Dr Pepper 160

Drax, Henry 83

drivers 55, 57, 66

Du Bois dataset 92, *210*

Duck, Captain Edmund 73

Dunn, Richard, S. 37, 52, 65, 72

Dutch colonies 30, 32-3, 35

Dutch occupation of Brazil 32-3

Dutch traders 32, 39, 81

Dutch West India Company 32, 81

Edward I 134
Efe people 3
Egypt 5, 8, 9-10, 11, 14, 131, 135
Eleanor of Aquitaine 130
Elizabeth I 34-5, 126, 132, 136
Emancipation Act 111
Emancipation Proclamation 124
English Civil War 37, 41
English colonies
  clothing 39-40, 54
  food 38-40, 45-7
  plant life 43
  social structure 39, 40
  trades and careers 39-40, 53,
    55, 71
  weather and climate 36, 38-9,
    41-2, 45
English crown 35, 54, 81-2,
  84, 154
English planters 38, 39-40, 46,
  49, 54, 60, 65-6, 70-2, 73-5,
  81-2, 83-84, 90, 91-2, 99-101,
  104-114
Enlightenment 100
enzymes 1, 10, 165, 193
Equiano, Olaudah 67, 69, 89, 90,
  92, 94-6, 97, 102, **102**, 104-6,
  112, 207, 211
eutrophication 179
Everglades 127, 180-1
evolution/behaviour/brain x, 1-3,
  143, 156, 164, 193
exploitation of workers 112, 128,
  182-3, 186, 190

factory food 142, 144, 146
Fairtrade 190
Fanta 222

fast food 163
fat consumption xii, 152,
  156-7, 159, 160, 164-5,
  168, 172
feminisation of products 170
Ferdinand II 22
fertilizers 178, 182, 189
fibre 172, 174
Fiji 113, 116, 151
fire branding see branding
First World War 149, 151, *221*
Florida 127-8, 180-182
Florida Crystals 181-2
Florida Water Committee 181
Food Standards Agency 171
Forme of Cury viii, 129, 131,
  133, *216*
Fox, George 99
Fox, William 102
free trade 54, 101, 103, 109,
  127, 141
freemen 83-4, **115**, 124-5
French Crown 74
French Revolution 74
fructose ix, 10, 165, 172
fruit juice x, 159, 167, 172
frumenty 46, 131
Fry's 147-8, 150
  Five Boys 147-8, **148**

Galen's theory of the Four
  Humours 8, 133, 137, 168
Gandhi, Mohandas 117
Gates, General Horatio 119
Genoese merchants 17, 131
Georgia 119
Glasgow 142
glucose ix, 10, 135, *193*

gold and gold mining 18, 25-6, 28, 30, 31, 34, 35, 38, 108, 137
Gold Coast 91
Gonçalves, Antam 18-19
Great Barrier Reef 180
Great British Bake Off, The 177
Guadalupe 23, 179
Gulf of Guinea 19, 30, 87, **88**
gur 8, 9, 190

Hadza 4
Haitian Revolution 74-79, **76**, 109-10, 119
Hall & Boyd refinery 144
Harlow, V. T. 34, 37
Hawaii 7, 127, 180
Hawkins, Sir John 34-5, 81
Heinz 173
Henry II 130
Henry III 130
Henry IV 132
Hershey, Milton S. 149
Hershey's 149
high fructose corn syrup (HFCS) 164-5
Himsworth, H. P. 168
Hinduism 8
Hispaniola 17, 22, 25, 27, 28, 31, 35, 55, 75
Home Office 185
homo sapiens 2, 5
honey vii, 1-4, 133, 138, 193
honey collecting 3-4, 3
honeycombs vii, 1, 3-4
honeyguide 4
Hospitallers 15
Hull 142
hunter-gatherers 1-4

indentured servants 40-41, 44, 46, 54, 66-7, 84
indentured servants, treatment of 54, 66
India/East Indies 3, 7-9, 21, 22, 101, 109, 113-4, 116-7, 178, 190, *194*
Indian workers 113-4, 116-7
indigenous people 18, 22, 24, 31, 86, 113, 115-6, 120, 127, 164, 179
Indonesia 7
Industrial Revolution 142, 144
infectious diseases 25, 31, 41, 78, 90-3, 104-5, 133
ingenio 16, 18, 19, 20, 21, 26-27, 30, 32-3, 57, 59, **61**, 62, 64, 185, *205*
insulin 165, 168
Irish workers 124, 126
irrigation 9, 10, 11
Islamic Empire
    in Europe 10, 13, 17
    medieval 9-12, 15, 130

jaggery see *gur*
Jamaica 36, 43, 45, 73, 76, 83, 179, 180, *200*
Jamaica Assembly 119
James VI/I 81
jams and preserves 133, 144-5, 149, 152

kanaka people 116
Kellogg, John Harvey 146
Kellogg's 158-9, 171-2
Kempe, Margery 130
Kent, Muhtar 178

Knights of the White Camelia 124
Knights Templar 15
Krispy Kreme 172
Ku Klux Klan 125

La Pantica 92
lactose ix-x, *221*
Leclerc, General Charles 76-7
Leeward Islands 70, 71, 73
Ligon, Richard 37, 41, 44, 46, 47,
    50, 55, 59, 69, 93, 97, 134
Lincoln, Abraham 124
Lisle, David 100
Littleton, Edward 60, 62
Liverpool 85-7, 103, 108,
    142, 186
    Africans and slaves in 86
lobbying 82, 83, 102, 106, 109,
    163, 181
loblolly 46
Locke, John 83
London 32, 81, 85-6, 142, 144
Long, Edward 64
Louis XIV 137
Louisiana 119-123, 126
Louisiana Purchase, The 78
Louverture, Toussaint 75-77, **77**

Macinnes, Peter 21
Madeira 12, 16-20, 26, 29,
    30-1, 65
malnutrition 118, 152, 169
maltose ix, 5
Manchester 85, 191
Mars 149
Mars, Frank 149
Martinique 23, 36
massapé 31, 55, 57

Mauritius 113, 190
McDonald's 163-4, 176, *221, 222*
McVitie's 146
medieval see Middle Ages
metabolic syndrome 165
Methodism 100
Mexico 28, 30, 182
Middle Ages 9, 112, 129, 138,
    129-33, 137, 141, *216-7, 218*
Middle Passage 92-98, **95**, 107,
    108, 114
Milkybar 173
milling the cane 4
Ministry of Food 153
Mintz, Sidney 115, 139
Mississippi 119
Mohammedoo, Dalla 88
molasses 62-3
mongoose, Indian **179**, 180
monosaccharides ix-x
Montesino, Anton 28
Mozambique 117
Mr Cube 154-5, **154**
mullato 51-2, 79, 203
Murad III 131
muscarrat 136
Muslim Empire, slavery in 12

Natal 4
Natal 116
National Health Service (NHS)
    154, 177
Nazi Germany *222*
Near East viii, x, 14, 16, 65
Nearchus 7-8
Nestlé 173
Nevis 35
New England 36, 37, 46

New England pioneers 36, 37
New Guinea 6-7, 11, 194
New Orleans 120, 124
New Zealand 116, 185
Newfoundland 46
Nixon, Richard 183
'no added sugar ' 172
Normans 13, 138
North Carolina 66, 119
nutritional information
      171-2, **172**

opioids 177
Orion, The 91
Ortelius, Abrham 133
overseers **33**, 41, 49, 51, 55, 58,
      60, 62, 68-9, 105

Palaeolithic man 3
Palestine 9
Paraguay 4, 28
Parliamentarians 82
Patout Estate 124
Penny Lane 87, 186
Penny, James 87, 186
Pepsi 159, 160, 178
Pepys, Samuel 83
Persian Empire 8-9, 16
pester power 156
pesticides 178, 179, 182, 189
pests 43
      caterpillars 17
      cockroaches 43-4
      mosquitos 43
      chiggers 44
      rats 56, 180, *204*
Phillips, William D. 12
Philippines 7

pirates and piracy 34-5, 36, 53,
      101, 104
Pitt, William, The Younger 99
Pollan, Michael 168
pollution 15, 143, 178, 189
polysaccharides x
Portugal 19, 22, 36, 49
Portuguese crown 19, 30
Portuguese plantations 17-8,
      30-33
prehistoric Britain 138
processed foods 157, 164, 172,
      178, 188
propaganda 90, 109, 154
Protestantism 99, 110
Public Health 176
Public Health England 173
puddings 133, 138, *145*, 146, 177
Pudsey, Cuthbert 30-1, 32, 64

Quakers 99-100, 150, 157-8,
      173, *202*
Queensland 180

racial segregation 116-117
Ramsay, James 53, 104-105, *207*
Rankin, F. Harrison 80
rattoon 57
Reagan, Ronald 184
Republicans 119, 125, 181, 184
Restoration, the 81
Richard II viii, 129, 135
Rillieux, Norbert 121
Road to Wigan Pier, *The* 166-7
Rochambeau, General
      Donatien-Marie-Joseph 78
rock and roll 186
Roundheads 38, 81-2

Rowntree 150
Royal African Company 39, 54, 83
Royal Commission for Sugar
    Supplies 150
Royalists 38, 82
rum 49, 55, 63-4, 69, 118, 150,
    206, *214*

saccharine viii, 169
Saccharum
    Genus 5-6
    origins 6-7
    S. officinarum 5-7, **6**
    S. robustum 6-7, *194*
    S. spontaneum 7, *194*
St Domingue 73-5, 179
St Christopher 35-6, 67
St Kitts see St Christopher
St Martin 35
Samuel, The 84
Sancho brothers 102
Santo Domingo 28, 34, 35, 74
São Thomé 16, 18, 150,
Schwartz, Stuart B. 13
Second World War 152, 163, 185
Senegal 87
serving size 172-3
setts 10, 31
Seven Years War 36
Sharp, Granville 100-1, 109
shipbuilders 84, 85
Sicily 8, 13
Siege of Acre 13, **14**
Sierra Leone 87, 88
Silver Spoon 153
slave
    festivals **48**, 89
    marriage 123

names 51
populations 19, 29, 50, 65, 66,
    70-1, 92, 98, 110, 122, 125
rebellions 70, 94, 99, 110, 120
revolt 46, 65, 71-3, 75, 93,
    101, 110, 114, 120-1, *208*
ships 38, 85, 86, 91-3, **96**,
    103-4
    conditions on 92-8, **96**
    disease on 91, 93
    rebellions on 94, 99
    waiting time in 90
trials and court marshals 70,
    71, 73, 110
slavery
    in court 100
    of Africans 19-20, 27, 29-30,
        31-2, 35, 41, 49-51, 54, 66,
        85-6, 89-90, 98, 104
    of West Indians 22, 25-27,
        28-32, 87
    abolitionist 80, 95-6, 100, 101,
        104, 109-11, 112, 190, *207*
    abolition 95, 100-2, 106-111
    anti-abolitionist 60, 107-9
    North American 119-124
Slave Trade, the xi
    Early 28-29
    Portuguese 18, 19, 29, 32-3,
        35, 38
    trade triangle 80
    transatlantic 80, 87, 90, **96**
    African 87-90
    abolition of 95, 95, 101,
        108-10
slaves
    and death rates 69, 80-1, 87,
        90, 91, 93-4

and sex 51
and their humanity 47, 50, 65-6, 99
as chattels 29, 41, 107, 183
as militia 73
as real estate 71
wages 114, 123
arrival on colonies 96-98
Brazilian 31-33, 57-8, 60, 112
capital punishment of 41, 67-8, 70, 72, 73, 120
capture of 88-90, 92
Christianisation of 47, 58, 70, 99, 101, 107, 123
clandestine trade in 83, 110, 126
clothing 66-7, 111, 123
compensation for 71-2, 111, 112
cost of 27, 31, 54, 83-4, 87, 92, 97
early freedom of 51-2, 70, 75, 100
emancipation of 29, 110-1, 112, 124, 125, 183
English descriptions of 37-8, 50-1, 203
exportation of 39, 81, 82-3
family structure of 28, 50
food and rations 46, 67, 87, 112, 117, 118-9
importation of 18, 26-7, 29, 32, 49, 54, 81, 125
injuries 60, 62, 63-4
Jewish child 18
Louisiana 119-124
music, song and dance 47-9, **48**, 94-5, 98, 123

packing on ships 95-7, **96**, *211*
pregnancy and birth 50-1, 112, 122
punishment of 18, 28-9, 33, 41, 51, 65, 67-70, **69**, 72, 73, 84, 108, 205
religious beliefs of 28, 47-8, 69-70
sex ratios 87, 122
Sloane, Hans 37, 44, 48, 51, 68, 71, 90, 135
smallpox 25, 31, 93
Smith, Adam 101, 103, 112
Smith, John 110
Society for the Abolition of the Slave Trade, The 101-103, 106, 108-9
soda drinks ix, 160-2, 164, 169, 172, 173, *223*
soda fountains 160, **161**
Solomon Islands 7
Sons of Ham 19
South Africa 113, 116-7, 151
Soviet Union 127
Spain 3, 10, 11, 17, **19**, 25-6, 29, 36, 49, 110, 125-6
    Muslim 13, 17
Spanish Crown 22, 25, 27
Spanish plantations 18, 25, 27, 38, 54, 74
    workers 126
Spirits, the 41
steam power 121, 125
Steel, Carolyn 160, 164, 175
strikes 112, 125
Strong, Jonathon 100
sucrose ix, 10, 56, 78, 164-5

sugar
  accidents in refineries 144
  addiction 2, 133, 136, 177
  and ADHD 177
  and behaviour 1-2
  and diet 139, 141-2, 146, 151,
    160, 165, 168, 170, 177
  and fecundity 135
  and nostalgia 146, 149, 177
  and obesity xi, 156, 160, 165,
    169-70, 173, 175, 176, 177
  and the British Empire x-xi,
    113, 115-7, 186, 190
  and wealth 33, 40, 86, 108,
    118, 136, 138, 190
  as a spice 129-30
  as medicine viii, 8, 10, 133-8,
    135, 147, 160, 168, 194-5
  banquets 132
  beet ix, 78-9, 149, 150,
    151, 153
  boycotting 109
  caster 135
  clarification of 26, 30, 60-1,
    62, 142
  consumption 74, 146, 148,
    149, 150, 151-3, 173-4,
    177-8, 188, *223*
  East Indian 101, 112
  etymology of vii-viii
  evolutionary adaptation x-xi, 1-2
  exporting 14-15, 32, 54, 74,
    78, 109, 122, 126, 149, 153
  Germany as producer 78, 149
  Hominids' love of 2-3
  importation 78, 131, 151-2, 155
  in Cuba/Cuban 17, 109, 112-3,
    125-8

  in Egypt 9, 11, 14, 131, 135-6
  in Hawaii 126-7
  in language vii-viii
  in Lent 136
  in orange juice 159, 172
  in the Old Testament ix
  in wine viii, 131, 134, 138, *218*
  loaves 26, **61**, 130, 131, 139
  mice 134-5
  monopolies 10, 17, 32, 39, 81,
    83-4, 103, 163
  muscovado 62-3
  organic sugar 189-90
  plate 131
  prices xii, 18, 26, 32-3, 54, 79,
    83-4, 101, 109, 127, 130-1,
    136, 141, 154-5, 163-4
  productivity 63, 124
  purging see clarification of
  purification of, see
    clarification of
  rationing 150, 152-3, 163
  refineries 15, 16, 18, 74, 118,
    126, 142-44
  sculpture see subtleties
  subtleties 131-2, **132**
  sources of 1, 5, 63
  sugar derived ethanol 189
  tobaccofication of 176
Sugar Board 153
sugarcane
  fields 10, 16, 26, 55-7, **58**, 88,
    120, 126, 179-80, 189
  in Madeira 16-20
  in the Mediterranean 10, 11
  juice x, 5, 8-9, 12, 17, 26, 58,
    60, 63
  weeding 10, 55-6

ecology 5-6, 18
genetics 6-7, 193
harvest 46, 54-8, **58**, **115**, 120, 122, **123**, 124, 128, 178, 189
juice boiling 10, 38
juice extraction 6, 11-12, 121
milling 11, 55, 57-60, **59**
planting 10, 38, 53, 56-8, 124, 189
Sugar Industry (Subsidy) Act 151
Sugar Reduction Programme 173
Sugar Report, 2020 178
Sugar Tax 174
suicide 70, 90, 93-4, 116
Sunny Delight 159
supermarkets 170, 174, 188, 190-1, *222*
supersizing 164
sweeteners 169-70, 188, 190, *224*
sweets and confectionery 8, 11, 85, 131, 138, 139, 146-9, 151, 156, 190
Syria 9-10, 14, 15, 16

Taino people 22-25, 26, 27, 28
Tanzania 4
Tate and Lyle 144, 153-5, **153**
tea 85, 136, 139-142, 144, 149, 152, 167, 169
teatime 139-41, **40**, 42
teeth, cavities and caries 136-8, 175
teeth, cleaning 138
teeth, fillings 137
Teutonic Knights 15
Thirteenth Amendment 183
Thoth, festival of viii-ix

tobacco 38, 39, 53, 116, 156-7, 159, 167, 174, 176-7
tooth worms 137
Toussant-Samat, Maguelonne 1
Treaty of Saragossa 17, 20, 30, 36
Trinidad 23, 113
Trujillo, Rafael 182
Trump, Donald 182
Turks, the 15-6
Twining, Thomas 139
type-1 diabetes 168
type-2 diabetes ix, 137, 156, 165-6, **166**, 168, 178, 188
Tyre 14

Unicorn grocery store 191
United East India Company 140
US sugar quota scheme 163-4

Valencia 3, 17-18
Venerable Bede, the 130
Venetian merchants 11, 15, 131
Victoria 150
violence toward African Americans 124-5, 184
Virginia 119

wages for workers 71, 101, 114, 116, 124, 127, 128, 190
Walvin, James 57, 118
War on Drugs, The 183
Watson, Tom 176
Wedgwood, Josiah 103, 106, 109, 110
West India Committee 107
West Indies 17, 20, 23-4, **24**, 35, 38, 45, 49, 54, 80, 83, 87, 113, 114, 180, 182, 185

Whigs 109
whipping as punishment 51, 67-8, 70, 94-5, *205*
Wilberforce, William 106, 108-9
William and John, The 37
Willoughby, Francis Lord 82
Windrush Scandal, the 185-6
Woodruff, Robert 163
Wordall, Thomas 52

World Health Organisation (WHO) 177
World Wildlife Fund (WWF) 178

yellow fever 29, 76-7, 91, 92
yoghurt 157, 173

Zong, The 104, **104**
Zululand 117